Whistleblowing

Whistleblowing

TOWARD A NEW THEORY

Kate Kenny

Harvard University Press   Cambridge, Massachusetts, and London, England 2019

First printing

Library of Congress Cataloging-in-Publication Data
Names: Kenny, Kate (Kate Marguerite), author.
Title: Whistleblowing : toward a new theory / Kate Kenny.
Description: Cambridge, Massachusetts : Harvard University Press, 2019. |
    Includes bibliographical references and index.
Identifiers: LCCN 2018036018 | ISBN 9780674975798 (alk. paper)
Subjects: LCSH: Whistle blowing. | Retribution. | Organizational behavior. |
    Organizational change.
Classification: LCC HD60 .K4822 2019 | DDC 174/.4—dc23
LC record available at https://lccn.loc.gov/2018036018

For my family

Contents

Whistleblowing

Introduction

A Whistleblowing Fairy Tale

Once upon a time, there lived a person who saw serious wrongdoing in the place she worked. She alerted her boss, who assured her that he would take care of it. He did nothing. She tried to tell his superiors. They did nothing. She found herself sidelined at work, given meaningless tasks to do. Her colleagues shunned her. She felt stressed out and isolated. She was upset because the wrongdoing continued, and it was causing harm to innocent people.

Frustrated, she spoke to a journalist who convinced her to go public with her story. She became known as "the whistleblower" and resigned from the organization when working there became unbearable. Wanting to discredit the claims she was making in the media, her organization launched an investigation into her past and a smear campaign against her. She got herself a lawyer.

She had to explain to her family that their income would be severely depleted; not only was the salary gone but she must now pay for legal representation and expensive counseling for the severe stress she was experiencing. Her loved ones began to feel the pressure.

Meanwhile, she was being celebrated in the press. She was seen as the brave whistleblower who challenged the big organization. And yet her legal case against her former employers dragged on for years. No firm would hire her; she was blacklisted in her industry. The lawyer explained that while there were laws to prevent this, they rarely worked in practice. She was ruined.

IF THERE IS something familiar about this tale, it is because it happens all the time. It could be set in any country in the world, in any sector: public, private, or nonprofit. Organizations can do bad things, and whistleblowers sometimes try to stop them. They have attempted to highlight problems in global finance that left entire nations bankrupt and suffering austerity. They have tried to speak out about breaches of safety protocols that caused devastating oil spills, space shuttle explosions in midair, passenger ferries sinking, and nuclear plant meltdowns.[1] Some whistleblowers are listened to, but more often they are ignored and sometimes punished for their efforts. The ones who are heeded save organizations worldwide millions of dollars each year.[2] Whistleblowing touches all of us who work; most employees will witness some form of internal corruption in their working lives, and most managers will have to deal with at least one incident of whistleblowing.

And yet the suffering experienced by many whistleblowers continues. The fairy tale that opened this chapter is a reality for countless people who go public with information about wrongdoing within their organization and experience retaliation as a result. There is little that is new or surprising about it. On the contrary, it is almost accepted as part of the experience of being a whistleblower. We shrug our shoulders, sigh that it is an awful situation for them, and talk about something else.

This book challenges this narrative and explores how we might change it. It proposes new ways to perceive the people who speak out and new ways to understand their struggle against powerful influences. For the purpose of this book, *whistleblower,* a term that has many different interpretations, is defined as an individual who speaks up about perceived wrongdoing in his or her organization, to someone who can effect change, and experiences retaliation for doing so.[3]

The opening fairy tale gives rise to some important questions that this book explores: Why did people not listen? Why was this woman isolated by her colleagues but also by others in the industry? Why is someone who is lauded as a hero allowed to be destroyed? The most important question is, why do we accept this story as more or less normal? Is there any other context in which a person providing such an obvious service to society would be left to suffer in this way? Through studying the experiences of people across the world who have been in this situation, I want to challenge this implicit acceptance of a story that is unacceptable, to rethink the way we perceive the individual at its core, and through this, to query the story itself.

I am a professor of management and organization studies. I am interested in organizations and particularly in how they affect our daily lives as employees and as citizens. My aim is to see whether new and innovative theories emerging in the field of organization studies might contribute to these questions.

Toward a New Theory of Whistleblowing

This book offers a unique perspective and contribution, one not yet found in existing studies of whistleblowing. In its chapters, I develop a novel approach to understanding people's experiences in their organizations and in wider society.

It is innovative for two reasons. First, it provides a new perspective on whistleblowing that challenges the current narrative by proposing that our accepted ways of perceiving whistleblowers focus too much on the whistleblower as an individual who acts alone. Academics, journalists, and advocacy groups all tend to describe her as a solitary actor struggling to achieve change. As the stories in this book illustrate, even whistleblowers themselves can unwittingly reinforce this view. These perspectives effectively stymie resistance to corruption in our institutions, not least because they discourage ideas of commonality and collective action. Therefore, it is vital that new theories of whistleblowing be developed. To this end, in this book I draw on critical organization theory, specifically the concept of affective recognition: a lesser-known but exciting perspective. Affective recognition helps open up our understanding of the self, seeing it as inherently connected to others rather than as autonomous and separate. This new concept of a radically social self offers us a way to see how the norms at work in the organizations and institutions that dominate our lives affect our sense of who we are. This has stark consequences both for whistleblowers and for people in contact with them.

This book is unique, second, because it features a detailed investigation of the experiences of financial sector whistleblowers in several countries. In doing so it moves away from previous studies of whistleblowing, which are largely quantitative and descriptive, and toward an approach based on in-depth, qualitative methods that yield a more nuanced understanding of people's experiences and enable new concepts to emerge. Viewing whistleblowing in this way sheds light on the famously ambiguous and poorly understood experience of speaking out, which is often accompanied by suffering and struggle. This analysis speaks to managers, colleagues, loved ones, and of course whistleblowers themselves by illuminating some of the complexities and ambiguities of their experiences. It offers a new way to understand whistleblowing.

Exploring Whistleblowing

This study began in 2010. As an Irish citizen, I was drawn to examining whistleblowing because I was outraged at what was happening to ordinary people because of misdeeds in global finance organizations. Two years earlier, like many countries, Ireland had been forced to pay out billions to rescue banks that had repeatedly misrepresented their balance sheets. Not just a little bit, an extra few euros on top of our taxes, but billions we would continue to pay for generations.[4] In Ireland the national pension fund was raided; money was taken from schools, health care, infrastructure, and many other services that had taken generations to build up. This meant a fundamental step back in the quality of life I was going to be able to provide for my children. The effects remain everywhere to be seen, as austerity economics have further widened the gap between rich and poor. Amid stories of friends who were emigrating and unlikely to return in the near future, close family members spending nights in hospital corridors on trolleys despite having paid for health insurance, and schools without the funding to mend a leaky roof in winter, I wanted to find out why this happened.[5]

Learning more about global finance and how cultures of complicity in its organizations contributed to the recent crisis, I became frustrated.

This was all the more difficult to bear because of the lack of evidence that anything was really changing in this industry. Despite talk of cultural reform, new laws, and tighter regulations, the sector retains many of the structural features that instigated the collapse; short-term incentives, outlandish salaries and bonuses, undue influence over political regulation, and a continuation of a rule-gaming approach.[6] It began to seem that as a society we were trapped in a cycle, tethered to a flawed yet powerful set of institutions that could call on us to pay their debts whenever their gambles failed to pay out.

One day I heard a radio interview with a man called Eugene McErlean, a soft-spoken Belfast native who was clearly unused to being in the spotlight. He described how, during his time at Allied Irish Bank in Dublin, he tried to speak up about business customers being ripped off and had been ignored. His story was part of a wider context of lax regulation of banks that ultimately was one of the leading causes of the financial crisis in Ireland and across the world. Realizing that there must be others like Eugene I wondered how I might learn more about them. I searched for people who had worked in financial services across the world, who had tried to speak out about the problems they witnessed, had been retaliated against and became known as a whistleblower.[7] From their stories, I learned about how difficult it can be to change problematic practices that are deep seated and systemic. I learned how intricate the cultures of such workplaces are: founded on strict rules of hierarchy, having a deep respect for money, and embedded in a society that tends to see banking as immune from interference because of its perceived importance.

So who are the whistleblowers I met? Mostly they are very ordinary people who have worked hard to forge a career in financial services. Some were in the United States, others in the United Kingdom, Switzerland, and Ireland.[8] Their roles varied: some advised wealthy individuals on where to invest their money, others arranged mortgages for ordinary people, and others sold credit card debt to collection agencies. I was struck by the similarities, despite the variety. Although the Cayman Islands are a long way from the cold Liffey waters reflected in the windows of the International Financial Services Center's buildings in Ireland, and although Texas and London lay thousands of miles apart, aspects of people's stories soon began to sound familiar. The majority of participants had been employed in watchdog roles; their formal job description involved finding and highlighting incidents of wrongdoing, whether this was as an internal auditor, a risk manager, a compliance officer, or an anti-money laundering officer. All occupied a senior position in their organization. Each whistleblower described witnessing significant wrongdoing and had attempted to raise the alarm, had not been listened to, and had begun to voice complaints outside the firm. A process then began in which the person found him- or herself isolated and stigmatized before being let go by the organization or forced to resign and finally becoming an outcast of the industry, unable to secure another job. There were similarities in people's situations too; it appeared that elements of a distinct global finance culture were shared and entrenched, in an industry spanning diverse countries and regions. This realization prompted the idea of putting these stories together—to try to show the richness and diversity in experiences and also the links between what whistleblowers had to say.

I was surprised at the outset by how difficult it was to find people who had spoken out but quickly learned that not everyone who does so welcomes the label whistleblower. Many people with whom I met explained that they were not in fact whistleblowers, although they had been called this name by lawyers and journalists. The notion of a whistleblower evokes the idea of someone who, during the course of doing a day-to-day job, observes some wrongdoing and then goes out of the way to raise awareness of it and stop it. In contrast, I was encountering people whose entire job description involved monitoring risk and safety. In some instances, they were legally bound by their regulatory authority to do this because signing off on unethical practices was illegal. The surprising thing is that they found themselves isolated, punished, and labeled whistleblower for simply trying to do the job for which they were being paid—for example, when they tried to alert senior management to practices that were risky or even fraudulent. Some participants told me that they rejected the label because of negative connotations it has gained in media reportage and in popular thinking; in many cultures, *whistleblower* has echoes of *informant* or *tattle-tale*.[9] Well-known tobacco industry whistleblower Jeffrey Wigand advocates using the phrase "person of conscience" instead.[10] At the same time, there are positive associations with the term; the Government Accountability Project, a leading U.S. advocacy group, uses the phrase whistleblower but defines it as representing "a person of conscience who uses free speech rights to challenge abuses of power that betray the public trust . . ."; they are insiders who speak up at great personal risk to themselves.[11] Other interviewees cited these kinds of interpretations and proudly called themselves whistleblower. Overall, however, whistleblowers in global finance were not easy to find.

There are simply not many people who speak out in this sector. We now know that, pre-2008, banks had significant problems and covered these up for years. Of course, the ideal scenario if you come across a problem in your organization is that you let your boss know, he or she deals with it effectively, and the problem is solved. The continual cycle of financial crises that includes what occurred in 2008 suggests that this does not always happen. Moreover, during the major scandals of the last twenty years, including AIG's insurance and accounting fraud in the United States, the Libor rate-rigging scandal, and the subprime crisis, the number of whistleblowers who came out to let the public know was negligible.[12] So where were all the whistleblowers? Surely plenty of people working in this industry objected and, when ignored, took their complaints outside the organization? Apparently not. Research tells us that people working in financial services are more likely than those in other industries to stay silent or even resign if they witness serious wrongdoing.[13] It is one of the most difficult industries in which to speak out for reasons explored later.[14] Financial services whistleblowers are scarce, which makes it all the more important to listen to what they have to tell us.

REPRESENTING THE WHISTLEBLOWERS

As an academic interested in organizational dynamics, my first step was to consult existing studies and theories to explore why people who speak up can find it so challenging to do so and why they are frequently stigmatized by others. These were very helpful for learning more about certain aspects of whistleblowing but did not always reflect the lived experiences of those I was meeting. I noted a tendency among researchers to reduce whistleblowing to sharply defined categories through the use of large-scale, quantitative studies. This approach is useful for putting numbers on aspects of whistleblowing—for example, the likelihood that whistleblowers will encounter retaliation given the kind of wrong-doing reported, their position in the organization, or their age. However, in this approach, the richness of people's experiences, which are surely complex and multifaceted, tends to be lost. Some researchers have used in-depth qualitative methods although detailed theorization of whistleblowers' experiences is rare.

Even within this body of whistleblower research, there remains a tendency to simplify and glorify this group of people. The familiar narrative of the whistleblower as a good and heroic individual who does the right thing and speaks up to challenge a clear wrong emerges in academic accounts as well as in popular culture, but amounts to a reduction of a complex process. Things seemed to be much less stereotypical once I began to meet with people who had found themselves in such situations. Certainly, all had a strong commitment to their cause and were incredibly brave in coping with retaliation that was sometimes brutal. I often felt in awe when listening to their stories, doubtful of whether, in the same situation, I would have the same resolve. However, they were not all good in that saintly, heroic mode that we see portrayed in Hollywood films but were, like us all, a mixture of dark and light, hope and bitterness, stoic with moments of weakness. Some were gruff, others dismissive of academics such as I for our apparent reluctance to actively intervene in real social problems. Yet others simply came across as a little bit broken, shaken, and regretful. I did not want to simplify their experiences after witnessing this complexity. Instead, it seemed important to build on existing research to see whether a richer approach was possible.

This led me to theories in organization studies that specifically examine contested and ambiguous identities, of which whistleblowing is certainly one. Deriving from critical theory, affective recognition compels us to rethink our idea of what a person is.[15] Rather than autonomous and separate, our selves are shaped both inside and out by desires to be recognized as worthy human subjects. These desires lead us to seek the affirming reflections found in the responses of others but also in aspects of social life, including the dominant social norms with which we live.

We identify with these aspects because they offer a sense of fulfillment and affirmation. This search continues, albeit often unconsciously, even when the identifications on offer cause us pain. As human subjects we are neither solitary nor autonomous; rather the boundary that we imagine between ourselves and others is porous, because we are constituted, through and through, by attachments to norms.

Affective recognition offers a deep and nuanced way of understanding how categories of identity, such as whistleblower or financial services professional, function in day-to-day life. It sheds light on how these are not neutral but can have powerful effects, not least because people form their identities in relation to dominant norms that exist in society—for example, becoming subjected to forms of power within global finance. Our organizations and the institutions that shape our lives have a strong grip on us, which we often cannot acknowledge or prefer not to. Making explicit these affective and desire-driven dynamics can, however, help explain the difficulties experienced by a whistleblower, where to speak out is to effectively threaten the institution that offers one a deeply desired sense of recognition. For the rest of us, our reliance on powerful organizations including those relating to global finance, for the control and certainty that they appear to promise, can perhaps lead us to abhor and reject those who challenge this protection.

These ideas have important consequences for whistleblowing; they help us understand the operation of our political and institutional structures, the cultural norms that maintain them, and the ways we might challenge these structures and norms. Only by highlighting that we are neither autonomous nor separate, and by no means in control of how we feel and how we live but are rather radically "other," can we begin to unpick these desires. We can start to question the institutional settings and scenes within global finance of which we are part and the repudiation of those who try to speak out. Affective recognition also shows how power can be productive; subjection can involve creating new categories of identity that people who speak out find comforting and helpful, and it can lead to the changing and subversion of existing ones. As will be seen throughout the book, different aspects of this theory help us understand some of the more subtle and lesser-known experiences of whistleblowing. They have some practical implications for how whistleblowers have been, and continue to be, perceived.

The book is set in the global finance industry, a sector that tends to privilege a relatively small subset of society and that has increasing dominance over our existence through the growth of financialization as a way of structuring social life.[16] Global finance repeatedly experiences cycles of boom and bust that are getting ever shorter.[17] In the last thirty years for example major events have included the savings and loan collapse of the early 1990s and the 2008 subprime mortgage crash. The busts are devastating, destroying people's wealth and wiping out the resources of whole cities and countries, and yet they continue. The 2008 crisis saw billions taken out of health services, schools, and the economy more generally.[18] This caused ongoing damage, including in the U.S. job market, where long-term unemployment rose fast.[19] Ordinary people in the United Kingdom ended up having to bail out their country's banks at an estimated cost equivalent to over £2,000 for every citizen.[20] In addition to wreaking this havoc, the relevant financial organizations failed their shareholders by promising long-term returns while behaving in ways that would ultimately destroy the value of their shares. Overall, global finance is a structure that veers from one collapse to the next, with some arguing that cycles of crisis are endemic to capitalist systems like ours. It is ordinary citizens who pay for each breakdown.[21] People are furious, and this anger is generally aimed at a generalized group of people, the bankers.[22] But some people working amid the toxic cultures of banking did try to stop the disasters from taking place.

The cases here are from among this group. For example, Eileen Foster's experiences at Countrywide were part of the very serious failures that led to the demise of Fannie Mae and Freddie Mac, which was at the center of the 2008 crash. Similarly, the story that features Paul Moore involved one of the largest UK bank collapses, Halifax Bank of Scotland (HBOS), in the credit crisis. Both whistleblowing incidents are of deep significance, for this sector and for each of us. Given their impacts, these events are pivotal in modern society.

Global finance is an interesting area for examining whistleblowing, not least because many aspects of this world actively work against employees speaking up. The 2008 financial crisis arose partly because of a new financial culture that had emerged in banking since the 1990s. This culture was known for its emphasis on short-term rewards, prioritizing profits at the expense of ethics, and perceiving rules as things to be gamed, obeyed only when they had to be.[23] These norms include specifically masculine ways of representation and behavior that echo the dominance of such approaches within global economic structures more generally. The culture was implicitly supported by organizations, regulatory authorities, and civil society, and it created the kinds of situations described throughout this book: well-known and reliable banks actively overselling loans to customers who were unlikely to ever repay, and selling products to people who did not need them. Toxic debts were parceled up and sold to sometimes unwitting others. The new financial culture was also known for its strong norms of complicity and silence that prevented people from speaking out.[24]

Ironically, even those who were paid to highlight problematic practices were prevented from doing so. As with any industry, financial services organizations employ people who act as safety valves. Working in risk, compliance, or audit roles, these individuals are tasked with spotting potential liabilities and alerting their organizations to them. As we will see, it was frequently impossible for them to do their jobs, even when mandated to highlight problems. The watchdogs were silent; the safety valve was not working—the system was broken. This dysfunctional situation did not threaten just the other stakeholders connected to the financial services industry; it threatened the organizations themselves, some of which were destroyed in the ensuing crisis. To understand what happened and how it might be prevented from happening again, it is vital to look at global finance from the perspective of those silenced watchdogs, of the would-be whistleblowers who tried to stop the last crisis.

Beyond global finance, the insights developed here can shed light on whistleblowing across a range of industries and settings. Whistleblowing is incredibly complex, often involving a lengthy process of trying to speak out and during which one's relationships shift and change—with one's organization, one's colleagues, and even one's self. Powerful elements, including the law and the media, influence this changing process. New theories such as affective recognition help make sense of this complexity. In exploring this, the book begins by detailing what has already been written from a scholarly perspective about whistleblowing in organizations, and I describe some areas for further development. Next, the new theoretical approach of affective recognition and concepts within it are introduced. After illustrating the context of global finance in more depth, the book then moves to presenting people's stories of speaking out in their organizations, highlighting the complexities and nuances of doing so, and weaving theoretical insights throughout to develop a new way of perceiving whistleblowing.

1

Speaking Out: What We Know

WHISTLEBLOWING RESEARCH is more than just an academic endeavor; it has wider relevance. Research findings can and do shape public debates. They feed into policies on whistleblower protection among others, both at national level and within organizations, and therefore have a tangible impact on people's lives. How we understand whistleblowers and what they do is important, and it is important to develop further.

Scholars approach the topic from perspectives as varied as political science, psychology, policy studies, law, and media studies. All tend to share the idea that a whistleblower is someone who discloses behavior that he or she believes to be unethical or illegal and generally agree that such individuals are important conduits for information about serious wrongdoing to come to light. After this, the commonalities are fewer.

This book takes an organization studies approach, drawing on research in the field of business and management studies. The study of organizations examines how people construct organizational structures and processes and how these shape the institutions that have such powerful influence over our lives and social relations more generally.[1] It is a vital perspective for understanding social settings, not least whistleblowing struggles, in which the tension between person, organization, and society takes center stage. In describing what has already been written in this area, it is helpful to think of three broad categories of research: studies of whistleblowing laws and policies and how these relate to organizations, descriptive approaches to whistleblowing in organizations that examine what happens when people speak out, and theoretical explorations of whistleblowing. As this chapter highlights, existing research is valuable but does not address the questions described earlier of why whistleblowing is so often unheeded, why those who engage in it suffer, and why this situation is accepted as more or less normal. Beyond some useful research reports, there have been few studies of whistleblowing in financial services organizations, and so I give examples from global finance throughout this book.[2]

Legislation and Organizational Policies

Much research in this area focuses on the legislative protections in place for whistleblowers, how they differ across countries, and their potential effectiveness. Without legal protections, whistleblowers are extremely vulnerable to being punished for speaking out and, as a natural consequence, will be less likely to do so. Of course, the result is that illegal and unethical practices may continue for years, unheeded.

Legal protections for people who blow the whistle have been in place in the United States since 1981 and have since been introduced in other regions.[3] These mandate that the whistleblower should be protected against retaliation and discrimination and that those who punish whistleblowers should be sanctioned. Unfortunately, whistleblower protection laws can fail to protect people who speak out for a variety of reasons.[4] Their implementation has, however, led to unintended consequences. These include organizations taking the initiative to change their internal disclosure policies rather than wait for something to go wrong, because of a fear of litigation. This has resulted in the reduction of whistleblower reports, because issues are addressed internally. It is not known whether perceived retaliation has increased or decreased since the introduction of whistleblower protection laws.

Another change in regulation involves the introduction of whistleblower reward, or bounty, schemes.[5] In the United States, for example, legislators revived Abraham Lincoln's False Claims Act, under which money is awarded to persons who give information to the U.S. government that will expose theft of government, and hence citizens', property.[6] The Securities and Exchange Commission now offers whistleblowers coming forward with information on fraud in financial services a percentage of the total recouped by the government after the successful resolution of a case, the IRS has a similar scheme for tax misconduct, and other sectors have recently introduced similar incentives.[7] Recent high-profile bounty recipients include UBS's Bradley Birkenfeld and Citi's Sherry Hunt, both of whom received significant payouts. This kind of scheme is currently being considered in other places, including the European Union. It is controversial, however, because the availability of a reward is seen to potentially compromise the motive of those who come forward to blow the whistle; the idea is that people who would not otherwise report will seek out opportunities to do so, to make money. In Europe, commentators frequently decry the inevitable stampede of bounty hunters that will result if such a reward is introduced. In reality, however, the number of claims that reach the first stage of investigation by the government is negligible, and success in the courts is even rarer. The presence of such laws does affect people's declared proclivity to speak up; in a 2015 survey of professionals in financial services, 90 percent of respondents indicated a willingness to report wrongdoing because of the Securities and Exchange Commission's protections and incentives. Equally striking were the similar numbers who would encourage a spouse or loved one to do this.[8]

Finally, new laws dictate that organizations must implement clear and usable processes for receiving reports of wrongdoing from employees.[9] Thus far, many organizations have operated under a de facto open-door policy, in which staff are advised that when they spot a misdemeanor, their concerns should be voiced informally to their line manager.[10] It has emerged that this is not enough, not least because of recent scandals in which employees were aware of serious problems and could have prevented disaster but did not feel comfortable raising the issue with their immediate boss.[11] For this reason regulatory bodies such as the Securities and Exchange Commission in the United States and the Financial Conduct Authority (FCA) in the United Kingdom have actively encouraged the organizations that they oversee to ensure that they put procedures and structures in place that encourage internal whistle-blowing.[12] In the UK financial sector specifically, the Prudential Regulation Authority, along with the FCA, requires that all deposit-holding institutions must have a senior employee who acts as a whistleblowing champion and receives reports of disclosures, and the National Health Service trusts require similar positions within the UK health sector.[13]

Moreover, organizations are increasingly aware of the advantages of implementing workable internal channels for reporting, and guidelines on how best to do this have been introduced.[14] Studies show that the presence of such speak-up arrangements yields more frequent disclosures by employees, particularly when multiple channels for raising a concern are available.[15] Even where these are in place, however, the implementation of new policies does not guarantee their adoption and use; speak-up arrangements within organizations have not always been successful.[16] Research into successful cases indicates that an organizational culture that does not invoke a fear of retaliation but rather supports employees in coming forward is essential if internal whistleblowing systems are to work properly.[17] A strong sense of trust between the discloser and recipient is vital.[18] More broadly, some critics argue that the institutionalization of whistleblowing through, for example, encouraging organizations to adopt internal channels deadens effective critique. For whistleblowing to have impact, for it to be heard and to make a difference, it must be outside existing systems and structures; it must provide a shock.[19] Anything else is merely institutionalized, impotent critique and not true whistleblowing. Recent analyses provide valuable recommendations of best practice in whistleblowing law, drawing on the experiences of the last thirty years or so.[20] Beyond a legal perspective, organizational scholars have long been researching the practice of whistleblowing itself.

Describing Whistleblowing in Organizations

Whistleblowers are few; most employees still fail to report observed wrongdoing.[21] Those who do are often studied using large-scale survey instruments. Such approaches dominate organizational whistleblowing research, and they typically examine how whistleblowing acts are influenced by variables, both organizational and individual.[22] They therefore study whistleblowing from a positivist, quantitative perspective and attempt to measure its prevalence and the contextual and structural features that accompany it. This has usefully shed light on many aspects of the topic.

LIKELIHOOD

Many scholars have examined how certain variables affect the likelihood of whistleblowing occurring. These include the nature of the industry; whether the organization is in the public, private, or nonprofit sector; the wider legislative framework in the country being studied; and whether the structural facilitation of whistleblowing is mandated in that country—for example, through formal speak-up arrangements.[23] Organization size influences the prevalence of employee disclosures, particularly in large multinational corporations, many of whom have policies in place even when the laws of the host country do not require them.[24] Features of the organization's formal structure are likewise seen as important: whether in-house organizational rules and procedures for speaking out exist and their nature and whether employee codes of conduct are in place.[25] Organizational culture is an important aspect, alongside the ethical climate that encompasses people's perceptions of the ethicality of their colleagues' and managers' decision-making processes.[26]

In addition to structure and culture, other variables more directly concerning the individual influence whether he or she raises a concern. Studies in this vein have focused on mapping the personal characteristics that whistleblowers present, with the aim of identifying exactly what kind of person blows the whistle in an organization. Early research into this area tended to focus on the distinct personality traits that make whistleblowers more likely to speak up.[27] Scholars have generally concluded that whistleblowers possess few common characteristics and thus there is little to be gained from this.[28]

Others have explored individual motivating factors; altruism is seen to be an important motive for blowing the whistle, as are religious convictions and the influence of past and future family relations, although research is as yet limited on these aspects.[29] Financial gain is cited as a reason to speak up, particularly in the United States, along with self-interest.[30] Often, and particularly relevant to this book, some employees work in jobs in which highlighting wrongdoing is part of the job description—for example, auditors, risk managers, and compliance officers.[31] As with research on organizational variables, although there has been significant focus on pinpointing the most prevalent motives, findings are typically ambiguous and mixed; for example, research evidence is lacking to show that whistleblowers speak out because of "moral reasoning or values," including faith-based ones.[32]

Nevertheless, there do appear to be particular contextual features pertaining to the individual that influences that person's likelihood to speak up, including his or her formal status within the organization's hierarchy and length of time in the firm.[33] A study in UK financial services showed that 37 percent of whistleblowers had been with their organization for two years or less.[34] Whistleblowers are often high-performing members of their organization prior to speaking up, and some studies find they are more frequently male, with higher levels of education and salary.[35] Another important influence is whether the whistleblower believes that he or she will be listened to, or initial expectations.[36] Many whistleblowers report beginning their journey with a naïve belief that once their boss or senior management hears their claims, they will be taken seriously and thanked for their efforts, even though they might meet with reprisal later in the process. The extent to which whistleblowers fear that they will bear the brunt of retaliation is an important influence on whether they are likely to report perceived wrongdoing. Although this research approach is important and interesting, it is very difficult and maybe even impossible to predict incidents of whistleblowing with any certainty. Moreover, each of the findings discussed earlier emerged from studies carried out in specific organizational, industry, and country contexts, and it is not always helpful to generalize.

PROCESS

Some researchers take a process approach, studying how whistleblowing incidents typically occur: what kinds of events happen between the initial spotting of the misdemeanor and the final resolution (or otherwise) of the issue.[37] On this view, it is important to see whistleblowing not as a one-off event that happens in isolation but rather as a sequence of interrelated incidents. Under a process perspective, the distinction between internal and external whistleblowing is important; the disclosure can be made either internally, to one's superiors in the organization, or externally, to authorities and groups outside.[38] This distinction has emerged as more complex in recent years, because the vast majority of external whistleblowers are known to have tried to speak up inside the organization to their direct manager, only moving outside when they did not perceive that the issue had been dealt with satisfactorily.[39] Research shows that nearly all external whistleblowing is, in practice, preceded by people speaking up internally within the organization: for example, a U.S. study reports that 97 percent of employees report internally first.[40] In any case, whistleblowing to external authorities is increasing; the FCA, for example, reported an increase in whistleblowing disclosures of over 800 percent between 2007 and 2015.

Renowned U.S.-based scholars of whistleblowing Janet Near and Marcia Miceli's early work focuses on modeling the process of whistleblowing to predict the likely stages that a whistleblower might encounter.[41] Building on this, Miceli and her colleagues propose that whistleblowing is a type of prosocial behavior aimed at enhancing the welfare of those it affects.[42] They describe a process encompassing varied stages of assessing a particular activity as the individual decides whether it is wrong and whether a decision needs to be made to speak up. Although this work has been influential among whistleblowing researchers, some argue that the process of whistleblowing is often too complex to model given that it involves many factors, such as the recipients of whistleblowers' disclosures and their subsequent responses.[43] Thus, it is important to see whistleblowing as not just something that the whistleblower does but rather as an interaction between the whistleblower and the person on the receiving end of the disclosure.[44]

RETALIATION

Whistleblowers can be subject to retaliations from others, including colleagues and managers.[45] This study is explicitly concerned with people who experienced retaliation. Whistleblower retaliation is defined as "undesirable action taken against a whistleblower—in direct response to the whistle-blowing—who reported wrongdoing internally or externally, outside the organization."[46] Research suggests that 18 percent of UK financial services whistleblowers contacting a whistleblowing charity had been dismissed after raising the issue for the first time. Although some research shows that the majority of whistleblowers are not retaliated against, other studies claim that it is common.[47]

A number of factors influence whether whistleblower retaliation is likely in a given situation.[48] People reporting an initial expectation that their immediate boss and those at the top of the organization will back them up are more likely to see their views heeded and less likely to be the subjects of reprisal. Retaliation is likely to be tougher and more oppressive when the observed wrongdoing is part of the day-to-day activities of the business; that is, when the very organizational practices are systemically illegal or unethical.[49] A widely used framework for understanding the likelihood of retaliation draws on the resource-based view (RBV) of the firm, a well-known management theory in which the comparable advantage of an organization depends upon the resources that it holds. Inspired by this scholars propose that retaliation will be proportional to the balance of power between whistleblower and wrongdoer.[50] Sources of power for whistleblowers might include their seniority or, otherwise, a formal role in which highlighting wrongdoing is mandated, and the support of their manager.[51] When the information held by the potential whistleblower is seen to be a serious threat to the organization—for example, if it relates to something that is potentially harmful to the public, to the legitimacy of the organization, or to its future performance—retaliation is more likely.[52] This is also the case when an external reporting channel is used.[53]

Types of retaliation vary, ranging from informal rejection and isolation by colleagues to situations in which the person is supervised very closely and micromanaged to create discomfort.[54] Privileges, such as access to the computer network, can be removed. The employee who has spoken out can be left with little autonomy and a work environment that is demoralizing. This is referred to as the "potted palm gambit."[55] More formal aspects of retaliation include being demoted or made redundant as a result of disclosing information about wrongdoing. In other instances, employees are referred to psychiatrists as a result of their disclosures.[56] Organizational retaliation can also involve the intentional prolonging of court cases ensuing from the speak-up incident as a means of depleting the whistleblower's resources, along with smear campaigns in the media with the aim of blackening the whistleblower's name. For these reasons, retaliation can be serious, leading to emotional problems, relationship breakdown, and financial struggles that last for years.[57]

Reasons for retaliation also vary; managers can perceive whistleblowers as a threat either to themselves or to their colleagues, and employers and coworkers alike can engage in reprisal in an effort to protect the reputation of the organization.[58] Retaliation can also be used to deter other potential whistleblowers in the organization and to publicly reinforce accepted norms of behavior and compliance, partly by isolating whistleblowers such that they become the subject of scrutiny and evaluation by coworkers.[59] In his well-known study of whistleblowing and how it relates to organizational power, C. Fred Alford draws on Michel Foucault's work on disciplinary norms to show how whistleblowers can be categorized as deviant, dangerous, and often mentally ill.[60] This effectively isolates whistleblowers from other employees, legitimizes retaliation against them, and helps control onlookers by discouraging them from speaking out.

PERSONAL IMPACT

Speaking out can have serious consequences for the whistleblower. For many, suffering continues long after they have left the organization in question or been fired.[61] Studies have found higher rates of anxiety, sleep difficulties, and depression among those who have reported wrongdoing.[62] Research into whistleblowing in nonprofit organizations shows that 84 percent of respondents "reported severe depression, anxiety, or general feelings of isolation" despite their being, prior to their disclosures, "generally high-achieving, respected, exceptionally committed members of their employing organization."[63] Whistleblowers whose names have become known can often find themselves informally blacklisted in their industry, struggling to find work in the area for which they have trained. Whistleblowing can lead to people losing their homes, paying for lengthy legal battles, and experiencing bankruptcy. Many end up with serious relationship problems, including marital breakdown.[64] Financial difficulties are common, associated with the loss of one's earning potential if blacklisted in the industry for which one has trained. The legal costs of pursuing a case can be crippling. For all these reasons, experts and academics tend to advise prospective whistleblowers of the importance of weighing their impulse to speak out against the potential reprisals they will face and the likely impact on their families.[65]

Not all research described here adopts a quantitative and positivist perspective; some draws on qualitative data, including interviews and observations. These enable a deeper understanding of how whistleblowers understand themselves and their experiences.[66] They usefully complement studies that focus on legal provisions and organizational policies, because they allow us to examine how these are enacted in practice. Typically presenting people's narratives one at a time, this body of work offers a detailed glimpse into people's lives, although in-depth theorizing around these stories and what they might mean is largely absent.

Theorizing Whistleblowing in Organizations

The approaches I have described are interesting and helpful. Often based on large-scale studies, they shed light on important areas of whistleblowing, including the prevalence of retaliation and the extent to which deep-seated, systemic corruption relates to the persecution of those who speak out. It is important, however, to broaden our understanding of whistleblowing. Theories are needed that highlight the rich and multi-faceted nature of this phenomenon as it is lived by people, to avoid an overall reductionism in scholarly approaches.[67] Some work is being carried out, and two major approaches are presented here. The first involves the question of why whistleblowers are perceived in such an ambiguous way: sometimes seen as heroes and other times as traitors. The second focuses on the whistleblower herself and how she experiences this ambiguity but speaks up regardless.

WHISTLEBLOWERS AND AMBIVALENCE

The ambivalence with which whistleblowers are perceived is an important area of research. It is seen as influencing the significant reprisals that can be experienced by people who speak up, and it contributes to the reluctance of others to do so. Opinion is famously divided on whistleblowers and their motivations. As a group, they are described as either "saints or rats."[68] For some, individuals who speak out represent "traitorous violators" of important organizational norms, including those of loyalty and secrecy.[69] They are therefore seen as somewhat suspicious individuals who have opted out of their commitments to their employer and to their colleagues. On this view, whistleblowing is perceived to be a "morally ambiguous activity."[70] For others, of course, whistleblowers are heroes who stand up for the interests of wider society when these are being compromised by their employing organization.[71] From this perspective whistleblowers are entirely correct in subsuming loyalty to the organization to honor more important values, including public health, environmental protection, or transparency in governance. They should be celebrated for doing this. Public perceptions of whistleblowing are therefore strongly linked to people's apparent reasons for speaking up: whether or not they can be deemed to have good or ethical motives at heart.[72] If a whistleblower reports on wrongdoing in his or her organization as an act of sabotage, say, or revenge on a boss or a coworker, this can be seen by some as problematic; it is not a valid motive, and therefore the whistleblower should not be taken seriously.[73] For others, the motive does not matter if the person's speaking up leads to a positive change for society.[74]

It is clear that whistleblowing is ambiguous, contentious, and poorly understood. In exploring why this is so, scholars propose that it is socially constructed—that is, interpretations of whistleblowing in any given time or place are based on other political, cultural, and economic forces; there is no objective truth of whistleblowing.[75]

As an example, perceptions of those who speak up are strongly linked to how their disclosures relate to dominant organizational norms and practices. For Nick Perry, whose 1998 article offers an innovative perspective on the position of the whistleblower within the organization, contemporary corporations operate under conflicting logics, and whistleblowers emerge as manifestations of these contradictions.[76] On the one hand, many organizations use scientific expertise and technological innovations in their work. These are considered fundamental forms of knowledge, in which something is either scientifically true or it is not or, in technology, it either works appropriately or it does not. There is apparently little room for manipulation of such knowledge by employees of the corporation. At the same time, however, organizations are intrinsically social systems involving networks of communication, relationships with powerful vested interests, and multiple personal agendas. Organizations are thus as dependent on rituals, myths, and ceremonies as they are on scientific and technical facts.[77] They operate under two different but equally important logics. This can place pressure on professionals to spin knowledge—for example, to manipulate how scientific results are presented or to selectively engage with rules of compliance: "the dilemma that such practitioners characteristically face is how to reconcile the perceived cognitive and technical necessities of their tasks with the social and political imperatives associated with their organizational positions."[78]

According to Perry, when employees find themselves caught between these competing logics, some refuse to betray what they perceive to be their professional responsibility to scientific truth or technological facts; they refuse to misrepresent the information. They opt out of engaging in the required myths and ceremonies and manipulating what they perceive to be objective truths. When such individuals find themselves forced to speak up about their refusal to cooperate, they are deemed whistleblowers. Perry points out that these people occupy a unique place within the organization because of their unwillingness to marry such organizationally important logics. They cannot simply be disregarded as other deviants might. They are seen as both valued professionals—masters of the science and technology on which the organization depends—and transgressors of essential organizational norms around how to behave. These whistleblowers represent a serious challenge to the prevailing logics of the organization: "not merely deviant but heretical, i.e. a challenge to the prevailing symbolic order, and through it to the social order itself."[79] It is for this reason that whistleblowers spark intense controversy and intense reactions.

Alford similarly sees perceptions of whistleblowers as influenced by their apparent fit with organizational norms and logics. He argues that whistleblowers elicit confusion and ambiguity because they have attempted to transgress organizational power, itself a significant force in today's society. For Alford, the organization is an autarky seeking total control over its internal environment, and whistleblowers potentially threaten this. In speaking out, they effectively step outside the prescribed "moral order," one that requires silence and acquiescence. Whistle-blowers are "inexplicable beings" from the perspective of the organization; they are "space-walkers," not of this world. The organization cannot tolerate such transgressions of its dominance and control, and it therefore attempts to destroy the whistleblower by any means possible. For Alford, whistleblowers' experiences of retaliation represent organizational power "in action."[80]

For Alford and Perry therefore, the ambivalence surrounding whistleblowers is a function of their perceived fit, or otherwise, with dominant organizational norms. Both suggest that the ambiguity of whistleblowers—variously perceived as committed professionals or as transgressors of implicit rules of silence—is premised on their lack of congruence with organizational logics and that this explains the extreme forms of retaliation that result from their actions. They are outside organizational norms and therefore inspire incredulity, misunderstanding, and suspicion. Building on previous research into whistleblowing, this suggests that the fate of the whistleblower not only depends on the laws that ostensibly protect her, and the organizational and personal variables affecting her situation, but also is inextricably interlinked with her position amid powerful norms.

These insights, although valuable, tend to remain at the level of the organization without examining the influences of other external institutions. We know, however, that whistleblowers are often not just radically excluded from their organizations, through isolation and sometimes redundancy, but cast out from their professions, with significant numbers unable to ever find work in their industry again. How to understand this broader exclusion of whistleblowers? That is the subject of this book's exploration. Building on the preceding approaches that focus at the level of organization and institution, it asks, what is the role of society in whistleblower exclusions? In addition this book is concerned with another level beyond the organization: the experiences of the whistleblower caught up in these contradictory logics.

THE WHISTLEBLOWER SELF

Scholars have called for a deeper examination of the person who discloses wrongdoing, adopting various theoretical and philosophical methods to analyze who the whistleblower is and why he or she speaks up, shifting the emphasis from the organization to the individual.[81]

In her novel analysis of whistleblowing, Alessia Contu argues that whistleblowers speak up not because they are compelled to do so by an external authority—for example, a god, a set of laws, or even a personal sense of "universal morality"—but because they experience a "pure desire" to follow through on an act of speech that is specific to a given situation and singular to the whistleblower; the act is one of "freedom" from the norms of consensus and conformity that surround them.[82] This, she argues, makes whistleblowing difficult to understand and difficult to generalize. She draws analogies between Antigone's famous self-sacrifice in the Greek tragedy and the plight of the whistleblower, noting that both characters eschew the influence of typical social norms in favor of a desire to act out a personal drive. Colin Grant likewise argues that whistleblowers do what they do not because of an adherence to universal morality but rather a "moral sensitivity that is peculiarly individual."[83] The act of whistleblowing often involves significant risk for the person who speaks out, therefore it is somewhat unintelligible in today's secular culture because it is seen as foolhardy. For Grant, whistleblowing goes beyond our mundane understanding of ethics as either adherence to universal moral principles or a "utilitarian" concern for others. Instead, it involves a spiritual realm akin to how the acts of biblical saints are described; whistleblowing involves a "single-mindedness through which the issue is posed with such crystal clarity for the whistle blower that there is no question abut what must be done"; this is a kind of "rugged individualism" through which the whistleblower experiences an intense personal challenge.[84] It is, Grant believes, more appropriate to understand whistleblowing in religious terms, as an extreme behavior that encompasses "radical self sacrifice." The only way to appreciate the true significance of whistleblowers is to see them as the "saints of secular culture" and to acknowledge the "respect and awe" that such acts deserve. They are different, he argues: "They stand out from the rest of us by such conspicuous courage and self-sacrifice."[85]

Returning to Alford's well-known study, he likewise theorizes about the nature of the person who speaks out. As do the preceding authors, Alford conceptualizes the whistleblower as a true "individual": a somewhat unique subject who is less constrained by group norms and a need to comply than are her colleagues.[86] Whistleblowers share some tendencies; first, they are people whose lives are based on constant engagement in "thought." Following Hannah Arendt, Alford conceptualizes thought as a continual dialogue with the self: an ongoing self-questioning of one's values, actions, and the impact of these.[87] For whistleblowers this is intertwined with a tendency toward "moralized narcissism," a concept for which he draws on Freud. Like all adults, whistleblowers are engaged in projects to sustain a coherent sense of self, or ego. For this group, however, it is essential that the self is moral; existence as a moral being is fundamental to whistleblowers. When this is threatened by their organization engaging in unethical practices, the experience is potentially devastating. It is for this reason, according to Alford, that whistleblowers will face even brutal retaliation to speak out about the wrongdoing they encounter and attempt to stop it; they are faced with a "choiceless choice" because their very sense of (moral) self depends on their actions. The act of whistleblowing becomes about "choosing the dread you will live for": the potential reprisals, "against the one you fear to die for" and the prospect of living a life that detracts from your core values.[88] The whistleblower is thus engaged in a struggle to reconcile her desires to be moral with the corrupt environment in which she finds herself.

In theorizing about the self, Contu, Alford, and Grant share an idea of the whistleblower as an individual striving for freedom to act on moral drives. These drives are particular to each person. This perspective emerges again in work that views the whistleblower as akin to the figure of the parrhesiastes from ancient Greece. Scholars draw on Foucault's interpretation of parrhesia as "free speech or frank truth-telling," adapting it for understanding organizational whistleblowing.[89] Parrhesia involves articulating the plain truth as one sees it. The person who engages in this practice is compelled to do so by a sense of moral duty.[90] For the parrhesiastes, her very sense of self is partially constituted by such truth telling; "as a mode of subjectivation, truth-telling enables the individual to establish a relation to a particular set of social norms and rules and to recognize himself as obligated to put them into practice."[91] Parrhesia is thus both an ethical practice and an identity position; the speaking subject comes into being through the process of engaging in parrhesiastic speech.[92] This practice often involves putting one's life at risk to speak the truth freely.[93]

For organization scholars, the idea of the whistleblower as a parrhesiastes is attractive.[94] It describes a compelling social identity for those who speak out. Parrhesia encompasses the risks that people experience, but the whistleblower as parrhesiastes also can be seen as a political actor. They speak truth to power freely and fearlessly and in doing so attempt to alter the status quo; they engage in political work. Seeing the whistleblower as a parrhesiastes allows commentators to move on from the ambiguity often associated with the category, in which they are seen as both heroes and traitors. Instead, an alternative, constructive, and theoretically grounded identity position is made available for this group of people. In addition, this concept fits with how the whistleblower self is described by Alford, Contu, and others; it emphasizes the person's compulsion to follow a particular, individual morality.

It is clear that a focus on the self of the whistleblower is important. We need to move beyond an explicit focus on the laws, organizational variables, and institutional logics previously described. Theories such as those presented here are helpful in exploring this. This brings us toward a more holistic understanding of whistleblowing, which attends to how people are positioned amid organizational norms but also how this plays out at the individual level. Some potential concerns emerge, however.

First, theories such as these tend to share the assumption that whistleblowers are extraordinary hero figures. Even authors who explicitly aim to dig more deeply and offer alternative ways of understanding whistleblowing experiences can replicate this problem. For example, Alford's framing of the whistleblower as a resister of organizational power ultimately points to a type of person who is unique, with a specific psychic makeup of moralized narcissism. Whistleblowers are, he notes, "sacred: blessed and cursed with a terrible knowledge."[95] They are highly unusual, individual, and driven, a depiction that is echoed by other approaches previously described, including those drawing on Foucault's notion of parrhesia. A problem emerges here because very few practical supports are available from society for those who speak out about wrongdoing and are fired from their organizations for doing so. Such individuals face significant personal, health-related, and financial pressures, and they are often left to suffer alone, despite having often risked their livelihoods by acting in the interest of the public. Academic research such as that described earlier, although helpful and nuanced, leads to what Perry terms "undue voluntarism" in depictions of whistleblowing, because it emphasizes the extraordinary autonomy, singularity, and freedom of the whistleblower.[96] This positions her as being quite different from ordinary people, somewhat superhuman, and therefore not in need of the kinds of supports that might be offered to others in a similar situation. Stereotypical classifications of heroic whistleblowers, even when these are theoretically rich and insightful, are unhelpful.[97]

A second issue is that current theoretical approaches effectively reinstate the widely recognized narrative of the trapped and tragic whistleblower introduced at the start of this book. Alford, Grant, and others continually invoke the notion of self-sacrifice, implying that there is little escape from organizational power and that the whistleblower will likely always fail in her struggle. They repeat and reinforce the classic tale of the whistleblower as a victim who battles the powerful organization and suffers as a result. There is a sense of fatalism inherent in this kind of theorizing; it implies that this is how it must be for whistleblowers. Even as they problematize accepted ideas around whistleblowing, academic commentators are often nonetheless tempted into reinforcing this sad story. This may be because of the romanticism that is associated with whistleblowing; describing whistleblowers as brave strugglers against organizational tyranny allows deskbound researchers the pleasure of vicariously participating in the sagas they portray.[98] The situation is further complexified by many whistleblowers themselves adopting these widely recognized cultural tropes of tragic, suffering hero when describing their own activities. For both researcher and whistleblower, it is easy to slip into these ways of thinking and describing, drawing on the frameworks and phrases that are commonly available to us.[99]

This is problematic because it reinforces the current situation that plagues whistleblowing. Stories of brutal retaliation against this group are now more or less accepted. Reprisals are denounced by media commentators and advocacy groups of course, but they continue nonetheless, and almost twenty years of antiretaliation legislation has not made much difference. Rather, we now have a situation in which "whistleblowing is partially protected by law but, nonetheless, is likely to be penalized with impunity."[100] The status quo is therefore that whistleblowers *will* be retaliated against, they *will* suffer, and laws will continue to fail to protect them. This state of affairs continues, and it effectively institutionalizes the tragedy of the whistleblower. Even the nuanced theoretical and philosophical proposals described earlier do little to change this.

Toward a New Understanding of the Whistleblower

In my research into financial sector whistleblowing, the studies described earlier were helpful for making sense of many aspects of people's experiences. They show the influence of macro forces, including laws, organizational structures, and the cultural norms within them. They shed light on what was happening at the level of individuals I met and how they were experiencing the struggles in which they were engaged. Even so, I was drawn to exploring whether it might be possible to further build on these theories in order to understand some emergent issues that seemed important.

How are individual whistleblowers affected, day to day, by these macro level influences, whether laws or norms? What are the dynamics by which they engage with the powerful institutional structures in which they are embedded? We know that whistleblowers are retaliated against, but what fuels the extreme and vitriolic nature of some reprisals, and how do whistleblowers survive such attacks? Finally, is the fate of the whistleblower predetermined, as suggested by classic narratives, or can it be altered?

To answer such questions, new ways of understanding the whistleblower are required and have been called for by leading authors in the field.[101] These would ideally highlight the contradictory and indeterminate nature of whistleblowing. They would not merely take the point of view of the whistleblower but would also account for how they are positioned amid wider social, economic, and political structures. They would show how macro and micro levels of social life intertwine and go beyond the organization to do so, thus viewing whistleblowing incidents as "constituted in and through the social order that generates them, the discourses that articulate them and the subject positions which realize them."[102] Building on the valuable research that has already been carried out in this area, such an approach would offer a valuable contribution to the study of organizational whistleblowing. It would enable us to perceive whistleblowers as complex, nuanced selves rather than clichéd, tragic heroes. In what follows, the potentially fruitful concept of affective recognition, emerging from critical theory approaches to organization studies, is described.

2

Whistleblowing: The Subject and Power

IN CARRYING OUT the research for this project, I heard many stories of how people had attempted to speak out about perceived wrongdoing in their organizations and been retaliated against for doing so. I could not help but feel shocked at the level of suffering to which people were subjected, often for simply doing their jobs. Here was power and domination at work, as organizations and institutions exerted their influence to silence individuals who posed a threat. It was important to me to understand how this power operated and how it was apparently shaping people's experiences, the lives of their families, and their very sense of self. Extant theories of whistleblowing were helpful but lacking, and so I was drawn to an emerging area of organization studies that takes inspiration from critical and psychoanalytic approaches to highlight the importance of affective recognition. On this view, our selves are founded on desires to be recognized as valid and legitimate. These desires compel us into complex attachments with dominant discourses in society, in our organizations, and in our institutions. The attachments are experienced affectively. As yet a niche approach, affective recognition is ideally placed to speak to the issues emerging from this study because it explores how and why people's lived experiences are influenced by structures of power both within their organizations and beyond. It highlights the complexity of such experiences and sheds light on why certain people can be deemed heretical and worthy of punishment and expulsion, as whistleblowers frequently are. It shows how desire shapes the ways people perceive whistleblowers and how they perceive themselves. Affective recognition therefore offers the potential to valuably add to our current understanding of whistleblowing.

Affective recognition is a concept that builds on the work of Michel Foucault, lately an influential author in critical organization studies, and that of philosopher and gender theorist Judith Butler, who valuably advances Foucault's ideas. Specifically, affective recognition draws on Butler's account of subjectivity as she has developed it over the last twenty-five years. Butler's approach is widely considered among the most significant contributions to social theory of this period, noted for its elegance in analyzing, critiquing, and destabilizing what we take for granted, including our assumptions about who we are as individuals.[1] Neither Butler nor those who engage with her work tend to use the specific term *affective recognition*. For the purpose of this study it usefully draws together aspects of her long engagement with poststructuralist, feminist and psychoanalytic theory to show how we as subjects are formed by, and formative of, power. Engaging precisely with the questions posed in the preceding, affective recognition enables an exploration of broader institutional and structural forces while also highlighting how these influence and are influenced by the day-to-day practices of people, alongside the contradictions and paradoxes that often result. In short, affective recognition links the micro level of the individual with macro considerations of power and domination in a nuanced and thoughtful manner. Of late, it has valuably informed a wide range of studies into subjectivity and power in organizational settings and shed light on labor conditions under capitalism, including precarious work.[2] In what follows, aspects of this theory are described. Norms are viewed as changing, and contingent, while people subject themselves to these norms in search of a stable sense of self through desire for recognition. There is a dark side to these dynamics; recognition can cause injury and pain to those left outside, and violence can result when certain outsiders find themselves in an abject position. Even as this occurs, normative structures are neither absolute nor determined but are continually open to subversion. Affective recognition has not yet been drawn on in the context of whistleblowing.[3]

Contingent Norms

Norms, or shared ways of behaving that are implicitly expected, are ubiquitous in social life. A classic example is the norm of the schoolroom; in a classroom setting most people will sit down and be quiet until told otherwise. What makes this happen is a set of shared assumptions about the particular context: the classroom and the behavior that is expected. This manifests in an implicit agreement to behave in a normatively required manner. Alongside shared ways of behaving, we have shared understandings of particular concepts, or categories, including categories of persons. These come with implicit assumptions about what it means to be a member. So when we encounter, for example, a teacher, a banker, or indeed a whistleblower, we might have certain assumptions about these people because of the label that comes with them.

Both Foucault and Butler are interested in normative categories, in unpacking and then questioning both the categories and the associated assumptions.[4] Butler asks why, when we encounter someone we associate with the label woman, do we tend to assume links with femininity, motherhood, and compassion? Why does this happen? What are the implications for the people associated with this category, either willingly or otherwise? Do these assumed attributes of a category relate to some sort of essential, foundational aspect of the self of the person in question?

Rather than seeing normative categories as stable and constant over time, under this view they are in fact contingent; a norm depends on how it is constituted within the particular social, historical, and cultural context in which it operates. The category woman is not an objective concept whose meaning remains the same at all times; rather, the understanding of this label intersects with "racial, class, ethnic, sexual and regional" discourses.[5] What it means to be a wealthy white woman in twenty-first-century Britain, for example, is vastly different from its meaning for someone living three hundred years ago in the slums of London. This means that it is "impossible to practically separate out 'gender' from the political and cultural intersections in which it is invariably produced

Coolanowle
Organics Ltd
Coolanowle
Ballickmoyler
Laois

TE?
M

BATCH:
INVOICE:
Date: 22
Time:
RRN:
AUTH NO:
AID: A0000000
APP: Visa D   t
TC: 7.3   09

TOTAL   35 UR

---CUS---

and maintained."[6] For any given category of person therefore, the task is to examine such intersections and see the different ways they inform the meaning of the normative category. The concept of discourse helps unpack this.

DISCOURSE

Power emerges and is sustained through accepted forms of knowledge and taken-for-granted truths, and Foucault uses the term "power/knowledge" to describe this. Categories, including categories of persons, are examples of power/knowledge in action.[7] Consider the way gender operates as an important category in society. Why do cultures all over the world see gender as so central? Why, for example, on the birth of a child, do people rush to ask whether it is a boy or a girl before seeking other information? Why is the male-female division the most common box to tick in public records? Surely there are other categories that could conceivably take priority. This elevation of gender is no accident; governments, and society more generally, are invested in ensuring that gender remains a primary category. Clearly distinguishing between males and females is necessary to support and uphold various social norms including patriarchy, phallocentrism, and "compulsory heterosexuality," all of which are important for the economic survival of the nation-state.[8] The overall pattern describes a particular discourse of gender distinction, in which *discourse* refers to "ways of constituting knowledge, together with the social practices, forms of subjectivity and power relations that support these."[9] The point is that many of the categories of person that we take for granted are neither neutral nor objective but embody particular interests and agendas. In one of the first studies to introduce Butler's work to organization studies, Professor Nancy Harding valuably draws on these ideas to interrogate the subject positions offered to practicing managers by business school textbooks published since the 1950s. She shows how discourses of law, rationality, and modernity, among others, "impregnate the language of management" within such texts with the promise that the use of management language will keep chaos at bay.[10] This compels readers to adopt particular managerial subject positions and Harding describes how this reinforces the dominance of the underlying discourses. In the cases of whistleblowing featured in this book, examples of influential discourses include ideals of professionalism in the sphere of global finance. Upheld by organizations, institutions, and wider society, such discourses tend to be taken for granted and can work in the interests of certain privileged groups.

SUBJECTION TO DISCOURSE

If we are to understand how problematic discursive categories continue to be maintained, despite their inherent contingency, it stands to reason that we should examine who it is upholding them day to day and why they do so.

Power is fundamental in the formation of individuals; it structures who we are and how we are seen by others. We come to occupy "subject positions" that are created and enabled by discourses of power, and because power is prior to our existence, the person cannot be thought of outside of her occupancy of such positions. This process, known as subjection, in turn shapes discourse. Power emerges as the outcome of the actions of a vast and dispersed network of people, whose practices of subjection cumulatively reinforce dominant discourses.[11] The subject position is thus a "structure in formation," a "site" that is occupied by individuals.[12]

Just because power relations influence the norms and categories we use in daily life does not mean that there is some person or group of persons who deliberately manipulates us. No central locus determines and defines dominant norms; they remain in use only so long as people adopt them and identify with the categories they yield.[13] Without this activity a norm would disappear. In the cases of whistleblowing described here, well-known whistleblowers subject themselves to powerful discourses to do with professionalism in banking as they articulate their positions. This in turn reinforces the influence of these kinds of knowledge.

Toward the end of his life, Foucault became interested in how the actions of people contribute to the reproduction of powerful norms that govern social life, such as norms of heterosexuality.[14] Despite his interest, he was "notoriously taciturn" on how and why this occurs, and so, to further develop his ideas on power, Butler takes up this question.[15] She draws on ideas from gender theory and particularly psychoanalysis to do so, because, she notes, any "account of subjection" that aims to understand why people identify with powerful norms "must be traced in the turns of psychic life."[16] By this she means that the psyche is always already inscribed by discursive power and the norms that accompany it. People cannot exist, socially, without the categories that offer them a place in the world. Her early work focused on subjection to discourses of gender, race, and sexuality and yielded robust and insightful ways of approaching subjection more generally. Following Butler, therefore, the *person* refers to an entity representing the meeting point or intersection of a variety of subject positions adopted at a given point in time. In her writing she refers to this entity as the subject.

It is important to unpack the dominant categories we use: to understand them as manifestations of power that are ultimately contingent. This enables us to continually problematize aspects of life we may take for granted, as Foucault recommended.[17] There is a further reason to do this. Real suffering can occur because of the ways particular categories operate, especially when people are invested in them and constituted by them. Powerful norms dictate the very "terms through which subjects are recognized," thus delineating which groups of people are deserving of recognition and who should be left outside.[18] This is described in detail next.

Ek-static Recognition

Why the attachment to these discursive categories? Can we not simply decide to opt out? As it turns out, we are intelligible as valid persons only when we can be recognized as subjects of particular dominant norms.[19] That is, we come into being under their terms. Building on insights from Lacan and Foucault through her engagement with Hegel and Spinoza, Butler argues that occupancy of legitimate subject positions is essential for our survival: "Our lives, our very persistence, depend upon such norms, or, at least, on the possibility that we will be able to negotiate within them [and] derive our agency from the field of their operation."[20] In the absence of this possibility of recognition, we are denied a valid position in social life: we become "impossible beings," nonexistent and irrelevant.[21] The "impossible" subject experiences itself as excluded, other to itself.[22] To be threatened with the denial of recognition, of a valid ontological status, is catastrophic, and people will avoid this at all costs.

This points to the power of norms and can help us understand the difficulties experienced by those who find themselves excluded from them, including those possessing a gender that does not fit the standard, male-or-female binary that is frequently insisted on by powerful structuring elements including law, psychiatry, and even social theory. The idea is particularly helpful in understanding the complex journeys undertaken by whistleblowers in global finance; industry norms provide a valued source of recognition, even for whistleblowers who openly critique the organizations and systems within which they work. This makes it incredibly difficult to go against these norms: to speak up, to risk exclusion, and to become "impossible."

What is the nature of the person who desires recognition in this way? Following the ideas presented in the preceding, categories of person, such as woman, are not essential, inevitable aspects of some inner self. Butler argues against the problematic concept of the autonomous independent individual that tends to persist in social theory and in practice. Its prevalence promotes a false sense of separateness from the other and ignores our mutual constitution as subjects. Instead, she offers a concept of the subject as ek-static. We depend on particular norms to exist socially, norms that are maintained through continuous reproduction by the actions of many diverse people in their mundane practices.[23] This means that what we might believe to be an "inner" psyche cannot be seen as separate from the social and political "outside" world.[24] Rather, the two are mutually constitutive because language is at the center of human existence and spans both the psyche and the social.[25] One's sense of self is not one's own; for example, "the terms that make up one's own gender are, from the start, outside oneself, beyond oneself in a sociality that has no single author."[26]

Of course, this turns the accepted perception of what a self is on its head. The subject is "radically external"; "power that at first appears as external, pressed upon the subject, pressing the subject into subordination, assumes a psychic form that constitutes the subject's self-identity."[27] Norms and discourses that might otherwise be presumed to exist on the "outside," external to the subject, shape what is perceived to be the "internal" psyche. Our persistent desire for recognition as valid means that to exist at all is to exist as a subject of power and thus to be "cast, always, outside oneself, Other to oneself."[28]

To say that the desire to persist in one's own being depends on norms of recognition is to say that the basis of one's autonomy, one's persistence as an "I" through time, depends fundamentally on a social norm that exceeds that "I," that positions the "I" ec-statically, outside of itself in a world of complex and historically changing norms.[29]

We actively desire recognition, but psychic investment in normative structures also takes place unconsciously and prior to our awareness of it, because we can only be known, and know ourselves, as subjects of discourse. In summary, Butler's person is a subject of power, who is neither agentic nor determined by structure, but rather driven by a power-inscribed psyche that emerges through patterns of past desires that have been variously fulfilled or thwarted. It is the meeting place of discourse, the "congealment" of former identifications and of losses that affect, but do not determine, the subject's psychic landscape.[30] This ek-static subject is not fully determined by the norms that offer recognition because the self is in a process of continuous transformation.[31] It is never the same at two successive points in time (as I describe later). Each encounter with an other transforms the subject in some small way; both subject and other are "cast forth into an irreversible future." Thus, the ek-static subject is always "at a temporal remove from its former appearance," albeit these temporal changes can be subtle.[32] These ideas have inspired scholars interested in understanding how employees in a variety of organizational settings, find themselves radically outside themselves: constructed in and through dominant forces within their places of work.[33]

Norms That Injure

In some cases, identification is painful. Even when we acknowledge problems and contradictions with a particular subject position, we can find ourselves compelled into subjection regardless; "Called by an injurious name, I come into social being, and . . . I am led to embrace the terms that injure me because they constitute me socially."[34] Our identifications with norms can therefore be ambivalent: our need for recognition forces us into what Harding calls a kind of "tug of war," in which desires for conformity and fear of exclusion confront a need to avoid hurt.[35] Unfortunately, we often have no option for escape; to exist socially is to depend on norms and therefore to depend on those others who confer them. The alternative is "symbolic extinction," and so it is sometimes preferable to "exist in subordination" than not to exist at all.[36] Thus, because of psychic subjection, even problematic and hurtful norms persist. Affective recognition has a painful side.

Within organization studies these ideas have been used to show how employees negotiate organizational norms, finding new ways of occupying subject positions even as they are injured or undone by expectations of how they should be and act.[37] Tyler studies the "dirty work" in which sex shop workers engage, finding that they experience stigmatization and a devalued sense of self because of the moral taint associated with the industry.[38] At the same time, however, the workers also attempt to undo their subjection to norms of gender, whenever they emphasize the novelty and potential of working in a sexually diverse culture and enable others to express themselves through transgressing norms. In addition to a focus on gender and sexuality, scholars show how other kinds of norms operate in organizations to circumscribe and define accepted subject positions around aging, ethical working, and management practice, highlighting how these can both affirm a person's sense of self and negate it, causing pain.[39]

SUBJECTION AND EXCLUSION

In addition to this compulsion to subjectify ourselves to norms that injure, there is a further dark side to the psychic life of power that fuels affective recognition. The construction of a subject position often takes place at the expense of those others who are excluded in the process. Butler draws on ideas from feminist philosopher and psychoanalyst Julia Kristeva and from anthropologist Mary Douglas to explore this. In *Purity and Danger*, Douglas studies the meanings of dirt in different times and places, in which dirt is considered any "matter out of place."[40] She is interested in the distinctions that are made between clean, unclean, and sacred. Douglas points out that societies uphold a notion of purity through rigidly separating themselves from those considered to be pollutants, or dirt. "A polluting person is always in the wrong. He has developed some wrong condition or simply crossed over some line which should not have been crossed and this displacement unleashes danger for someone."[41] Clear boundaries are marked out along the line that "must not be crossed." The expelling of those impure others helps the society itself cohere around a shared understanding of what is happening, yielding a strong sense of unity.[42]

Inspired by these ideas, Julia Kristeva develops her concept of abjection through reading Douglas's ideas via Freud and Klein to better understand subject formation.[43] Abjection refers to separating one's sense of self from an aspect of the self that causes horror and is deemed intolerable (the abject). The abject represents the "impossible within."[44] Specifically, Kristeva argues that early development in a human child requires initiation into the world of language, norms, and symbols, or the Lacanian symbolic order. Here, the law of the father dominates, and the maternal remains outside and excluded.[45] The maternal thus haunts the border of the symbolic, in a taboo non-place that is neither thinkable nor tolerable. Evoking feelings of disgust and repulsion, the subject feels compelled to repel this abject maternal, despite it representing an inescapable part of her psychic makeup. The body of the mother is thus rejected. For Kristeva, therefore, the development of the subject is founded on the exclusion of the maternal body and the resultant boundary between the self and this abject figure. The feelings of toxicity and disgust that emerge come to be projected onto other elements in the symbolic, including other people and groups. These entities are relegated to a place of non-existence within the terms offered by the symbolic.

These ideas from Kristeva and Douglas inform Butler's account of how the formation of the subject can be accompanied by a casting out of repudiated others. She analyzes contemporary forms of homophobia and sexism, arguing that certain sexualities and gender positions are deemed to be dangerous, a polluting force that threatens the norm.[46] Not quite lives, those in such groups exist in a shadowy state of suspension. For Butler, these dynamics of exclusion can be fueled by melancholia.[47] Early attachments to non-normative ways of being (homosexuality in a culture in which it is taboo, for example, or non-binary gender identifications) become subsumed and repressed as one moves into adulthood and is compelled to conform with acceptable norms (e.g., heterosexual identifications and "normal" ways of doing gender). In such cases, it becomes imperative to separate oneself from those who represent the disavowed identification. The subject continuously strives to "discover and install proof of that difference." His "wanting will be haunted by a dread of being what he wants, so that his wanting will also always be a kind of dread"; to overcome this dread, he continually reinforces the boundary. "What is repudiated and hence lost is preserved as a repudiated identification," and thus the subject works hard to deny this connection.[48] These early identifications therefore never leave the subject but persist in the unconscious as a melancholic incorporation: a deeply held but "disavowed" grief for what one has once loved but has now lost.[49] Melancholia is therefore an effect of power; the subject must engage in active and aggressive refusal of these earlier attachments. Butler analyses displays of homophobia and sexism from this perspective. One effect of melancholia involves the subject's turning back on itself, berating the self for failing to live up to normative ideals. A second effect is the resultant strengthening of the boundaries around dominant norms and the concomitant exclusion of others. In the example given here, heterosexual norms (and norms relating to gender) are all the more entrenched because they are constructed and upheld through melancholic incorporations. Ensuring the continued repression of these incorporations means excluding the others that represent them.

This framing also sheds light on racism. Contemporary Western subjectivities can be, Butler argues, premised on exclusions of certain non-Western others, exemplified by the way Muslims were inexplicably vilified amid recent antiterrorist hype in the United States and Europe.[50] In an earlier example she cites the lives lost from AIDS in Africa, arguing that these were more or less ignored by Western media because of this dynamic.[51] These cast-out others occupy a "zone of uninhabitability," a site of "dreaded identification," that is both feared by the subject and constitutive of it.[52] In the context of organization studies, Harding's work on the discourses of management found in textbooks highlights how the language of management that such books espouse "brings into being subject positions that depend for their existence, ultimately, on abjected and subjected others."[53] These insights help explain a somewhat awkward finding within the accounts of whistleblowers I present here: for many, constructing a sense of self as a true whistleblower involved a sometimes stark othering of those colleagues who also witnessed wrongdoing but who stayed silent.

Ironically, of course, these abjected others are essential to the constitution of the subject; a norm relies on expelled non-subjects to sustain itself.[54] Representing the conditions of possibility for the subject to come into being, these impossible entities "form the constitutive outside to the domain of the subject."[55] As Butler points out,

> If construction produces the "domain of intelligible bodies," must it not also produce . . . a domain of unthinkable, abject, unliveable bodies? This latter domain is not the opposite of the former, for oppositions are, after all, part of intelligibility; the latter is the excluded and illegible domain that haunts the former domain as the spectre of its own impossibility, the very limit to intelligibility, its constitutive outside.[56]

Again we see a blurring and questioning of the distinction between self and other. Because the other is instituted through expulsion of what is disgusting within the self, those "excremental passages in which the inner effectively becomes the outer," the border between us and them, is not as clearly defined as we might have presumed.[57] For Butler, the commonly accepted boundary is merely "tenuously maintained for the purposes of social regulation and control."[58] Instead, the abject is within the self—it is essential to its very formation. Not easily cast off, a remainder is always present. Butler draws on psychoanalytic insights to understand how this manifests in the subject's "engaged preoccupation" with the abjected other, that which represents the "most debased and defiled" about itself.[59] The subject finds itself locked into a continual struggle to repel this aspect of the self that it cannot accept, a struggle that is ultimately futile. Thus, paradoxically, the cast-out other must be kept close; it represents a "most treasured source of sustenance," vital for the subject's very existence.[60] Even so, the impulse to repel the other need not always result in their exclusion. It is possible for us to acknowledge deep-seated aggression that appears to be part of our constitution as subjects, but yet find other more integrative ways of being in relation to this other, as described in Butler's recent work.[61]

Scholars of whistleblowing have long sought to explain the visceral antagonism that people who speak out seem to evoke in others, a reaction that often seems disproportional and unfair given their apparent motivation to simply correct a wrong. This antipathy can be shown not only by colleagues but also by complete strangers. As will be explored later, the concept of abjection helps us see how the figure of the whistle-blower might represent for others an idealized childhood self that once enjoyed a purer sense of right and wrong. This notion must be repressed to ensure the survival of the powerful entities that represent a treasured source of identification for so many of these onlookers: the organizations and institutions of global finance.

CENSORSHIP AND IMPOSSIBLE SPEECH

In her book *Excitable Speech,* Butler extends her work on recognition to considering speech acts: what makes some acceptable and others not so.[62] Censorship acts as a matrix of control; it constrains people from uttering certain kinds of speech, but it also produces categories of subjects: those that engage in "legible" speech under the dominant "norms of speak-ability" and those that must be excluded because their speech is consid-ered unacceptable and "impossible." Censorship therefore produces boundaries that distinguish viable "candidate(s) for subjecthood" from others who cannot be recognized. Their illicit speech is deemed to be "precisely the ramblings of the asocial, the rantings of the 'psychotic,'" and the culprits are excluded from viable subjectivity.[63] In this way "cen-sorship produces the parameters of the subject."[64] These ideas inform discussion of how hate speech proliferates and, in the context of organ-ization studies, for example, how certain styles of leadership are accept-able and others are not.[65] From speaking with whistleblowers, I found that global finance norms give rise to certain kinds of acceptable sub-jecthood. Through engaging in speech about corrupt practices that were known about by many in their organizations but rarely discussed, people transgressed these norms, and their statements were deemed illicit. The result was a denial of recognition for these transgressive speakers, which was often violent.

VIOLENCE

More recently, the ideas encompassed in the concept of affective recog-nition have been used to understand how violence emerges in various forms—specifically, how violence is legitimized against the other who has been excluded.

It is important to note that this approach differs from other theorizations about violence against an other; it is not simply about oppression of another subject but something more fundamental; "to be oppressed means that you already exist as a subject of some kind . . . but to be unreal is something else again. To be oppressed you must first become intelligible."[66] The shadowy others that occupy the zone of unintelligibility Butler describes are unreal. They are not considered human: they cannot speak as such, and they cannot be recognized as such. Violence against this shadowy figure, the non-subject that haunts the boundaries of accepted norms, is easily justified because this figure has already been symbolically excluded and repelled. Violence against "those who are not quite lives . . . leaves a mark that is no mark." This is because, ultimately, "there have been no lives, and no losses" and "no common physical condition, no vulnerability that serves as the basis for an apprehension of our commonality."[67] There is neither acknowledgment nor recognition, and so violence is not seen as violence. This insight has helped inform critiques of organizations and their role in social violence. Butler has inspired discussions of corporate violence in developing countries, with a recent study showing how the Coca-Cola corporation utilized social and discursive processes of "derealization" of the inhabitants of an Indian town, such that their lives were deemed "ungrievable" and violence against them was accepted by observers.[68] In addition to sometimes extreme violence that whistleblowers experienced as a result of engaging in illicit speech, this book highlights another aspect: self-violence on the part of those who, despite having left their organizations and being in dispute with them for long afterward, remain deeply attached to them and to the norms therein. These norms include prescribed silence in the face of wrongdoing and the attendant exclusion of those who do not comply and speak up regardless. Paradoxically, whistleblowers are themselves not immune, because of their deep-seated organizational attachments. They can internalize this normative rejection. Such aggression, turned inward, can lead to painful and anxiety-inducing struggles around one's sense of self-coherence. It can yield continual self-questioning about whether one has done the right thing. Butler's ideas on guilt and violence shed light on these complex and painful experiences.

Throughout her work, Butler asks whether the unreal subject can resist this designation, altering the symbolic, or whether resistance is merely subsumed and incorporated by the dominant order. She draws on political challenges by those occupying new gender positions to show how something powerful can occur when the unintelligible, excluded subject nonetheless "lays claim to reality," a point I return to later.[69]

Performativity

Categories of person are powerful. They have significant consequences for subjects who find themselves engaging with them. Are they static, unchangeable features of society, or can they be altered? A well-known aspect of Butler's work involves her ideas on how norms are "performative"; they can shift and alter and be "re-cited" in different ways. Recognition, therefore, does not preclude subversion. The notion of performativity draws on Lacan to show how the ideal subject position implied by a particular norm is always just a fantasy; the ideal does not exist. There is no perfect, stable, and integral exemplar of the category woman, but rather each instance of the label being taken up by a subject is a little different from others, because it occurs in a different context, by a different person. Each performance intersects differently with race, class, culture, and other aspects of identification; every manifestation of a normative label is slightly different from the last. The notion of an objective, unchanging ideal of woman, therefore, is fantasmatic. This insight defuses the power of the normative ideal.[70] Attempts to identify with it are futile because it does not exist. This opens up and problematizes categories of identification that might have previously been assumed to be integral, stable, and an essential feature of some individuals. This way of problematizing gender introduced in *Gender Trouble* led to Butler's reputation as one of the more important contributors to feminist theory in recent years and, beyond this, to the study of subjectivity and identification.

In this account of performativity, each time the norm is enacted through a subject's attempted identification, it is altered slightly. This idea draws on Jacques Derrida's concept of *différance:* the temporal time lag between successive iterations and instances of a given social structure leads to it shifting and altering in the process.[71] It is within its very re-citing that the "apparent ideal" represented by a particular category of subject can "elide, slide, alter, [and] shift."[72] "Becoming" a subject in the terms of a dominant category does not therefore involve a straightforward repetition of the norm but rather an "uneasy" and unstable process.[73]

Within this unpredictable enactment lies the potential for subversion, and Butler discusses the potential undoing of misogynistic aspects of contemporary culture. Reenactments of gender have the potential to queer, or denaturalize, accepted norms of, for example, womanhood. They highlight their contingency, destabilize their apparently foundational and unchangeable natures, and mobilize them in new directions.[74] In *Gender Trouble* Butler famously explores the role of parody in prompting such risky, unstable re-citations. Parodic encounters can lead the observer to question the norm that is being cited, thus opening it up for potentially thinking otherwise. Drag, for example, throws one's previously held certainties into question: the moment when the viewer thinks it is a woman but then realizes it is a man problematizes the idea of an original and thus the reality of both genders. It leads viewers to question the knowledge that informs their initial assumptions regarding anatomy and clothing and to see how such knowledge is not a given but rather has become naturalized through a process of normalization and repetition.[75] Thus, the parody problematizes the very notion of an original at the heart of either gender norm; the reality of gender is placed in crisis.

Overall, therefore, parody shows how accepted, foundational norms in social life are, first, dependent for their existence on the repeated performances of diverse subjects, and, second, open to alteration and perhaps even subversion in each successive attempt at reenactment. Importantly, subversion is not an inevitable outcome of re-citation via parody; only some kinds of repetitions are "effectively disruptive" and "truly troubling" to the norm.[76] Nonetheless, these ideas have been drawn on by activists outside the university and by scholars within organization studies.[77] Researchers have shown, for example, how comedy shows such as the BBC's *The Office* prompt a parodying and questioning of dominant gender norms, effectively queering how we think about gender in today's organizations.[78] The potential for transformation through performativity offers an interesting new perspective on global finance whistleblowers. I found, for example, that many people I met had learned to laugh at the category of whistleblower itself, despite it causing them pain. Other people find different ways to rework it and perform what it means to be a whistleblower. These practices sometimes appear to open the category up for subversion, to defuse its power and lessen its ability to cause pain.

Affective Recognition

Bringing together these ideas, affective recognition represents an account of subject constitution that offers us a new way of understanding the self. This self is neither separate nor autonomous from others and does not fully belong to oneself, but it is instead radically social, crisscrossed with desires for subjection to powerful discourses and histories of affective attachments. But is this a new concept? After all, the self that seeks recognition from others is a common notion in social theory, from Hegel onward.[79] In other approaches, however, including the political theories of well-known recognition scholars Charles Taylor and Axel Honneth, the self that seeks recognition is conceived of as somewhat separate and distinct from the other that offers it. This position is challenged by more poststructurally oriented critical theorists.[80] With this in mind, others develop theories of the self in which it is founded on a deep-seated and inherent relationality with an other.[81] However, for Butler and others, ekstatic recognition is yet more radically external than suggested even by the notion of relationality, because the latter implies a harmony within the self-other divide that does not exist.[82] The relation is always in tension because of struggles around abjection described earlier and because of its continual iteration and thus is always in danger of rupturing. In this way, affective recognition represents an account of being in relation that encompasses complex, sometimes ambivalent attachments that are open to change over time.[83] It also emphasizes the role of power in these attachments, which can be overlooked in other theories of recognition.[84] Affective recognition therefore overturns common assumptions about the self within social theory.

The approach is not without its critics, including those who argue that Butler's account of subject formation denies any agency on the part of the subject.[85] Such critiques tend to be based on a limited reading of her work, overlooking her frequent problematization of the notion of agency itself. There is no self that exists prior to, and separate from, subjection to power. We come into existence via the norms and categories that offer us a sense of place in the social world; power "assumes a psychic form that constitutes the subject's self-identity."[86] This does not mean that we are determined by social structure either; the complexity of subject constitution and the layers of past attachments and losses that comprise it mean that ways in which the subject engages with the world cannot be predicted.

A POSTSTRUCTURAL APPROACH TO EMOTION?

Affective recognition offers us a theory of subjection that is compelling and somewhat unique; the self is both constituted by discourse and inescapably interdependent. This interdependency means that we are attached to others around us, and this attachment is experienced affectively. We feel its pull in ways that are underscored by our desires for recognition; the subject "responds to reflections of itself in emotional ways, according to whether that reflection signifies a diminution or augmentation of its own possibility of future persistence and life."[87] Desire for recognition within the symbolic order thus emerges in the "passion and grief and rage we feel," affects that "tear us from ourselves, bind us to others, transport us, undo us, and implicate us in lives that are not our own, sometimes fatally, irreversibly."[88] Affective attachments are an unavoidable accompaniment to our embeddedness in others. Moreover, they are a requirement of life itself; from an early age we become aware that "there is no possibility of not loving" and that "love is bound up with the requirements of life."[89] These insights enrich Foucault's work on subjectification to power, which tends to actively downplay and occasionally ignore issues of passion and emotion.[90]

The question remains, therefore, what are these affects? How do they manifest in social life and can they help us understand the subject's relation to power? And how do they fit with the poststructural inflections of affective recognition? Beyond Foucault, a disregard for emotion is common to poststructuralist thinking more generally. The concern is that to examine the emotions that people ostensibly feel is to invite two new problems. First, emotions are socially scripted; expectations of proper emotional displays are an active part of the experience of subjection. In other words, the emotions that a person is expected to feel and to display in any given situation are normatively prescribed, dependent on one's location amid subject positions relating to gender, race, profession, social status, and so on.[91] A woman may be expected to display innate maternal concern in the presence of a crying child, whereas these expectations might be less rigid for a man. Meanwhile, for the same woman, more masculine emotions such as anger might meet with disapproval. It is clear that such prescribed emotional scripts are both hierarchical and exclusionary; they determine who may and may not act in particular ways. Normative emotional demands are part of our subjection to discursive categories: integral to the ways we perform our selves. What this means is that emotions are not to be trusted as indicators of anything beyond subject positions being performed as prescribed.[92] A researcher that focuses on the emotional displays involved in a given setting typically reinforces the status quo and further enhances the power of the categories she uses. We see similar dynamics in whistleblowing; it is common for whistleblowers to act emotionally in response to finding themselves a target for scrutiny in the public eye, blacklisted in their industry, and unable to support themselves and their families. People can get anxious and angry. This is often used by a retaliating organization engaged in refuting a whistleblower's claims in the media. Displays of emotion are presented as evidence of the person being unreliable and mentally unsound and exploited to disparage the person speaking out.

A second and related danger in relation to the study of emotions, from a poststructuralist point of view, is that they tend to reinforce the idea of an inner, sovereign self. Herein lies the reason that many poststructuralist authors eschew psychoanalytic approaches, because they are assumed to invoke a view of the subject as an autonomous individual; emotions, including anxiety, are said to emanate from deep within this internal space. This concept is antithetical to poststructural thinking, because a focus on the individual tends to distract from powerful influences pertaining to a given situation.[93]

And yet, despite these concerns, affective recognition invites a reintroduction of the emotional even as it embraces the idea of the decentered self.

How might emotions be attended to while retaining a commitment to the radically externalized subject at the heart of this approach? Here, a rethinking of what we mean by the concept of emotion is required, one that first, draws on the notion of the self as constituted by discourse and continually becoming, and second, that moves us beyond the idea of emotions as either representing an essentialized inner self or as being socially determined.[94] In this, two points are key relating to Butler's understanding of emotions—or affects—as simultaneously social and psychic.

First, affect is not static but rather is continually reproduced in moment-to-moment instantiations, each of which holds the potential for discrete alteration. So even as certain emotional scripts are called on when we are compelled into subjection to a particular social norm (for example, the maternal concern previously described), we perform the affect inasmuch as we perform the subject position. The performativity of subjection also involves our re-citation of prescribed emotional scripts, and this process is imbued with possibilities for these scripts to be re-cited differently, including in ways that might sabotage or resignify them. What this means is that both the norms that make up the subject and the pattern of affects by which we perceive him or her are continually exposed to possible subversion and transformation. Emotions are not static but are performative and potentially open to iteration.

Second, in addition to being social in origin, emotions operate through psychic processes. Again, Butler follows a poststructural reading of psychoanalysis following Lacan.[95] Under this view, affects emerge from a surplus force that supplements and overdetermines all social and discursive processes.[96] This can manifest in emotional slips that are un-planned and perhaps unwilled and that effectively destabilize a partic-ular scene. Thus, affect is a force that is felt and embodied but can also disrupt. Affect can disturb an assumed sense of self-coherence and con-trol on the part of the subject and decenter her, not least because this force is "generated from a realm beyond that of the ego . . . [it represents a] psychic remainder that emanates from a rupture in the 'constitutive outside' to the subject."[97] Affect can upset the expected performance of a given subject position.

Bringing these ideas together, this felt force is both social, in the emotional material it draws on that prescribes how and what the person may feel, and psychic, as it emerges to rework this material in unforeseeable and indeterminate ways. Butler's more recent work calls for attentiveness to these embodied and visceral feelings and how they are performed. In this, she departs from Lacan and other poststructuralist thinkers in their clear disdain for a scholarly focus on people's "affective . . . lived experience."[98] Butler acknowledges their mistrust, based as it is on the lure of imaginary interpretations of emotions, but for her the force of affect cannot be overlooked. In her later work, she increasingly replaces a cool, detached tone with one that urges an attentiveness to how this lived experience is replete with feeling but in a way that neither privileges the social nor disavows the psychic. Under this view, what is important from an affective recognition perspective is what emotions and passions do—their performative effects. As Butler describes it, this force is what transforms the self. To be ek-static means,

> literally, to be outside oneself, and this can have several meanings: to be transported beyond oneself by a passion, but also to be beside oneself with rage or grief. I think that if I can still speak to a "we," and include myself within its terms, I am speaking to those of us who are living in certain ways beside ourselves, whether it is in sexual passion, or emotional grief, or political rage.[99]

Affect is a force that threatens the autonomy of the subject. It decenters her, not simply in the abstract and theoretical way described by poststructural scholars but also by encompassing the embodied and visceral manner in which we feel the sudden and unwilled ruptures to our sense of coherence and composure. On this view, emotions can hold a "disruptive, possibly even transformative potential, contrary to their socially-determinist framing."[100] Affect is therefore a "force that follows its own logic" in that it subjects us to a "radical and irreducible alterity" that we can never fully understand, control, or even predict.[101] This force emerges from a psychic life that is always ongoing but that has no single and agentic author, least of all ourselves.

These ideas suggest a new form of ethics, based on the challenges posed by the radically social, ek-static self to traditional ways of understanding personhood.[102] For Butler, to focus on the individual self, as though it is disconnected from others, singular and autonomous, is problematic:

> The idea of the unitary subject serves a form of power that must be challenged and undone, [it signifies] a style of masculinism that effaces sexual difference and enacts mastery over the domain of life.[103]

The very concept of the "unitary subject" is illusory and leads us to think that we are more independent of each other than we actually are. It creates the false view that we are in control, when we are not. Moreover, it has ethical implications:

> Ethical and political responsibility emerges only when a sovereign and unitary subject can be effectively challenged and . . . the fissuring of the subject, or its constituting "difference," proves central for a politics that challenges both property and sovereignty in specific ways.[104]

Political approaches that retain a primacy on the sovereign subject cannot be ethical, a point explored in Butler's more recent work.[105] In contrast, affective recognition compels us to acknowledge that our very survival depends on the other, and thus we have no choice but to defend this other within from injury.[106] Precariousness is a condition we share; we are exposed in different ways to others and their suffering.

Organization scholars have drawn on these ideas of late. For example, Fotaki discusses how market logics and consumerism within contemporary health care systems tap into fantasies of invincibility, showing how Butler's work on the precarity of subjectivity and our shared vulnerability to others can inspire alternatives.[107] Elsewhere Fotaki applies these concepts to public health provision, and pedagogy within business schools.[108] Throughout this book, affect appears to accompany subjection. Affective recognition from others—whether proximate (family and friends) or distant (those from whom one is temporally and spatially separated)—helped people construct a livable position. More than simply involving an intersubjective exchange, however, constructions entailed people feeling more than themselves, blurring the boundaries between themselves and others. They evoked their presence within a larger collective self, one that granted a sense of validity and coherence. Finally, it might be that an awareness of affective desires for recognition helps us at least problematize our deeply held attachments to the organizations and institutions pertaining to global finance to which we belong: attachments that can perhaps influence the severity with which whistleblowers are often treated. This might alter our current approach to understanding and supporting those who speak out, which is somewhat deficient.

The concept of affective recognition introduces a valuable emphasis on passionate attachments: displays of emotion and affect and how these can help us understand "the possibility of apprehending the fundamental sociality of embodied life": its ek-static nature along with attendant subjection to power.[109] This has implications for people engaging in empirical research; if we want to better understand how subjects engage with power, we need to be attentive to the subject's "emotional ways" of responding to it.[110]

AFFECTIVE RECOGNITION AND WHISTLEBLOWING

Affective recognition offers new and interesting ways to theorize the subject and its relation to power. Concerned with how, for example, norms and categories affect and are in turn affected by subjective identification, it enables us to retain a focus on what is happening at the wider level of social structures and institutions while we also examine what is taking place at the micro level of day-to-day life. This lens emphasizes the power of normative frameworks but also the potential to resist and subvert them. It shows how we are compelled into desiring recognition from these categories and frameworks. Thus, affective recognition provides a concept of the subject as fundamentally social in nature, albeit with a complex and often problematic relationship to the external other that paradoxically lies within the self. It is clear that affective recognition is a useful lens by which to analyze organizational dynamics. What this can add to whistleblowing research is an interesting but also valuable perspective that considers desiring human beings, in all their contradictions and complexities, as being embedded in the social structures that define them in important ways.[111] Affective recognition is ideally placed to help us understand aspects of whistleblowing, and this book explores how it can.

In addition, this approach has clear implications for the methods used in this research. The study explores the experiences of people who spoke up about perceived corruption within global finance, who became known as whistleblowers, and who were retaliated against as a result. As is clear from the preceding, however, knowledge is not objective but rather is constituted through discursive power. In asking people to take part in this study as a whistleblower, I was drawing on existing norms around whistleblowing and inevitably positioning people alongside these. Rather than an objective account of the experiences of whistleblowing, therefore, this text is necessarily a co-construction among various subjects: me as researcher, my interviewees, authors I was reading, people who have commented on the book, and eventually the person reading it. It is not an explanation of the truth of whistleblowing but simply an interpretation of what occurred when certain persons were asked to speak from the position of whistleblower and others listened.[112] Moreover, the production of the resulting book is inevitably infused with my own desires for recognition, including as an academic and an author; being in the position of researcher by no means leaves one immune from such needs.[113] A further issue emerges in the construction of research findings, including those presented here. There is a strong temptation to adhere to norms of structure and argument and in so doing to downplay the complexities, paradoxes, and inconsistencies that arise in any in-depth study of social life. These are the restrictions of empirical academic research, and so in carrying out this study, I was inspired by the numerous authors who have drawn on the concept of affective recognition in the context of studying organizational life. Drawing on Butler's ideas, studies have shown, for example, the many "signifying economies" that work in today's organizations to define and differentiate employees and how this categorization can lead people to seek recognition as subjects amid painful and exclusionary norms.[114] Inspired by such work, I have attempted to enable these complexities to emerge and also to be as explicit as possible about different choices, exclusions, and positions adopted in the research and writing of this book.

WITH THIS in mind the book explores whistleblowing through the lens of affective recognition. It is essential to understand wider institutional, social, and economic discourses prior to such an analysis, and so Chapter 3 outlines the empirical backdrop to the study. The financial services industry is described and illustrated with the story of whistleblower Eileen Foster, along with the impact of whistleblowing in this sector on our daily lives. Chapters 4 through 10 follow the trajectory of whistleblowing typical for many who speak up, beginning with the initial observation of misconduct and raising of the alarm in one's organization, illustrated by Chapter 4's Paul Moore at HBOS bank in the United Kingdom. The chapter details how, having spoken up and suffered retaliation, he took on the subject position of whistleblower partly because his lawyer assigned it to him when Paul challenged the reprisals. The chapter focuses on how he emphasized his reputation as a committed professional albeit one who had been naïve in trusting the organization. Recognition as such helped him cope with this new position of whistleblower and the challenges that accompanied it. Ironically, the very system that he was critiquing—financial services—is what offered him recognition as a legitimate, professional, whistleblower and enabled him to continue to speak out. This was the case with many other participants.

Chapter 5 asks why extreme forms of violence against people who disclose wrongdoing, often as part of doing their job, can persist. It focuses on Olivia Greene in Irish Nationwide Building Society, a member-owned financial institution, who spoke up in defense of her colleague. In Olivia's experience, occupying the position of whistleblower was accompanied by strong responses; she was isolated, was excluded, and became the target of retaliation. In exploring why this was, her status as an "impossible," censored subject is described, along with how this legitimized violence against her by others in her bank.

Chapter 6 continues on the trajectory of a typical whistleblowing struggle to highlight what can happen when people go public with information about wrongdoing, making disclosures to parties outside their organization. The majority of whistleblowers are ignored, and only some gain a public voice because they have been legitimized as valid truth tellers with important information to impart. Rudolf Elmer's story of his struggle against retaliation from his former Swiss bank employer reveals how recognition as a legitimate whistleblower is contingent on ancillary norms and discourses that operate in the wider geopolitical context. Realizing this about his situation, Rudolf traveled to the United Kingdom, where he gained an audience and reconstructed himself as an important figure: a valid subject. The chapter concludes by asking whether it is possible to avoid the violent reprisals often meted out to whistleblowers when one has attained legitimacy in this way.

In Chapter 7 another side of public whistleblowing is described: violence against whistleblowers, previously inside the organization, can be taken up by those outside. It highlights how people who speak up can be isolated and targeted by third parties, who focus firmly on the individual whistleblower and not on the wrongdoing or on the system that enables it. Returning to the story of Paul Moore, among others, the dynamics of this are discussed alongside its dangers. Contributors include the media, industry recruitment circles, and friends and colleagues. Surprisingly, we see that whistleblowers themselves can be unwittingly complicit in this targeting for scrutiny; they are forced into a spiral of individualization once their stories are told in the media, and they participate by sharing personal details to make their claims stronger. They find themselves compelled into an injurious position that ultimately aggravates their suffering.

Chapter 8 deepens this interrogation of how whistleblowers are subject to violence by highlighting the role of the whistleblower herself as she internalizes the exclusionary discourses that cause it. Whistleblowers are participants in organizations and in social life, and so they are not immune from the kinds of abjection to which organizational outsiders are subject. Here, however, the self is the target. Ambivalent and unsure about the very position that one is forced to adopt, feelings of guilt, self-doubt, and confusion emerge as these exclusions are turned inward, on the self. Stories from Allied Irish Bank's Eugene McErlean and others illustrate this. The chapter explains how retaliation against whistleblowers can lead to anxiety and stress, noting that any display of emotions can be used to further demean and diminish their claims.

The focus of Chapter 9 is on how people cope with such exclusions. Participants drew on affective recognition from other parties to cope, as illustrated by UK and US whistleblower Martin Woods. In people's accounts, the boundary between the whistleblower and the others providing recognition is blurred and porous. The necessity of others for survival in harrowing circumstances places the whistleblower outside herself; this subject position is radically ek-static. The dynamic of speaking up cannot therefore be seen as an individual experience but is instead inherently social. A darker side to this dynamic exists; people's self-constructions as whistleblower were complex, sometimes involving a distancing of self from cowardly others.

Chapter 10 continues this investigation into how the label of whistleblower can enable affirmation and survival even as it simultaneously isolates and harms people. It shows how this position can shift and alter over time, and can be performed in different ways. Specifically, we see how this category is reworked and re-cited by people who have been painfully interpellated within its terms. First, people begin to reconceptualize it away from the idea that successful whistleblowers must be those who prevail and bring their organization to justice. Rather, we see them alter their positions to being the winner of small victories. Second, the category becomes something of a joke, a thing to laugh at and not to be taken seriously. This requires that people step outside their current position, letting go of long-held fantasies of defeating the organization and seeing whistleblowing as others see it. Both approaches involve subversion of the taken-for-granted narrative of what whistleblowing entails and both help people survive.

The book concludes by asking what the implications of this new way of perceiving the whistleblower are, both for people who speak out and for others who are complicit in the disproportionate reprisals experienced by this group. The chapter returns to the role of global finance in today's society and the continued difficulties in challenging its dominance, including attempts to speak up by employees in this sector.

3

Global Finance:
Norms of Complicity

WHEN CONSIDERING whistleblowing it is important to look at the context in which it occurs. Many studies tend to examine whistleblowing as an experience that remains the same regardless of the industry backdrop, and indeed there are many similarities across cases. However, different sectors offer different environments for speaking out about wrongdoing. The experiences of whistleblowers are heavily influenced by the particular organizational, institutional, and societal contexts in which they take place. These contexts give rise to norms: practices and beliefs that are implicitly accepted. As French critic and philosopher Michel Foucault would tell us, such norms are contingent. They do not appear out of the blue but have a history; they are closely related to other forces at work in society, and they can change. This study focuses on financial services whistleblowers, and so it is important to explore the norms of this sector, their features and contingencies, to gain a more nuanced view of the backdrop to people's stories. In doing so, three key levels are described: the organization for which the whistleblower works, the regulatory setting, and the wider society in which global finance is located. To introduce these points, and to highlight the effects of complicity within this sector and why it affects us all, let us hear Eileen Foster's account of speaking out at Countrywide Financial.

One Whistleblower's Story: Eileen Foster, Countrywide's Fraud Watchdog

During the 1990s a new financial culture in banking was gaining prominence across the United States and Europe. It was characterized by excessive incentives for short-term thinking, a general lack of transparency, and light-touch regulating by nation-states that adopted a hands-off approach to policing the sector. In relation to speaking out, or whistleblowing, these features came together to create an effective culture of complicity within the industry. They were evident in people's accounts of whistleblowing, including that of Eileen Foster. She spoke out about mortgage fraud at Countrywide Financial, a large mortgage lender in the United States. After months of trying to make contact, I was fortunate to speak with Eileen. In many ways her story exemplifies why whistleblowing in financial services is so difficult, how attempts to speak up even by watchdogs can be severely punished, and also how this difficulty has significant impacts not only on the stakeholders of the institution involved but also on ordinary citizens of the United States and of the world. To introduce the concept of speaking out in financial services, her story is helpful.

SPEAKING OUT AT COUNTRYWIDE

Eileen Foster was caught up in something that would not only threaten her livelihood but also cost her fellow U.S. taxpayers billions of dollars, contributing to the closure of health services and schools. She is an example of a person who attempted to stop the carnage wreaked by systemic problems within the new financial culture in mortgage banking. Eileen joined Countrywide in 2005 and by March 2007 had been promoted to executive vice president, leading the company's mortgage fraud unit. It was a turbulent time for the firm; house prices were beginning to wobble and news of customer defaults was growing.[1] The number of staff assigned to her unit was dwindling too, with experienced fraud investigators having been recently laid off. Hers was an important position within the bank, not least because Countrywide had recently been warned by the U.S. regulator, the Securities and Exchange Commission, that its internal systems for investigating customer complaints were not working. It was Eileen's job to rectify this. Three months after her promotion, an anonymous call came into Countrywide's fraud hotline. It was an employee who had been recently dismissed from a Boston branch office that dealt with subprime loans. Serious fraud was taking place there, he said: "You need to go take a look at that region." People were being given loans they could not afford and were not qualified to take out. The anonymous caller told Eileen that he had protested and was fired for doing so.

Investigating the claims, Eileen examined files and emails relating to the Boston office. It appeared that something was up. She called up the company that looked after paper disposal and shredding for Countrywide in Massachusetts. She asked them to hold off on destroying their current load and to discreetly store paperwork at a secure location until she could examine it. Upon arriving in Boston, Eileen's team spent hours digging through the paper recycling and shredding bins, finding borrowers' pay stubs and comparing the figures to those recorded on the loan documents. They discovered that loan officers had forged hundreds of statements of income, claiming that borrowers were earning more than they did and sometimes inflating incomes by more than 800 percent.[2] In other loans, borrowers' incomes did not qualify them for mortgage financing, and they were switched to another kind, a "no-doc" loan, which required no documentation. One mock-up document had the address for one home cut out and glued onto a property appraisal for a totally unrelated asset. To complete the process, a borrower's signature would be cut and pasted from the original application, made in good faith, onto the doctored one for approval. This document would then be photocopied and faxed to make it look authentic.

Eileen's team organized a series of interviews with staff at the Boston office. Rather than cooperate, as they were obliged to under company policy, many people simply resigned. At the time, the job market was robust, and so this group found similar roles quite easily. Some people who remained and were interviewed pointed out that in fact they had been reporting the fraud for years but through official channels. Those who had repeatedly spoken out about the problem had been fired.

Reporting the extent of the Boston office fraud, Eileen and her team saw their work contribute to the closing of six branches that were judged to have been involved. This had not been easy. Some officials were not pleased with what was happening. One manager emailed his Massachusetts employees to warn them ahead of time that the fraud unit was on the case, thus preventing Eileen's team from doing their job effectively. The email told Boston workers not to put anything in writing, email, or messages that could someday incriminate them. During the branch closures in Boston, another executive phoned her to say that he was "g—d—ed sick and tired of these witch hunts." Later the same executive pointed out that the system used in the Boston branches was not aimed at misleading customers but was designed to speed things up so that people would have their loans approved more quickly and efficiently. "This is jaywalking," he noted, "not murder."[3]

Even with the branch closures, and the dismissal of forty-four out of the sixty staff involved, Eileen felt uneasy about how the fraud had been dealt with. Those who had been removed were generally low-level staff. The managers who had surely overseen the widespread forgery remained in the organization. Moreover, she began to hear reports that boxes of Wite-Out and other tools of forgery were not limited to Massachusetts' Countrywide branches.[4] Rather, systemic fraud seemed to pervade the organization. From Boston to California, Florida to Alabama it had become Countrywide's way of doing business.[5]

At first glance it all seemed to make little sense: Why would Countrywide loan officers spend so much time forging signatures and doctoring forms, just so that the company could lend money to someone who was unlikely to ever repay it? Eileen had known for a long time that there was a strong culture at Countrywide of making as many loans as possible, with little regard for the quality. This quantity-not-quality imperative arose from the CEO himself, Angelo Mozilo, who had set the audacious goal of dramatically growing his company to gain almost a third of the entire U.S. home loan market by 2008. For this reason, employees were strongly rewarded for selling as many loans as possible; their pay and bonuses were linked to meeting outlandish targets.

But why would Mozilo chase a goal like this, one that could ultimately hurt the mortgage lender? The answer was simple. Companies like Countrywide could package loans in complex bundles and quickly sell them to Wall Street investors and bankers, and *these* groups would take the hit should a borrower default. So the company was not going to be hurt directly.[6]

As she learned more about the systemic fraud, Eileen began to hear about employees in Countrywide who had tried to report the wrong-doing by following protocol for reporting internally. Investigating why her team had been informed about only a fraction of these, she learned that there were a number of reasons.

First, fraud investigation in Countrywide was not centralized; each division looked after its own fraud reporting processes. For example, the Countrywide subprime mortgage unit had an in-house fraud team, whose members would report problems to the sales manager in charge of the division. It was this person's responsibility to pass relevant information to Eileen's office, an action that was likely to prompt an investigation into his or her own department. This rarely happened. Her office had learned about the Boston fraud only because the anonymous caller had broken with protocol by calling it instead of his own fraud unit or the Employee Relations Department. Eileen had put together a proposal in 2007 to reengineer the structure for dealing with fraud, but it was turned down; she was told that it "wasn't the right time for a reorganization."[7] A second factor was that complaints often failed to reach her office because staff in Employee Relations had kept the information to themselves. Eileen wondered why.

It was then that Eileen began to hear more and more stories about internal whistleblowers being punished and sometimes fired for raising concerns. In fact, internal reporting channels were used to identify and isolate potential whistleblowers rather than deal with the problems raised. In effect, people who were just doing their job—protecting Countrywide from potential prosecution as well as protecting the money-borrowing public—were being watched, singled out, and punished. As she would later note, she believed that Employee Relations was "engaged in the systematic cover-up of various types of fraud through terminating, harassing, and otherwise trying to silence employees who reported the underlying fraud and misconduct."[8] Staff in Employee Relations, she said, had "the ultimate power to silence the whistleblower. They were the controlling factor. Without them, it wouldn't work."

Eileen was incensed to hear about whistleblowers being punished in this way. Moreover, by now, fraud appeared to be causing serious problems; by the end of 2007 Countrywide was almost bankrupt. Despite having become the largest mortgage lender in the United States, one third of its loans were in foreclosure. Eileen's work was, in effect, to help stanch the flow of bad loans that were contributing to this increasing current of debt and loss. She describes how she felt that something had to be done, immediately. Her efforts had already met with some success, and she had kept the company from running into serious trouble. She was doing her job as effectively as she could.

In May 2008, Eileen asked for an investigation into the flawed reporting procedures for fraud and into the firing of those people who had tried to speak up. An investigation was indeed begun, but not the one she had requested. Unbeknownst to her, interviews were carried out with her own staff members, and the topic of the investigation was Eileen Foster. One man would later complain that investigators had kept him for almost six hours, in two sessions, aggressively questioning him in a style that prompted him to answer in a certain way and say negative things about Eileen. This kind of investigation was highly unusual; her direct supervisor had been neither consulted nor interviewed about it, and it came without any of the usual precursors for disciplinary action— being reported, suspended, or in any way disciplined. In fact, Eileen was formally considered to be "a high-performing employee with no history of poor performance or conduct issues."[9] Once she discovered that such tactics were being used, she worried about her chances of being able to carry out her work on fraud within Countrywide and the support that she could expect from senior colleagues.

By mid-2008, the tide seemed to be turning. Countrywide was to be bought out by Bank of America. This promised a change in the toxic culture of the organization and, for the first time in years, Eileen began to feel optimistic. Surely the renowned Bank of America would not wish to carry on the legacy of fraud that had brought Countrywide to the position of needing to be bought out at a fire-sale price? Adding to her sense of hope, she was promoted to the position of senior vice president heading up the new, combined mortgage unit. She was formally invited to discuss Countrywide's processes for reporting suspicious activity with federal regulators from the Office of the Comptroller of the Currency.

Eileen describes how she interpreted this as a vote of confidence in her work. She felt that it was symbolic that Bank of America was placing so much trust in her, a manager well known by now for the tough line she took on fraud. A new era was coming. To add to this, the Employee Relations Department was formally stripped of its power to carry out investigations such as the one into Eileen. She had come to believe that the new Bank of America management would not ascribe any weight to the accusations from Employee Relations. It looked as if change was in the air.

Eileen describes how, at 7:45 a.m. on Monday, September 8, 2008, she sat at her desk as always. She believed she had been doing a commendable job, spotting irregularities in certain departments at Countrywide. It was her fifty-first birthday and she could hear her staff planning a "surprise" party outside the door. Waiting for the celebrations, she worked on the spreadsheet she had prepared for the federal regulators—it detailed how the subprime division was regularly underreporting claims of suspicious activity. She was also reflecting on the phone conversation she had had the day before with a colleague, who had briefed her on what to say and what not to say at that meeting. She smiled to herself, thinking that she would do what she always did—tell the story straight. Her telephone rang at 8 a.m., and because she was expecting a scheduled call from a Human Resources official to discuss her staff's salary structures, she greeted the caller pleasantly. Before the conversation could begin, the door to her office opened suddenly.

She recognized the two women who entered as Countrywide Employee Relations staff. One informed her that the call she had just received from Human Resources would be a conference call—she should switch to speakerphone. She could see two security officers standing across the hall. Eileen was presented with a fourteen-page document outlining an agreement that offered her $228,000, almost a year's salary, in exchange for her silence about how work was carried out at the company. She became angry and refused to sign. The conversation changed tone, and the women began to discuss her dismissal from the firm. It was to be immediate. It had been determined that she was unsuitable for a management position, and unfortunately, no other role was available at the time. They asked for her identity badge and the keys to the office. In mere moments, she was escorted from the building by the security officers. An email message she later received from the company was that she had been let go because of her "inappropriate and unprofessional behavior" and "poor judgment as a leader."[10] Eileen was not alone in being fired for speaking out at Countrywide; many others were persecuted in similar ways, as extensive investigation by journalist Michael Hudson subsequently revealed.[11] Court cases remain outstanding at the time of writing. Eileen consulted lawyers, who told her she was a whistleblower and that she had a valid case under U.S. law.

BANKING AND FINANCE: NORMS OF SILENCE

Eileen's story shares a context with the other whistleblowers appearing in this book; they all took place in financial services organizations between 2000 and 2010 in the United States and Europe. Although people had different roles, from anti-money laundering officers to audit and risk personnel, the organizations that they worked for shared some cultural norms. It is useful to set the scene by describing these.

By the late 1990s a new culture had emerged in global finance, characterized by an overriding emphasis on short-term speculation and equity-based compensation against a backdrop of weak and ineffective regulatory oversight and ratings agencies acquiescing to the banks and financial institutions they were supposed to be judging.[12] This particular flavor of finance had become deeply embedded in how our banks were run. It was partly supported by a "wall of silence" that tended to surround misconduct, described as the "silence in the City" of London's financial services center, for example.[13] These features contributed to the global financial crisis of 2008, which had crippling consequences for people across the world.[14] Trained professionals including many of Eileen Foster's colleagues did not, or could not, speak out about the problems they saw. In response to the crisis, demands for changing this culture have been repeatedly made, albeit detailed research on speaking out in financial services remains somewhat rare.[15]

Complicity in Organizations

During this study, it became clear from speaking with the whistleblowers I met that acquiescence with wrongdoing was a norm in many of their banks. It was just the way things were done. People often commented that many of their colleagues were similarly troubled by what they saw, but such worries were rarely discussed. Why the silence? Cultural norms such as this do not emerge by themselves; it is helpful to explore the specific organizational contexts that gave rise to this ethos of complicity.

SHORT-TERM INCENTIVES

Malpractice is rewarded. The linking of short-term performance with pay is now synonymous with banking. In many financial sector companies large bonuses are awarded for performing well over a short period. Common practices are to link rewards to an increase in the company's share price over a year or award bonuses for hitting a six-month sales target. This short-term approach leads people to focus on only the immediate future to the detriment of the longer term. So what is the problem? Research shows us that providing incentives for short-term results can lead to people acting in corrupt ways.[16] Excessive bonuses and compensation schemes continue to have a detrimental effect on the financial services sector today, with almost one in three professionals reporting pressure to engage in illegal or unethical practices as a result.[17] Compensation measures like these put a bank and its customers at risk.

Martin Woods exposed laundering of significant sums of drug money from Mexico through his bank, Wachovia. He talked about the effects that inflated salaries and bonuses had on people's willingness to speak out about malpractice in their organizations, giving the example of a senior colleague. When Martin approached him with evidence that the bank was involved in processing money from Mexican drug cartels, at a time when U.S. authorities were punishing competitor banks for exactly this crime, thoughts of his bonus seemed to distract the colleague, making him unable to listen and deal with the problem:

> In fairness to [my colleague], he was challenged as to which way to deal with this [evidence]. Ultimately, it turns out that he backed the wrong horse, he should have supported me, and he would be in a better place now. But he was like most bankers: he was [a] short-term [thinker].[18]

Martin felt that this man's every move was focused on achieving short-term goals:

Everything he did consciously and subconsciously, he was thinking [of] how this impacts [his] bonus this year. Everything was very short term, and it was also very self-centered.[19]

Martin was convinced, coming as he did from a policing background into this new world of banking, that there was a very different mind-set in these organizations. Short-term incentives led to a drive to make money at all costs:

Some bankers in my experience—and I've been at three different banks—all they look for is the excuse as to why they can [allow suspicious transactions to continue under their watch]. . . . The best news banks get about the commercial transaction is good news. Good news means, "I can go make money." . . . So they often look at these transactions through opaque glasses to find the good news and wish to dismiss the bad news.[20]

At times, however, the financial incentive structures were more complex than simply promoting individual greed. Sometimes rewards for meeting short-term targets were dispersed, so that people who turned down an opportunity to make money because they were aware of some wrongdoing would let down others. If a mortgage or loan salesperson made a sale, for example, the bonus would be shared with the team. This incentive structure helps maximize sales, but it increases the pressure to make decisions that are not in the best interest of either the customer or, in the long term, the bank. In summary, pay and rewards for meeting short-term goals can be substantial in financial services, and there are strong incentives not to articulate problems. Subtle interpersonal attachments support this; Martin felt the informal pressure, and others were influenced by colleagues' dependency on them.

The practice of banking has not always been thus; lending money and protecting savings are activities that have a long history, one in which short-term avarice was not a distinguishing feature. As former Citigroup leader John Reed noted, in 1965 the Citibank he joined was very different from today. Banking was seen as an important function of society, a public good, with attendant responsibilities.[21] The industry was strongly regulated, almost as utilities are. The customer came first, and excessive profits were not considered a goal of the organization.[22] By the late 1990s, however, people were paid well for meeting short-term targets and to stay quiet about the risks involved.

Complicity with perceived wrongdoing can attract rewards, but surely it goes against the rules? Policies dictate that when financial services employees see something amiss, they must report it. Rules are not always taken seriously in this industry as was the case in Countrywide. In her ethnography of Wall Street, another corner of the global finance world, Karen Ho describes the cultural peculiarities of the trading floor, noting that there is a sense of being chosen among the traders she worked with, who feel that they are special and in some way evolutionarily and intellectually superior to those outside finance.[23] This special status supports the view that banks must regulate themselves, because bankers are likely to be the only ones who have the knowledge and authority to do so. It also encourages the notion that outlandish levels of compensation and bonuses are morally justifiable and duly earned. Finally, it supports the idea that rules, including those prohibiting silence about wrongdoing, can be gamed. This means that only rules that are absolutely necessary to follow, so as to avoid trouble, are adhered to. Harvard Business School professor Malcolm Salter describes the ubiquity of this à la carte rule-following approach to regulation within financial services, drawing on examples such as Citigroup.[24]

As many who participated in this study noted about their firms, banking regulations are often perceived as obstacles to be dealt with rather than guidelines to promote sound ethical standards, leading to a phenomenon known as regulatory arbitrage. Ex–Lloyds Bank employee-turned-whistleblower Ian Taplin described how, "[People in retail banking] think regulations are a pain in the arse. . . . They have to deal with [them], but they don't like it because it stops them making money."[25] Regulations were not taken seriously. Gaming of the rules is described by Graham Senior Milne, who spoke out about life insurance policyholders being unfairly deprived of their entitlements at his UK retail bank. From his experience, he felt that it was the risk of being caught, rather than the ethical issue, that was a deciding factor:

In a lot of cases of course, people [who discover wrongdoing] may take a gamble, and they get away with it. They say, Well, okay, there is a potentially serious problem here, what is the likelihood that if I don't do anything about it, it will actually get found out about? If it gets found out about, what is the likelihood that it will, you know, be taken a step further? Well, if an investigation will be . . . soon, . . . you know, what is the likelihood that we will be found culpable, and even if we are found culpable, what will the damage be to the company or to me personally?[26]

In his experience, therefore, rule following was tantamount to a cost-benefit assessment that hinged on the eventual implications for bank workers themselves.

ETHICS ABSENT

Surely people would feel compelled to speak up because it was morally the right thing to do? Many participants in this study, reflecting on their workplaces, noted that ethics did not feature strongly in their organizations. On the surface, ethics are supposed to be built into the regulatory guidelines governing bank work—for example, the UK Financial Services Authority (FSA) principles that ostensibly regulated work practices at Ian Taplin's bank.[27] Trainee bankers were required to learn these. He described how this worked in practice:

You would have to learn the FSA principles. Before you get into the bank, you have to take the basic exams. You do a regulatory exam, which says, Please explain the twelve principles and what they mean, etc.; please explain what *this* means.[28]

As he went on to discuss, the actual ethical content was rarely considered or understood, however:

But the actual ethical side of it—they [my colleagues] don't talk ethics. *Ethics* is not a word that is probably ever really mentioned. They don't talk ethics; they talk regulation, and regulations aren't there as an ethical protection. They don't see it like that.[29]

Again we see the social side of this culture of complicity, the influence of colleagues; people tend not to speak about ethics, and therefore it tends not to be seen as important.

Research tells us that workers in financial services tend to stay quiet about wrongdoing because they possess a distinct lack of faith in their organizations' willingness to follow up on perceived problems, even if they were to report them. Employees in this sector also tend to have a greater fear that they will be retaliated against for reporting wrongdoing than those in other industries.[30]

Within financial services organizations a complex web of influences including short-term thinking, the gaming of rules, absence of discussions of ethics, fear of retaliation, and employees' sense that they will be ignored for speaking out, contribute to reasons people remain silent. Organizational cultures do not exist in isolation, however; they are supported by wider institutional norms, not least regulatory ones.

External and Regulatory Silences

Financial services organizations obtain their license to operate from what is ostensibly a greater authority: the state. In return, national governments are expected to regulate the activities of such firms, ensuring that they do not endanger their customers, their employees, and the wider society in which they practice. On paper the system is well governed by nation-states, with plentiful avenues for people to speak out. Various factors alter this ostensibly simple relationship.

THE WATCHDOGS?

The state places personnel inside the bank whose job it is to ensure that laws and regulations, such as those upholding shareholder interests, are obeyed. These watchdogs include risk managers, compliance officers, internal auditors, and fraud officers like Eileen Foster. All have a responsibility to ensure that certain rules are followed; they are there essentially to act in the interests of the country's taxpayers (compliance officers) and the bank's shareholders (risk managers), to represent their interests from within the bank. Paid a salary by the bank, they have a duty of loyalty to their employer, a situation that can naturally lead to conflict.[31] These people monitor day-to-day operations in the firm, such as lending practices, accounting methods, and investment strategies. All the while they must remain knowledgeable about the latest regulations and legislation.

Importantly, people in this role are legally obliged to ensure that laws and industry regulations are complied with. This task is not always fulfilled.

Lax compliance practices have significantly contributed to successive financial crises.[32] In exploring why, culture is again key. Watchdogs can find themselves undesirable people within financial sector organizations. Graham Senior Milne described people's attitudes toward internal compliance officers and auditors in the bank in which he worked:

> It is more difficult when you are an auditor, because in a sense, it's your job to find a problem. And on top of that, people think of internal auditors as potentially finding things they have done wrong or, you know, things they should have done that they didn't do as well as they might have done. So there is an automatic problem. . . . Other people in the company can be pretty defensive in their approach to an auditor, you know, which can range from being just not as helpful as they could be to downright obstruction. That can even happen at the highest levels in a company.[33]

We see such defensive reactions toward watchdogs throughout people's accounts in this study. The watchdog is attempting to stand in the way of a strong cultural preference for a lax approach to the rules. Paul Moore described what this was like from his perspective as a senior risk officer in the UK's Halifax Bank of Scotland (HBOS), when the culture encouraged excessive loan sales at all costs:

> The retail bank [of HBOS: Halifax] was going at breakneck speed and an internal risk and compliance function feels like a man in a rowing boat trying to slow down an oil tanker. I'm not saying that there were any bad intentions in that but it was difficult to slow things down.[34]

Paul appealed for assistance to a superior. He sent an email pointing out that this cultural climate prevented his risk-monitoring team from doing its job; the bank was at risk as a result. Paul described this cultural climate as

> a sentiment that constantly questions the competence and intentions of GRR [Group Regulatory Risk] carrying out its formal accountabilities for oversight, plus the ever-present need to be able to prove beyond

reasonable doubt as if we were operating in a formal judicial environment. The more we adopt this approach, the more adversarial it all becomes, the more emotional it becomes, the more personal it becomes and the worse the relationship becomes. It becomes a vicious circle, which needs to be broken.[35]

It is not at all easy for watchdogs to do their job fully and insist on the rules being followed.

In addition to being a cultural issue, the difficulties experienced by watchdogs relate to the structure of many financial services organizations. Even though adherence to rules is clearly vital for the bank to survive long term, risk and compliance officers are often found at a relatively low rung in the organization's hierarchy. This means that the opportunities to directly report up the chain to senior management can be limited. One must go through one's own boss, who will then decide whether to take it further. The result is that serious problems might never reach the board of management, particularly when they involve the discloser's line manager. This was the case with Paul Moore who, despite having the role of head of Group Regulatory Risk at his bank, was not given a regular seat at the board. He was required to raise issues through his immediate superiors.[36] Eileen Foster similarly struggled to reach senior management despite her position. Wachovia whistleblower Martin Woods described how this worked in relation to his role as anti-money laundering officer in a large international bank. He had no direct access to the board:

> There were times I was allowed to communicate, and indeed I had to communicate. I presented to the board regularly on issues, but I recall once asking [a manager] if I could inform the board of a certain issue. And he said, no, I wasn't allowed to, which is a really serious move.[37]

He went on to describe the problems inherent in this kind of structure:

> In a vertical line of management . . . and many firms have been criticized for having vertical whistleblowing processes, it's almost a pointless thing to do. . . . So you are going to blow the whistle to your manager about a problem in his department or her department? That's probably not going to go down too well, because who is in charge of that department, and who therefore does that impact and reflect upon?[38]

For watchdogs, therefore, there are clear cultural and structural reasons why it is difficult to do their jobs. This is compounded when risk and compliance officers' compensation plans are linked to the overall performance of the group or organization, which sometimes happens. Martin Woods noted how this could compromise his compliance colleagues:

> The bonus quite rightly can be used as an incentive for people selling, and [it] is based upon the profit and loss of the division they work in, or their own sales. But within compliance and other areas, including risk, all too often it's not used as an incentive; it's used to compromise you. [The bank] had one single control mechanism for [compliance] staff, and that was money. . . . I do not believe that compliance officers should be part of a bonus structure.[39]

This linking of compensation and compliance is clearly problematic, interfering with people's official obligations to their role.

In every sector, safety officers are present. These people are tasked with pointing out situations in which risk-taking has reached dangerous levels. In many financial sector settings, the general distaste for following rules was projected onto those individuals who represented the rules; they became a target of disdain. People in this study who occupied risk and compliance positions felt apart from the rest of the organization and sometimes stigmatized, long before they spoke out about malpractice. In addition, formal organizational structures, hierarchies, and compensation schemes supported these informal, cultural features. Justin O'Brien discusses this shift in attitudes toward compliance within the global finance industry, referring to the new regime as "creative compliance."[40] The function of risk management has been demoted within banking organizations, he notes, and has come to be seen as a cost center, a drain on profits rather than an essential feature. Under this new attitude, creative compliance means that an organization will try to get away with the minimum in terms of following rules, doing only what is necessary to remain on the right side of the law.[41] The very people employed by the bank to ensure that the laws are followed and that the bank does not risk its own long-term survival for a short-term gain are often restricted in what they can report and to whom, denied a voice on the company board. In addition, watchdogs can be incentivized to keep silent even when they perceive wrongdoing; like their colleagues, they are rewarded well when

sales volumes are high and compensated generously for short-term gains.
The organization is effectively shutting off its own safety valve.

LIGHT-TOUCH REGULATION

A culture of light-touch regulation pervades the finance sector, with government pressure being its chief driver.[42] In the United Kingdom, for example, the FSA was under pressure to remain hands off in its approach to enforcing banking regulations in the years prior to the 2008 crisis. The aim was to foster international competitiveness in the financial services industry. According to Gordon Brown, chancellor of the Exchequer in 2005, he planned to eradicate excessive red tape, adopting "not just a light touch but a limited touch."[43] As one result of this limited touch, the United Kingdom saw a PPI (payment protection insurance, which is sold with a loan) scandal unfold in the latter half of the first decade of the twenty-first century.[44] Sales of PPIs generated very high margins for senior executives and so were a lucrative source of income. The regulator had been aware that contracts were being inappropriately sold as far back as 2005, when it warned the banks of the danger and began overseeing these sales. UK banks ignored repeated FSA warnings and continued to sell the contracts until 2010, in clear defiance of a regulator that was in no way feared.[45] Similarly, the U.S. regulator was aware of Wachovia's role in drug money laundering for years before it prosecuted.

Light-touch regulation affects whistleblowing in this sector. Many people contacted for this book had approached their country's regulator after their claims had not been listened to internally. The law requires anyone in a compliance position who witnesses wrongdoing to report it. For many, however, the regulator's response was unhelpful. In Martin Wood's case, although he complained to the FSA about the behavior of Wachovia, he claims that the organization never updated him. Instead, he says that they gave him the number of a charity, Public Concern at Work. The FSA showed little interest:

> Bear in mind [that] they compel you to blow the whistle, to have an open and cooperative relationship with your regulator, which is what I did [have]. . . . [But] they don't support you as a whistleblower; they dump you.[46]

According to Michael Winston, a senior executive at a different branch of Eileen Foster's Countrywide, he brought his claims about both mortgage loan malpractice and the physically toxic office buildings in which Countrywide employees were working to the regulatory authorities in the United States. He was similarly ignored. Around the time of the banking crisis, many national banking regulators issued declarations that encouraged whistleblowers to come forward and share information; people were actively advised to blow the whistle. What people found again and again was that when they did there was no assistance available. Woods continued,

> I sent them an email in early 2009, and I said, I need to talk to you. And they sent me an email back, and—now bear in mind, I haven't said what I need to talk to them about, right? I could be saying, "Look I'm going to commit suicide"; they don't know that; they haven't got a clue—they sent me an email back and said, "We don't need to talk to you and so we are not going to talk to you." And that statement there says, "We don't want your intelligence and information." Intelligence and information is the most important commodity in the markets and yet the FSA don't want it.[47]

Woods went on to describe to me how he, like others, had important information: this time about billions of dollars being laundered from Russia and Eastern Europe. Woods is not alone in condemning the UK authority for its coldness and apathy in relation to the potential whistleblowers it encourages to come forward; the organization came in for criticism from many.

In the United States, people expressed frustration with the Department of Justice and the Securities and Exchange Commission. Bradley Birkenfeld, who spoke out about tax evasion schemes that enabled U.S. citizens to hide their assets in offshore accounts, was convinced that as soon as reasonable people saw his evidence they would be overwhelmingly on his side. His information would turn out to contribute $20 billion to the U.S. tax take. Bradley approached the relevant authorities but was immediately prosecuted for his role in the activities he was reporting and spent thirty-one months in prison.[48] Eugene McErlean in Ireland went with confidence to the Irish regulator, sure that his report of Allied Irish Bank's overcharging its business customers would draw immediate attention. He was asked by the regulator to withdraw his accusations.

Regulatory inaction can be linked to the reputation of the authority in question and how it is perceived in the wider banking and political environment. At the time that some prominent financial services whistle-blowers were contacting Ireland's financial regulator, for example, it was already in trouble with its European counterparts, having been warned for having an overly lax approach to overseeing the international firms occupying Ireland's International Financial Services Center. Pub-licly following up whistleblowers' complaints and thus amplifying sug-gestions of wrongdoing may have been an unwelcome proposition.

Related to this is that banking regulators tend to have something of a confused mission in relation to speaking out about wrongdoing. Ire-land's regulator, for example, has the overall financial stability of the country as a core objective and as part of its mission statement. The fi-nancial regulator must avoid overregulation that might "threaten the competitiveness and viability of financial businesses." On the other hand, the regulator is tasked with "the setting of regulatory requirements . . . that must be complied with by regulated financial services providers" and the "supervision of financial services providers."[49] That this leaves regu-latory authorities with something of a contradictory purpose was con-firmed by a senior regulation officer in Ireland interviewed for this book who prefers to remain unnamed. He pointed out that in Ireland regulatory authorities tend to encourage increased competitiveness and a looser approach to regulation. The same is true for other financial reg-ulators in countries studied here. When it comes to potentially exposing a major banking scandal that might destabilize the system, we can see how the first objective, to support the stability of the banking system, can be in direct contradiction to the second, the enforcement of regula-tions. When a whistleblower arrives at the door, how does a regulator respond? To act on the news could seriously disrupt banking in the country in the short term. There is therefore a major paradox in the way that regulatory authorities are set up. A tendency for silence, in relation to systemic corruption, results. On the other hand, this contradiction is a distinct advantage to banks who transgress regulatory guidelines, in-cluding those mentioned here. Critics also point to the revolving door system as a key conduit of influence between banks and regulators, in which ex–senior bankers are hired by the regulator and vice versa, retaining friendships and old allegiances.[50] Finally, regulatory authorities in the banking sector are notoriously understaffed, in Ireland, the United Kingdom, the United States, and elsewhere, and this adds to the pressures on them.[51]

SCALE

Even so, surely organizations that clearly break the rules can be punished. Why do states not simply revoke the license that misbehaving banks have been issued? The sheer scale of financial institutions has shifted the balance and created a dependency. Changes to regulation in the United States and elsewhere since the 1980s have facilitated the emergence of megabanks through merger and acquisition activities. The size of these institutions means that they are deeply embedded in the economies of the nations in which they operate. In the 2008 financial crisis many failing banks, organizations that in any other industry would have been allowed to go bankrupt, were fully rescued by country governments, using taxpayer money.[52] These bailouts were reported as being done in the national interest to prevent further crisis; banks must be supported at all costs.[53] To destabilize the sector would be tantamount to destabilizing the economy itself. As the head of the UK Prudential Regulation Authority stated in public, many large retail banks are simply "too important to fail."[54] U.S. Attorney General Eric Holder in March 2013 also expressed his worries about big banks to a congressional committee: "I am concerned that the size of some of these institutions becomes so large that it does become difficult for us to prosecute them when we are hit with indications that if we do prosecute—if we do bring a criminal charge—it will have a negative impact on the national economy, perhaps even the world economy."[55] If an entity is too big to prosecute, it is thereby protected by state and society working together. What this means is that banking is given a special place, and banks, to a large extent, are allowed to decide how to organize their own practices and regulate themselves.[56]

Scale also affects our ability to hear criticisms of this industry. When faced with stories about massive fraud running into billions, we often struggle to comprehend them. The fraud is simply too big, and as humans, we are cognitively limited in what we can cope with in terms of the scale of a problem.[57] To seriously listen to whistleblowers such as Eileen, to accept and acknowledge that wrongdoing is going on at the scale they seem to be saying it is, is a huge cognitive challenge.[58] The easier thing to do is to close our ears and stop listening.

INFLUENCE

The predominant norm of complicity within financial services regulation is often supported by strong lobbying organizations demanding input into laws that govern the sector.[59] A classic example of this kind of gaming of the system involved powerful organizations lobbying for repeal of the Glass-Steagall Act after the 1998 merger of Citicorp and Travelers Group. This meant that banks no longer had to separate their investment banking from retail banking functions. For many commentators the repeal of the Act was a key cause of the 2008 banking crisis.[60] As another example, a head of the U.S. Securities and Exchange Commission, Mary Schapiro, notes how she and her fellow regulators saw the need for reforms of money market funds for a long time before this came to the public's attention. Her call for change was not listened to and drew strong opposition from the banking industry and indeed from other members of her commission. In this case, the regulator knew about the wrongdoing but could do nothing.[61] In the United Kingdom, strong lobbying by financial sector interest groups led to increased deregulation of certain sectors in the years leading up to the crisis.[62] Politicians were complicit in this partly because the huge profits generated in the City of London were considered central to the UK economy, and they were in awe of the unprecedented rate of growth of this expanding sector. Postcrisis, this activity continued; the U.S. Volker Rule, a piece of legislation that strongly curtails banks' ability to trade in derivatives using their own capital and thus reduces the risk to taxpayers and some clients, has been the target of intense lobbying since its proposal.[63] Lobbying can be more subtle too; for example, U.S. government officials enjoyed discounted mortgages from Eileen Foster's Countrywide, being classed as "Friends of [CEO] Angelo"—a special status.[64]

Importantly in the context of this book, this dynamic is particularly prevalent in relation to laws governing whistleblowing in financial services. After changes to whistleblowing laws were proposed, lobby groups representing the banking industry in the United Kingdom, United States, and Ireland were influential in dictating how these laws were written.[65] Influence can also affect how laws are applied to whistleblowers in other ways. Countrywide senior executive Michael Winston had experienced severe retaliation, and had been dismissed, for speaking out about mortgage fraud and health and safety violations. He brought a wrongful-dismissal and retaliation suit against the company. A month of testimony followed. During this time, a senior human resources executive testified that he had been "a problematic employee and not a team player."[66] This was despite her writing a performance evaluation, shortly before the company's retaliation against Michael began, that said he had "done well to build relationships with key members of senior management and [continued] to do so. . . . Michael [strove] to be a team player." Other senior managers similarly gave testimony that contradicted their earlier praise of his work. As one juror (a former human resources manager at General Motors) reported, "There was no doubt in my mind that the guys at Countrywide had not only done something wrong legally and ethically, but they weren't very bright about it." He went on to note that the bank officials testifying against Michael "didn't have a lot of credibility'" and their evidence was contradictory. The jury sided with Michael; he won his case. However, Countrywide, which by this time was owned by Bank of America, fought back and appealed. The bank argued that the jury made a mistake: Michael had been dismissed because of difficulties with senior management at Countrywide, there had been no job for him at Bank of America when it took over, and the jury had been "swayed by emotion" in the earlier case. Despite being featured in the *New York Times* as the man who "conquered Countrywide," and David Dayen of *Salon* describing him as having a "stellar record" Michael's verdict of wrongful dismissal and retaliation was overturned.[67] Not only was the jury's decision reversed and his claim for compensation denied but Bank of America then went on to pursue Michael personally, placing a lien on his home and demanding over $90,000 in court costs. A trillion-dollar company was chasing an unemployed whistleblower for legal fees, and Michael took his complaint to court. His complaint was denied on the fantastical grounds that he "failed to prove a disparity in resources" between himself and Bank of America.[68] Michael's struggle and those of others in this book highlight the influence that financial organizations

can have over powerful institutions not least because of the disproportionate resources that they possess. Wider forces are at play in ensuring
that silence and complicity persist in our banking sector.

Complicit Society

The entities described here—organizations and regulators—clearly play
a role in people tending not to speak out about corruption within financial services. But this is supported by society more generally. Corruption would not be allowed to continue if public opinion was sufficiently
strong and if there was a widespread demand for reform or dismantling
of this clearly out-of-control sector. Why do we accept and contribute
to the silence in financial services, and why are we apparently comfortable with the idea that a self-regulating entity like the institution of
banking is allowed to continue in this way, costing us so much money?

First, journalists are typically reluctant to report on financial corruption. This reluctance relates to the difficulty in actually understanding
what is happening in global finance. The practice of banking is opaque;
it comes with its own complex terminology (CDOs, option swaps, and
so on), mathematical formulas, and implied assumptions, and to even
attempt to understand it one needs to have high numeracy. To examine
and critique the practices of banking, one must speak the language, and
this is something that many people outside the industry find too difficult. Journalists struggle to make the mathematical story behind a financial scandal legible for the average newspaper reader. Courts often fail
to find jurors to serve in trials of white-collar financial crime because
very few people are capable of even beginning to understand the tech-
nicalities of such cases.[69] Even industry insiders struggle to comprehend
the complexity of today's financial services systems, with a recent U.S.
secretary of Treasury stating that neither he nor any regulator overseeing
the financial sector could claim to understand the vast and interlinked
connections within this industry.[70] Here we have a situation in which the
banking system that has developed over the last few years is too compli-
cated for anyone to fully understand. Even those who use the complex
technical instruments and formulas daily do not fully understand them.
The links between banking, politics, and journalism are deep seated
because of mutual dependency in areas like advertising.[71] In addition,

journalists tend to focus on short-term stories in the main, often missing bigger trends. They can also be reluctant to report major systemic wrong-doing, especially in sectors that are central to the economy of the nation, as finance is. To do so can result in being vilified as a traitor to the nation, as happened to economists like Ann Pettifor and Morgan Kelly who were among those predicting the financial collapse of 2008. Raghuram Rajan who later would become governor of India's Central Bank, was in 2005 called names such as "luddite" for his alternative position on the finance-driven boom that was taking place.[72]

Second, we feel a need to trust the banks. People are reluctant to accept that banks can be the bad guys, even after decades of financial scandals. The institution of banking has an important function in our world. Given the ubiquitous nature of money and that we live in capitalist societies, albeit of different flavors, money is a commodity at the forefront of peoples' minds. We believe that we need it, and quick access to it, to live our lives. And it is this lifeblood—money—that is at stake; it has been entrusted to the banking system. We feel a strong need to maintain faith. We need to believe that these institutions are solid and stable, that they have our best interests at heart, and that our money is safe in their hands. Banks for years have recognized this and have promoted a strong image of trustworthiness: banks occupy venerable old buildings in the center of town and their suit-wearing executives are steady and conservative in personality as well as work practice. The industry has carefully cultivated these social markers that keep the circle of faith intact, that maintain the illusion of trustworthiness. Philosopher and social theorist Michel Foucault comments on the process by which certain groups of professionals, including doctors and lawyers, create an image of themselves and their work that invites public respect and trust.[73] Knowledge is shaped through the exercise of power and through this, problems are formulated that only experts of the profession can solve, as with the legal system. Opaque, difficult-to-understand language contributes to this, and the status of the profession in society remains unchallenged. Foucault notes that this gives the profession in question a strong position of power, because most people do not understand its practices but are told to respect it. With its complex terminology and tendency to create problems that only it can solve, finance is not dissimilar from the kinds of professions that Foucault describes. Perhaps the best evidence of the strength and longevity of this institution lies in it continuing to be more or less preserved and upheld by society and the governments it elects despite the significant reduction in public confidence in banks and bankers in recent years.[74]

When situations arise that potentially shake our trust, it makes us nervous. British sociologist Anthony Giddens depicts this sense of unease as a feature of living in modern capitalist society. Today we put our faith in many systems that are too big and too complex for us to comprehend, including insurance, finance and health care. Large institutions are responsible for important aspects of our lives but we often cannot see or even picture them; we do not know where they are located or who is running them. These institutions that govern how we live have become disembedded from our ordinary conceptions of place and time; they are increasingly becoming abstract entities. For example, the company that sells us our insurance policies and mortgages is frequently not the same company that ultimately owns and operates these products; they get passed around in a complex system we do not understand. And there is often no physical building for us to visit in the case of a problem, nor a human being at the end of the phone line. This abstraction creates a sense of unease. For Giddens, living in modern Western society often feels more akin to "being aboard a careering juggernaut . . . than being in a carefully controlled and well-driven motor car."[75] Although we do not understand these faceless systems, we need to trust them, and so we close our eyes and hope that they will work in our best interests. We are aware of the risks built into them, and how our inability to directly access them increases the risks, but we cannot cope, or do not want to cope, with the implications. As citizens of contemporary societies, our very sense of security depends on maintaining a level of trust in the world we encounter—including such institutions. Today, therefore, this sense of security is frequently built on blind faith in a system of abstract, faceless processes that are ultimately beyond our control. We prefer to maintain the fantasy that banking remains a social good operating in a stable fashion with our interests more or less at heart.

A third reason that society tends to comply with these norms of silence in financial services relates to the inherently gendered structure of this industry. Its powerful institutions have historically favored certain categories of person—specifically, white Western men who are relatively wealthy. In financial services and in other global industries, male bodies are equated with power and authority, and it is such bodies that we tend to find in positions of leadership.[76] In finance, this equating of authority and responsibility with maleness is supported by how organizations in the sector cultivate an image of trustworthiness; for example, banking has long been portrayed as a gentlemanly activity.[77] Global finance has traditionally been founded on the idea of a male role model: the venerable, conservative gentleman banker who exudes a sense of responsibility and control over a chaotic environment.

The gendering of global finance is not simply related to the uneven distribution of men's and women's bodies within the industry. Ways of seeing and representing the world have emerged that are specifically masculine (and that are not necessarily exhibited by male bodies only) and that give primacy to a particular world view. Studies have shown that financial commentary in magazines such as the *Economist* tends to be replete with images of manly prowess and domination. Extreme risk-taking in finance is portrayed as "heroically and glamorously masculine."[78] Activities such as capital investment are described through metaphors evoking invasion, occupation, and colonization, as the "masculine conquest of virgin territories."[79] Other kinds of financial transactions are depicted as "the operations of masculine agents called on to act boldly in the face of panic, irrationality and 'exuberance.'"[80] Knowledge and language within this industry is imbued with ideals of conquest and domination: specifically masculine tropes. Because of the growing influence of finance on other sectors, this masculine language has become a global standard for business.[81]

The emergence of the new financial culture represents a further intensification of masculine ways of seeing, within this setting. As British geographer Nigel Thrift notes, the short-termist, irresponsible, and forceful behaviors that are associated with this period, and that are celebrated and rewarded, are founded on a "certain type of male role model," one that celebrates aggressive rent-seeking and risk-taking.[82] An assumption that control over a complex world can be attained dominates, and other ways of seeing the world and of making decisions are ignored.[83] In-depth studies of financial services organizations have provided fascinating insights into how these assumptions influence daily life.[84]

In addition to the predominance of male bodies and masculine world-views within organizations in global finance, the gender effects of the sector are felt outside its institutions by the people it affects. Decisions made by financial markets can often overlook the concerns of those most impacted by poverty and powerlessness across the globe, a group that disproportionately includes women.[85] Specifically, the singular pursuit of profit at the expense of other considerations encourages quick-hit economic restructuring and other practices that ensure that production becomes cheaper for investors and owners. Such decisions have been shown to exacerbate the feminization of poverty.[86]

This suggests that global finance is structurally gendered in the representation of women within its ranks, particularly at senior levels; that it is also culturally and symbolically gendered in terms of the language and assumptions that have become normal in this sector; and that its cyclical crises continue to have disproportionate effects on women worldwide. Exacerbating this gendered structuring are the ways that financial instruments and strategies are represented and portrayed, which tend to occlude their social and cultural roots in particular forms of exclusion.[87] The gendered heritage of global finance remains hidden, while the impacts of its strategies on real human beings are rendered invisible.

Surely the 2008 financial crisis, with the extreme effects it had on people, led to challenges to this clear concentration of systemic power in a small group of elites? In fact, this financial shock merely exacerbated the illusions of mastery and control that had become endemic to global finance.[88] The period since the crash has seen a growth in managerialist perspectives—the idea that through the correct application of management strategies, elite business professionals can successfully control their environment. This shift has merely strengthened support for masculinist ways of thinking.[89] Financial language dominates as governments attempt to describe both the crisis and the planned recovery. Implications for real people tend be downplayed in favor of almost exclusively economic explanations for the crisis and analysis of its effects. Nations now strive for "high levels of market liquidity," "low global interest rates," "low capital costs," and other neutral-sounding goals. These apparently benign phrases mask the crippling strategies of social austerity on which they often depend.[90] They are abstract and technical, devoid of relation to actual people, and their very ambivalence makes them difficult to challenge. Meanwhile, women disproportionately bear the brunt of austerity. Attempts to ensure gender equality in organizations are typically postponed during intercrisis periods of recovery.[91] This weak system that favors a particular group of people continues to exclude others—women but also feminine ways of seeing the world. It effectively hides this exclusion. And as a society we continue to support this status quo through our implicit support for global finance, despite its inherent instability and despite the inequalities that it continues to perpetuate. Our complicity in accepting this unequal and outrageously skewed system may well be grounded in deep-seated acceptance of the patriarchal authority and masculine power on which global finance is built.

For these reasons, among others, banking tends to be left to do its own thing. Both the nation-state and the wider society therefore support a generalized impunity for the financial sector.

Impacts of Complicity

The features that make up the new financial culture within the sector are clear, as is their role in fostering complicity with wrongdoing. But what impact does this actually have on our day-to-day lives? Finance is simply one sector of the economy; why should we be concerned with what happens in it?

Eileen Foster's story exemplifies the effect of silence. Ordinary Americans who had nothing to do with mortgage fraud ended up paying for it, through their increased taxes in the years that followed the banking crisis, and cuts in funding at their children's schools and local hospitals. While Eileen and her colleague Michael Winston were raising their complaints, Fannie Mae and Freddie Mac were buying loans from Countrywide, packaging them into securities, and selling them to investors. Rather than reviewing and examining these loans, the banks simply relied on statements from Countrywide that they were up to standard. Loans that should never have been made were granted in the name of U.S. taxpaying citizens. Despite attempts by Eileen, Michael, and others, the problems within the firm continued for years. Countrywide, at the time a significant provider of mortgages in the United States, found itself at the epicenter of the 2007–2009 financial crisis. As the housing market collapsed, a full third of the loans it had made went into foreclo-sure. When so many foreclosures take place, effects are widespread: fam-ilies are pushed out of their homes and the value of the surrounding homes decreases, which further fuels the collapse of prices.

In 2008, Fannie and Freddie were effectively nationalized, having almost collapsed from losses related to mortgages such as these. Coun-trywide had cost them $1 billion, because they were liable for the de-faulted loans resulting from the kinds of fraud Eileen Foster and her colleagues saw and tried to stop. Since then, U.S. taxpayers have paid al-most $170 billion to support Fannie and Freddie and are likely to have to continue paying.[92] In Europe, too, Eileen and Michael's counterparts were trying hard to alter this dangerous culture, because they saw the impending problems. And they too were punished for it.

Eileen Foster, Michael Winston, and the few colleagues who joined them in speaking out could not have been the only people at Country-wide to realize the wider impact of their organization's fraudulent prac-tices. And yet most remained silent about it. Why was this? As Eileen herself puzzled, "How did it get to this point? How do you get people to go to work every day and do these things and think it's okay?"[93] There are plenty of people working in the financial industry with what most would consider a strong moral fiber; not everyone would take risks and jeopardize customer money just to meet targets and potentially secure their bonuses. Many such people were disturbed by the kinds of things that threatened customers' and the banks' futures but remained silent for compelling reasons.

Conclusion

Whistleblowing is a complex and contradictory process that takes place amid "discursive, institutional and structural forces" that are made man-ifest in such incidents.[94] Global finance is a sector built on layers of complicity. This is upheld by a network of forces that traverse organ-izations, the nation-state, its agents, and each one of us. They do not operate at some macro, structural level but have a strong impact on our lives because we are forced to pay the debts of corrupt organizations. They affect our sense of security. They make it difficult to speak out in this sector, or about it, not least because they shape the subjectivities of those employed in it and alongside it. People working as regulators, journalists, and bankers all depend on financial services to some degree to offer a stable sense of self—as a valid professional with an important job. To speak against it is to state things that do not fit with the culture, as happened with Eileen, Morgan, Raghuram, and others. To exist at all in relation to this sector, therefore, has a price: complicity.

However, as Foucault notes, no such structural arrangement is static and unchanging. Every system contains within itself the potential for subversion and resistance, although this rarely happens in a straightforward way. In financial services, every so often someone emerges, often from a watchdog role, who breaks with the norms of complicity. Doing so is not easy. In what follows we examine in more depth the push and pull of forces as whistleblowers such as Eileen Foster struggle with their contradictory positions as professionals within this industry, and their desires to see it changed.

4

The Whistleblower as Professional: Subjection to Norms

WHAT MAKES PEOPLE like Eileen Foster persist in speaking out, even when they realize that they are acting against the wishes of bosses and colleagues? In exploring how whistleblowing is experienced by the person involved, it is useful to begin at the very early stages, when he or she becomes aware that something is wrong in the organization and tries to alert others to it. At this point, the whistleblower has not yet gone public; she is a regular member of staff. What compels people to continue to speak out, even when they are aware that their actions are increasingly unpopular among colleagues and managers? The well-known case of Paul Moore illustrates the somewhat surprising dynamics involved. Like others, Paul did not think of himself as a whistleblower when he made his claims. He survived the process, he explained, by reinforcing his position as a professional, albeit a professional that would speak out when his ability to act as such was challenged.

Paul at the Halifax

Paul Moore worked for Halifax Bank of Scotland (HBOS), one of the United Kingdom's largest banks and a core institution there.[1] He had come from the legal profession into banking. A specialist in risk governance relating to financial sector regulation, he joined HBOS as head of regulatory risk for the Insurance and Investment Division in 2002. His role in the bank was to ensure that the rules were being followed. Paul would turn out to be an important witness and source of information in the parliamentary and media investigations that followed the UK banking collapse of 2008.

With a long history in banking and finance, he had been a partner at the audit firm KPMG and worked for major financial firms, including American Express. Since he began the job, he had become aware that the culture of the Halifax Bank was changing; people were encouraged and indeed rewarded to take more risks. One example of this related to sales of a particular financial product, corporate bond funds (CBFs).[2] When yields on their standard deposit accounts decreased, customers were advised to switch their money over to these accounts. The risk involved was seldom explained; customers often believed that they had moved to another safe fund. If a customer did so, this was good news for the banks because they received higher margins for CBFs than for standard deposit accounts.[3] Bank advisers were actively encouraged by their bosses in sales to increase the volume of customers signing up for these lucrative CBFs. Strict targets were imposed.

Customers were being encouraged to jeopardize their savings. This also put the bank's health at risk of course; customers did not understand the gamble they were taking, and HBOS itself would be exposed if the market suddenly turned. As Paul explained,

> So you have risks to customers. You also have risks to colleagues. And you have risk to the whole system because you're obviously going to need more liquidity to cover the volume of business that you're actually doing.[4]

This flurry of CBF-related activity in the sales department began to cause concern in other parts of the bank. As HBOS's own asset management division's CEO communicated to Paul Moore,

> The reality is we are being forced to invest in lower quality bonds because [the sales force for insurance and investment products] wants to sell more product. Now that's what I call risk![5]

Even the regulator, the Financial Services Authority (FSA), expressed a worry about CBFs when it carried out its complete risk assessment of the whole HBOS group in 2003. In fact, it emerged that the CBFs were just a small part of a larger problem; the FSA presented to the HBOS board a long list of concerns that it had about the bank's operations. This declaration of concern on the part of the regulator was an example of the light-touch regulation approach dominating the UK banking sector at the time, in which regulators did not actively police financial services institutions. Instead, perceived misconduct was dealt with by conducting reports, issuing cautions, and appealing to the organization to address them.

It was decided at HBOS that a complete review of risk practices in the bank would be needed. Given the praise and recognition that he and his group had been receiving for their work, and his good relationship with the regulator, Paul was chosen to lead this. In August 2003 he was asked to take over the top job as head of Group Regulatory Risk for the entire bank. Before doing so, he expressed his reservations to his manager. By now he had realized that a distinct culture was in place at the bank: "I have been doing this since 1984, and I could *smell* the control issues, I could smell that what they cared about was sales and nothing else."[6] In addition to a focus on sales at all costs, Paul knew that certain units at the bank were not particularly open to investigation or challenge, something that would be a problem for him in his new role:

> I already knew that the culture inside the retail bank was a "West Yorkshire bully boy culture."[7]

So in accepting his promotion, Paul was well aware of the excessive risk-taking that had become a cultural norm within certain sections of HBOS. Moreover, he knew how resistant his colleagues might be to the investigation that was so badly needed and that he was to lead. Nonetheless, he began investigating the CBFs. This task was a small part of a larger project that would lead to his eventual termination at the bank: the full review of HBOS's sales culture.

RESISTANCE TO RESEARCH

Paul's team began their work in late November 2003. The report took four months and brought its own challenges, as he would later describe:

"To say that doing the work was like going behind enemy lines might be an exaggeration but it certainly was not far off."[8] The team encountered resistance from many sources. It turned out that just under a quarter of customers of the fast-selling CBFs did not know that investing in this fund carried any risk to their initial capital investment at all. They were under the illusion that it was another form of a deposit account, with a higher interest rate.

In March 2004, it was time to compile the findings and circulate the report to be checked and signed off by different people in the bank. Paul said,

> The extreme "argy bargy" that took place in trying to finalize the report itself was upsetting to my team and to me. . . . On quite a number of occasions, my team carrying out the work reported that they were being threatened.[9]

Resistance to the report's findings came from several areas, including the sales team in charge of insurance and investment products. He notes that people actively lobbied senior management to force him to alter his findings, so that they would not reflect so badly on the bank. A distinctly adversarial relationship was emerging between his Group Regulatory Risk team and other divisions, including sales.

By this point the FSA had become concerned that the sales culture had got out of balance with controls at the Halifax; it appeared as though staff in the bank were becoming overly focused on sales at the expense of proper management of risk. The regulator issued another warning. In response, a thorough review of the entire sales culture at the bank was commissioned, again headed by Paul.[10]

The aim of the review was to figure out whether risks to customers through the sale of financial products by the HBOS retail division, alongside risks to the bank itself, were being managed in an appropriate way. It would examine specifically whether sales practices were being governed properly and within a cultural environment that respected the rules laid out by the FSA and HBOS itself. The review was comprehensive; between April and June 2004, Paul's team met with over forty senior managers in the retail division, nonexecutive members of the board, and others. More than thirty branches and contact centers were visited across the United Kingdom. To assess the organization's culture, focus groups were also carried out, and over a hundred frontline staff members were interviewed. People were given the opportunity to open up about the worries they had been harboring for some time. The research was revealing; as Paul said, "It was like taking the lid off a pressure cooker."[11]

Examining the results as they emerged, Paul was amazed and concerned. With characteristic English understatement, he later commented that things seemed to have become "a little pacey" at the bank.[12] Bank managers appeared to be focused solely on the quantity of loans, with appropriate checks being regularly ignored. This had become a real risk. He saw customers being persuaded that they should take out another loan—for example, to upgrade their kitchen—simply because they had received a mortgage. Alongside this, unnecessary payment protection insurance was sold.[13]

For Paul, this was going against the fundamentals of banking, which in his view included judgment and prudence: "Ordinary people when you offer them extra money find it very difficult to resist, that is why you have to be prudent. You have a fiduciary duty to your customer."[14] Paul was seeing this sense of duty being diluted. His colleagues all seemed to be subject to a new kind of pressure; incentives were high and bonuses were linked to sales volume. To meet the targets, rules were being overlooked. There was little oversight in place. Paul said,

> One woman put it like this: It's impossible to sell ethically and hit our sales targets. [There was] a huge focus on targets and a culture of fear if you didn't [meet them]. Put these together and you have a very heady mix.[15]

Reflecting on the causes, Paul could understand why this was happening; the Halifax was expanding rapidly in the retail market and the pressure to sign as many customers as possible was intense. He understood his chief executive's approach to growing the bank:

> When you have a strategy, that in a supermarket environment would be described as "stack 'em high and sell 'em cheap" . . . you have to sell a lot of them, because you have lower margins.[16]

The pervasive focus on meeting sales targets in the overheated environment of the retail bank, however, meant that adherence to safeguards for risk and compliance suffered: "The entire organization was focused on selling, selling, selling. But not on risk management. I was flabbergasted."[17] Paul was concerned that his bank was changing in a dangerous way. New cultural norms threatened not only the Halifax but also its parent HBOS, its shareholders, and its customers. The dramatic switch in culture to one focused on generating profits at the cost of risk was not unique to HBOS and echoes practices at Eileen Foster's Countrywide in the United States. These are just two instances, of many, of the cultural shift taking place across the global finance sector at the time.[18]

TENSIONS MOUNT

The emergent culture of HBOS had implications for rule following at the bank. People were being paid well to overlook them. Risk management professionals were struggling to do their jobs. When Paul reported to a Group Audit Committee meeting in June 2004, this was the main concern he raised. He talked about the report on the sales culture he had prepared, which detailed the "cultural indisposition to challenge" at the bank:

> I would not want the Committee to be under any illusion as to how strong the tensions were as GRR [Group Regulatory Risk] carried out its oversight work. And I have to say that there have been some behaviors which I would consider to be unacceptable.[19]

He expressed a hope that the organization would deal with this problem culture. Shortly afterward, he was called to meet with a senior sales executive. The meeting had been arranged in the hope that the ever-mounting tensions between the sales department and Paul's regulatory risk division could be discussed. Perhaps the resulting difficulties might even be resolved. Unfortunately, this was not to be. Paul described an exchange that took place:

> Before we had begun to discuss any of the issues, [the senior executive] lent across the table and pointed her finger at me and said, "I'm warning you, don't you make a fucking enemy of me." Later in the meeting she taunted me by asking if I would be embarrassed to learn that my report on Sales Culture was being re-written over the weekend by [two senior executives].[20]

Paul was due to present his sales report to the overall HBOS board, but before he got the chance, another sales executive took the report and summarized it. Reading the new version, Paul felt that some important points were left out. He decided to state these orally at the board meeting. He spoke with passion about the tensions between the risk and sales divisions, telling the directors present that the tensions "were almost unbearable and did not promote a good working environment." The FSA had been correct to worry about problems in the sales culture. Paul then went on to outline some solutions.

Despite his exertions, these points were not included in the minutes of the meeting. On realizing this, Paul spent a lot of time contacting the relevant people to demand that they would be, but he was repeatedly turned down. Even so, there was reason for optimism. His message seemed to have been surprisingly well received. Many meeting attendees had congratulated him for his hard work and for his bravery. One of the auditor managers who had been present at the meeting joked that Paul must have "a death wish" to have stood there and spoken so frankly about the problematic tensions within the bank.[21] Paul recalls the chairman of the Group Audit Committee thanking him for sharing the full report and noting that he "now understood how serious the issues were."[22] Worn out from his extensive research, Paul went on a summer holiday with his family. He relaxed and took the time to reflect on how well things had gone in the end. He would return to a HBOS that seemed dedicated to building a new culture. His bank would be considered a leading light of ethical behavior.

Paul returned refreshed and ready to help lead a new era in banking at his firm. One of his first meetings was a pleasant one; he was once again openly thanked for his work on the dangerous sales culture at the bank. A month after his holiday, Paul was summoned to the office of the chief executive, Sir James Crosby. He expected another discussion about his future plans for building and strengthening the regulatory risk division's function at HBOS. At the meeting Crosby started to talk about the planned restructuring of HBOS. Paul nodded along, waiting to learn where he would fit in. Apparently, he would not. Crosby informed Paul that he was to be made redundant; his role was no longer required because there was no role for him in the revised structure of HBOS.[23] According to Paul, Crosby was dismissive in his manner. He gave few reasons other than to point out that both executives and non-executives had lost confidence in him. Paul was stunned:

> I felt absolutely devastated. I went outside and I cried. I actually cried on the street. . . . [I had] a million thoughts: "What will I tell my wife? What will I tell my kids? Everyone knows I am a lunatic. . . . Betrayal after trust, for telling the truth. . . . The betrayal of it—there's nothing in it for me."[24]

Dana Gold, a consultant at the U.S. whistleblower advocacy group Government Accountability Project that represented banking whistleblowers Eric Ben-Artzi, Eileen Foster and others, describes how, "Employees get fired all the time for blowing the whistle. We see it so much; it's a predictable phenomenon."[25] Eileen Foster had likewise been dismissed for her attempts to speak up.

Paul decided to challenge the decision. Upon meeting with his lawyer he learned that he was, under UK law, a whistleblower. People in the United Kingdom who are fired because they tried to disclose information that relates to illegal practices taking place in their organization are protected under the Public Interest Disclosure Act legislation. This means that if an employment tribunal agrees that such a disclosure was attempted, it is up to the employer to prove otherwise. Paul's solicitors were confident that his efforts to draw attention to repeated breaches of FSA regulatory guidelines meant that his case was very strong. Moreover, as head of Group Regulatory Risk, he represented what the FSA deemed an approved person; any attempt to silence someone in that role is treated very seriously by the regulator. He therefore assumed that the FSA would be a strong supporter in what was now considered to be his whistleblowing case.

Motivation or Subjection?

What compelled Paul to keep on speaking up, even in the face of so much opposition? Even when he realized just how unpopular he and his team were becoming by raising awareness about the cultural changes within the bank, he persevered. Why would he and others like him go to such lengths, risking their jobs and their livelihoods? Many scholars aim to explain why people blow the whistle by examining the motivations that drive individuals. A consideration of Paul's experiences suggests a problem with this approach. It implies that motivation is a simple thing: that whistleblowers wake up one day and decide to blow the whistle for a specific reason. As Paul's story illustrates, many so-called whistleblowers are simply doing their jobs, albeit in a very committed and often outspoken manner. When this persistence goes against the norms of the organization and people are retaliated against for their commitment, they can be given a position of whistleblower, after the fact. In Paul's case, it was under the terms of UK law that this label came to be assigned to him. To defend his claim, he adopted it and, as we see later, used the whistleblower tag to speak out about wider cultural problems in UK banking. Eileen Foster's adoption of the label was also retrospective. Taking on the whistleblower subject position is something that people frequently do post hoc and often for tactical reasons. What they are actually doing, when they are going through the experience itself, is not whistleblowing but getting on with their work.

Rather than search for motivations for blowing the whistle therefore, a more interesting and potentially fruitful direction is to explore the processes of subjection at play. This means unpacking the norms that are being drawn on when someone adopts the label of whistleblower and accounts for actions taken under this category. The preceding statements from Paul are taken from TV, radio, and print interviews and my interview with him. In all these interactions, he was compelled to speak as a whistleblower. In constructing himself as such, Paul reinforces his position as a dedicated professional. He emphasizes this aspect when accounting for his actions. He frequently cites his extensive experience in risk management—for example, describing his ability to "smell the control issues" and sniff out potential problems, the core work of a risk professional. Paul also presents himself as extremely knowledgeable about the financial services industry more generally, as he details the "stack 'em high" strategy of the Halifax. He describes his initial response to learning about the problematic sales culture at the bank as being "flabbergasted," implying that these practices offended his professional status. Paul has been hailed as being an exemplary representative of his profession, and here it appears that highlighting and emphasizing this status helps him withstand harsh retaliation and aggressive resistance, including the "extreme argy bargy" he faced from a senior sales executive when he was trying to do his work.

Complementing this professional position, Paul adheres to his commitment to banking more generally, specifically to an idealized view of it in which ethics is paramount. In an interview he reflected on the history of the Halifax Bank and how its organizational culture was traditionally quite different from the one he witnessed. He recalls that the Halifax emerged in northern England during the Industrial Revolution as a way for ordinary people in communities to come together and organize, manage their money, obtain credit for families and businesses, and save for the future. It was a public good, founded on clear principles that considered people's well-being. For a hundred years, the Halifax helped many people and, prior to demutualization in 1997, was run in a somewhat conservative manner, focused on its members' needs.[26] For Paul, this is the kind of banker he is:

> The essence of a bank is prudence. You have a fiduciary duty to your customer. . . . Taking bets with other people's money doesn't fit within the definition of banking. A firm must act with integrity; a firm must act with due skill, care and diligence. A firm must have adequate systems and controls. . . . A firm must pay due regard to the interests of its customers and treat them fairly.[27]

Paul thus underlines his position as a consummate professional, committed to the original ideals of banking.

He explains that this commitment was so strong that it led to naïveté when he began to speak out. He describes how he had faith in his organization, believing that if he only worked hard enough, gathered evidence of sufficient quality, and took it to the right people, senior management would share his outrage and right the wrongs. In an interview some years after he left HBOS, he was asked whether he realized the danger he was in, when he continued to raise his head above the parapet:

> No I didn't—maybe I was good at all other forms of risk management except for risk management of my own personal circumstances. I felt very strongly that if I was able to demonstrate through evidence,

through the rigorous audits that we were carrying out, that things were going wrong, that I would be listened to. Even if I wasn't listened to by the executive, that I would be listened to by the non-executives, and also the FSA.[28]

He positions himself as a faithful employee, albeit noting that this faith was misplaced. Paul's self-construction as a naïve professional echoes that of other whistleblowers. Eileen Foster described her response to the fraud taking place at her retail mortgage bank:

> You'd think that the correct behavior for a regional manager would be to align *with* the corporate fraud group, to say, "Hey, if there *are* employees in my region committing fraud, I need to know about it," not going out and warning his employees and saying, "Hey, they are onto us!" And that was one of the things that shocked me more than anything else.[29]

Eileen drew on her sense of self as a professional, which led her to be shocked at what was happening:

> I never think people really understand how significant *that* was. I mean, that is the opposite behavior that you would expect, and yet when I would say that to Employee Relations or anybody else, nobody else was acting shocked. And I was like, "Why does this not bother anybody?"[30]

She went on to describe how she was full of hope when Bank of America took over Countrywide. She believed that the new management would listen to her complaints about the thousands of mortgages that were based on fake documents and see the extent of the wrongdoing. They would surely then get rid of the people who had facilitated the systematic mortgage fraud she witnessed, rehire her, and fix everything. She soon learned that Bank of America was not only aware of the fraud but was happy to let it continue. Describing her position in all this, she said it was a case of "rose-colored glasses. I guess I couldn't believe that corruption was *that* widespread." As with Paul, this hopeful view was what kept her going: "That's kind of what was powering me there. . . . I still thought I could fix it."[31] Of course, other elements emerged in people's narratives as they constructed their "I" in relation to the label whistleblower. People often described how their pursuit of the truth was influenced by the wrongdoing they witnessed affecting people they knew and cared about. Others spoke out because the misconduct threatened their own freedoms, should they be implicated in the wrongdoing. If it was uncovered and it turned out that they had known, because of their watchdog responsibilities they might be liable for a fine or jail time.[32] Even so, implicitly seeking acknowledgement as a professional is a recurrent feature of people's narratives. Their profession represents something of an authority, offering a strong and reliable identification. Drawing on it helps them make sense of what has happened. It must be noted here that whistleblowers are often disbelieved or seen as having suspicious motives, and most are aware of this danger. It is therefore tempting for them to use the best means available to attain validity in the eyes of others. Without this, they might not be believed.

Rather than attempting to determine the motivations of people who blow the whistle, it is interesting to hear their accounts of what they did and consider what kinds of power relations act through such self-positioning. First, recognition under the terms of dominant norms can come with a price. Whistleblowers, such as Paul, when presenting themselves as committed adherents to the profession of banking are also upholding another kind of authority. Although on the surface they appear to be speaking freely, unfettered by the strong cultural norms of their organization that command silence and acquiescence, in defending their speech they draw on another set of norms relating to the banking profession. Constructing the self as an idealized professional banker enables people who speak up to make sense of what has happened. Ironically, this means citing but also reinforcing the very industry and system that is ultimately responsible for the retaliation and suffering they receive. Philosopher Judith Butler describes this aspect of subjection; we are often led to embrace the terms that injure simply because they constitute our very sense of self.[33] Perhaps adopting its own terms in this way works to reinforce the authority of global finance as a system in society, causing it and its representative organizations to be even more entrenched and difficult to challenge. What might seem a benign identification is therefore problematic. On the other hand, it might entail a reworking of what it means to be a finance professional. Here we see the construction of a true professional as representing, overall: a person who adheres to the rules despite the lure of excess compensation for ignoring them, has sufficient skill to see the wider impacts of their actions on society, and has the ability to step outside the position of being a bureaucratic cog in the machine. This may result in a recasting of the position of finance professional as denoting a person who resists, a point returned to later.

A second issue relates to how we research whistleblowing and the methods we use. Other whistleblowers I interviewed espoused a similar position of naïve professional when describing their role in speaking out. Indeed, researchers who study whistleblowing often reiterate this concept when depicting their research subjects, noting that they are not disgruntled dissenters as is often assumed but rather people who strongly identify with their organizations, have pride in them, and hold great faith in their willingness to listen.[34] They are committed, albeit thwarted, defenders of the ideals of their profession. Similarly, whistleblowers often report a deep understanding not only of their role in the organization but also of the impact their organization has on the world. They can see the wider implications of the wrongdoing to which they are connected by their work activities and how it affects others in the organization and society beyond.[35] Ethics scholar Colin Grant terms this the "crystal clarity" of vision displayed by such individuals.[36] What such research tends not to examine, however, is that in asking a person a question in an interview or survey setting, they are implicitly inviting them to adopt a subject position, and a story, in response.

This returns us to research that attempts to discover whistleblowers' motivations; there exists an underlying assumption that speaking up is driven by clear, identifiable factors such as altruism or clarity of vision. Such factors are elicited by the researcher who, through either interview or survey, approaches the person known as whistleblower after the event and asks what compelled him or her to do it. This assumes that people are able to step outside their past selves and objectively point to reasons for speaking out. It is problematic because it overlooks the post hoc rationalization that comes with any research-generated narrative and that can be exacerbated by people who have engaged in traumatic actions like whistleblowing.[37] It also ignores that we tend to draw on culturally available ways of making sense of the world, not least when we are trying to explain complex and confusing situations. When journalists, researchers, politicians, and regulators approach someone they know as a whistleblower, they are implicitly asking him or her to speak from this subject position and to account for him- or herself as whistleblower. In such cases it very tempting to reiterate popular ways of understanding whistleblowing when trying to explain what happened.

When we are called to describe who we are and what we have done, we work with what is available. When we articulate our selves and the positions we hold, we are not in charge of the identifications we present. These are written for us elsewhere; "the one who speaks is not the originator of such speech, for that subject is produced in language through a prior performative exercise of speech: interpellation."[38] Norms are powerful, not least because we construct our identifications in relation to them; we perform ourselves against a backdrop of discursive power because of our desire to see ourselves, and have others see us, as coherent, valid subjects.[39] Positions of professionalism exist and compel the whistleblower into accentuating their occupancy of these spaces because they appear to offer the existential security whistleblowers desire.

In his in-depth study of whistleblowing, C. Fred Alford found whistleblowers adopting certain well-worn tropes when describing what occurred.[40] Whistleblower stories, he finds, often follow similar scripts. We can see how this happens. "The language the subject speaks is conventional and, to that degree, citational" as Butler points out.[41] By positioning ourselves alongside existing normative frameworks and articulating our selves in this way, we are citing the same norms, ensuring they remain alive. In whistleblowing, taking on such identities as naïve professional, particularly in public interviews, makes these available for other, future whistleblowers. This challenges existing theoretical work on whistleblowing that portrays the person who speaks out as uniquely free from normative influences, able to step outside the pull of culture and speak truth at will.[42] It also suggests that in exploring whistleblower motivations it is vital to unpack how these are articulated and what discursive forces are reinforced as a result.

Conclusion

Rather than search for factors that motivate people to speak out, it is helpful instead to examine the ways the subject position of whistleblower emerges. The ability to construct oneself as whistleblower in a manner that makes sense to oneself and to others is vital. The subjection to power required by a search for recognition as valid enables people such as Paul and Eileen to continue their efforts to speak up, even in the face of severe and violent reprisal. When asked to tell their stories and account for their actions during the early phase, being a whistleblower was not on their minds; this is a label that came later. In describing what they did and why they kept going in the face of harsh criticism by colleagues and bosses, adopting the position of whistleblower-professional was helpful. This was not straightforward but involved subjections to other kinds of authority including, ironically, those very institutions that they were trying to critique. Moreover the reinforcing of the position of professional as a source of identification can necessitate drawing a clear boundary around it, one that excludes others, as is explored in Chapter 9.

5

Whistleblower Retaliation: Impossible Speech and Violence

PEOPLE CAN EXPERIENCE retaliation when they begin to speak up about perceived wrongdoing in their organization. It can involve being isolated from colleagues, having their job reduced to menial tasks, or informal bullying. We tend not to be surprised when we hear of such reprisals; we have come to associate them with whistleblowing not least because of depictions in newspaper reports and in films. There is an implicit acceptance that it is okay, that whistleblower retaliation is part of life. When it occurs we don't intervene. Given that people are ostensibly speaking out with good intentions and with the aim of rectifying problems, are these reprisals really acceptable? Are they even understandable? In this chapter the concepts of exclusion and censorship help us see how an economy of recognition emerges in certain situations to classify whistleblowers' statements as *impossible speech* and how violence against such persons is justified as a result. Drawing on Irish whistleblower Olivia Greene's experiences, the chapter explores why whistleblowing seems to prompt such violent responses and what makes violence against whistleblowers so acceptable to onlookers.

Scapegoat: Failure of an Irish Financial Institution

Everyone in Ireland knew about the charismatic and powerful Michael Fingleton, who had grown a tiny organization into one of Ireland's largest lending institutions, Irish Nationwide Building Society (INBS).[1] He famously ran INBS in a personal, autocratic style, paying himself a salary of over €2 million in 2008.[2] One year earlier, Olivia Greene had provided evidence in court against him and became known internally as the whistleblower. The story captivated the Irish public.

Olivia had held a senior position at the building society since 1998, working alongside Fingleton as a loan supervisor. By 2007, her boss had begun to worry. The massive lending institution was running into serious financial difficulties due to the volume of loans it had made, many of them granted personally by Fingleton to high-profile journalists, politicians, and artists in Ireland, often without the appropriate documentation or collateral.[3] He had hoped to have sold the business by now, but it was 2007, the market was turning, and it did not look as though there were many buyers.[4] As yet, however, nobody knew of the scale of the exposure, so Fingleton had time. He began choosing senior executives to scapegoat.

One such scapegoat was Brian Fitzgibbon, whom Fingleton openly blamed for having lent large sums of money to two solicitors, loans that Fingleton himself had directly authorized, often in "an entirely informal process."[5] Regardless of the facts, Fingleton ordered that Brian be suspended from work. In turn, Brian brought an unfair dismissal case.

Brian was a friend of Olivia's and asked her to help him. She had been party to the loans and so had the proof he needed to clear his name in court. She gave evidence at an Employment Appeals Tribunal that Fingleton had authorized the loan. She was to feel the effects of this decision very soon. Olivia recalls what she was doing on the day Brian's case was heard:

> Fingleton was having a meeting with the board and a few branch managers. I was out for lunch, . . . and one of them rang and said, "Fingleton is after finding out [that] you signed the affidavit. You are after signing your death warrant." And after that, things became impossible; life became impossible.[6]

There was a culture of silence at INBS: Fingleton's staff were so loyal to the organization, or so cowed by Fingleton's often aggressive management style, that no one would speak against him even after serious scandals arising from his style became public knowledge. In 2009, when Olivia gave a controversial interview on RTE, the national broadcaster, the TV station asked over two hundred of her former colleagues to come and speak on the program. The station promised to provide anonymity by obscuring faces and altering voices. Not one person agreed to join Olivia in publicly criticizing Fingleton and highlighting the wrongdoing at the firm.

BULLYING

After giving evidence in court and thus openly disclosing the corruption at her organization, Olivia became known as the INBS whistleblower to colleagues and to others outside the bank. She remained working there for six months before conditions in the office became too difficult to bear. Sometimes Olivia was bullied in ways more suited to a children's playground than a professional workplace setting including physical aggression. One day she was about to pass through a door, walking behind her boss. To her surprise, Fingleton held it open for her: "I thought, Oh, things must be getting better now, he has held the door for me! But he slammed it back, and I got the door full in the face."[7] In another instance, at a credit committee meeting,

> I was by my chair, and Fingleton came in late. And because there was only one chair free, and it was beside me, he sat down in my chair. And one of the guys said, "Actually, that's Olivia's chair."
> "Oh, is it?" [said Fingleton].
> I had all my documents and everything, and just with one sweep [he knocked them to the floor]. Everything. In front of everybody. I had to go around on the floor, picking up—all the paperwork! Nobody would help me.[8]

The bullying ranged from such petty acts to more serious accusations of poor work practice. Interest-only mortgages are widely considered to have contributed to the demise of Ireland's banking sector that happened shortly afterward:

At a meeting [Fingleton] started saying that I introduced interest-only mortgages to the society; that it was all my fault. [He described] how I introduced the one-year fixed rate, so that was all my fault. . . . So eventually at one of the meetings, I said, "Hang on one second, I will be back," and I came back up with *his* paperwork where he had signed it off. . . . And it was still my fault! . . . It was just pure bullying: harassment.[9]

Not all the bullying she experienced was at the hands of Michael Fingleton. Other times, it was a continuous stream of belittling statements emanating from some of his closer colleagues:

There were a few older guys, managers within other departments. Grown-up men, in their sixties, who should have known better. [They] used to come down [to my office] and do Fingleton's dirty work as well! I remember saying to one guy, he was ready to target me again, you know, because he used to do it in front of all the staff, really, really trying to belittle me. . . . So he was [saying], "You did this wrong, you did that wrong."

And I said, "How long are you here?" And he said, "Three years."

I said, "I am ten years here. I am running this department. You are running the other department upstairs. Can I give you a bit of advice?" Now, this is a man in his sixties! [*laughs*]. [I said,] "Why don't you get back up to your own department and run it, and do what you are being paid to do?" . . . You just sometimes had to get as ignorant [rude] to them as they were to you, even though it is not in my nature.[10]

Olivia's little act of defiance did not go unheeded:

So he went and reported it to Fingleton. Then all of a sudden this guy—I wasn't allowed to run my department; this guy was running the department. I had nothing to do. He used to call a meeting at ten to nine on a Monday morning, knowing I wasn't in until nine or half nine. I would come in and then he'd target me about my attitude, how I wouldn't give anything in meetings. And basically he just used to pick and put me down.

Now, I was giving as good as I got. All the time. Yes, I would go outside and cry my eyes out. I would go out and ring [my husband] on the mobile. But I would never let them see me do it.[11]

Even though she was tough, the bullying got to Olivia. As did Paul Moore and Eileen Foster, she drew on her professionalism to describe how it was to occupy the position of whistleblower and to deal with the aggression that it seemed to compel from others. She recalls reinforcing her status as a competent professional, confident in her ability to run her department.

Reports of aggressive, bullying behavior by employers and by colleagues were common among whistleblowers interviewed for this study. Before he was dismissed, Paul was threatened not to make a "fucking enemy" of a senior colleague, and Eileen found herself the subject of an internal investigation into her "inappropriate and unprofessional behavior" and "poor judgment as a leader."[12] Few of the bullies were ever reprimanded for their actions, but rather some whistleblowers described how they had watched with dismay as the careers of these people flourished.

ISOLATION

In the six months before she left the bank, Olivia's job changed completely. She was being watched and monitored as though she were an entry-level clerk in her late teens: "HR [staff] were monitoring me: monitoring, monitoring every move. If I was here, then I should have been there."[13] Gradually she was coming under pressure to adhere to the smallest rules associated with her contract. She had to be present on Monday mornings by 9 a.m., even though she had had a long-standing informal agreement that, because she lived outside Dublin, on Mondays she could be a few minutes late.

Olivia was effectively demoted; all power and responsibility that she had previously held was taken away:

> I was watched, stripped of everything, stripped of a job, stripped of any power. . . . I couldn't sign things off anymore. I couldn't agree [approve] a loan, couldn't decline a loan; I couldn't give a party release. . . . I could do absolutely nothing. And that's what they wanted me doing. I had to turn up and be watched and scrutinized.[14]

People who speak out about wrongdoing often describe being sidelined at work and given a new, diminished set of responsibilities.[15] Senior managers are unwilling to fire these people but want to remove them from their senior role and try to ensure that working conditions are uncomfortable. Such a move sends a clear message to other staff and keeps the person out of the way. This is nicknamed a "potted palm" position; the resulting job is as useful and interesting as the office plant's.[16]

During the months that she remained at INBS after having given evidence in court, Olivia felt increasingly isolated by colleagues, as well as by management. This isolation was felt in formal gatherings such as the mundane credit committee meetings that she was now required to attend regularly. She described her perception of these:

> It was nearly like I was exposed, and they were all ready just to pounce. And because they were all sitting around the table like this [*gestures at the other end of the table*], I ended up sitting at the top of the table with all these people looking down at me.[17]

Even outside such formal settings, Olivia began to feel more and more alone at her work in headquarters.

> People at head office were afraid of even speaking to me because I was the black sheep of Nationwide. Staff that I had a relationship with would barely talk to me. . . . There were only a few people that [I] could speak to, like [my husband, who also worked at INBS] and a few guys at the branches.[18]

After ten years of running her department, this was hard to take.

> You'd actually see people that you thought maybe were friends, even out in branches and everything—seeing the managers, and they'd started doing back-track stuff. Towards the end, I'd say there was about eight good people I could trust within. And there wasn't one of them within head office, they were in branches. . . . And if you exclude [my husband], that's seven people.[19]

Experiences of isolation are common among whistleblowers.[20] Like Paul Moore, Martin Woods was a banking watchdog. An anti-money laundering officer, he blew the whistle on billions of dollars from drug dealers in Mexico being laundered through his bank, leading to the most significant charge levied at the time under the U.S. Bank Secrecy Act. He described the response that one can expect from colleagues after having blown the whistle in such a situation:

You have taken action that others determined not to take. And by the action you have taken, you have jeopardized their position, because they might lose their job. And if they keep their job, they are probably going to have to work twice as hard now, because you have highlighted these problems that now will take a lot of fixing. And also some people think you are just cocky and just think you a smartarse.[21]

Isolation is very difficult to cope with at a psychological level. Work attachments inevitably form, simply by being in the same environment as other people. Suddenly these connections are broken, and the person is cast into solitude.

Eventually, in May 2008, Olivia handed in her notice, resigning under duress. Soon after, her husband was temporarily suspended from the bank and later fired; the targeting continued even after she was gone. Olivia was not alone in losing her job as a result of speaking out; this has happened to many other whistleblowers, both in financial services and in other industries.[22]

Exclusion, Censorship, and Violence

The whistleblowing literature can explain this to some degree. Retaliation often occurs because managers feel threatened by whistleblowers, as happened with Olivia and also with Paul and Eileen.[23] Fingleton and the close colleagues who apparently retaliated on his behalf reacted strongly to Olivia because of her publicizing his misdemeanors; she posed a threat. Research also tells us that the strength of retaliation that a whistleblower experiences, in any given setting, tends to be proportional to how deeply embedded the wrongdoing is in the system.[24] When the wrongdoing is directly related to normal, everyday ways of doing business, therefore, the resulting responses can be very aggressive indeed because revealing it threatens the entire organization. This occurred for Olivia. At the time that she was speaking out, people in her bank had begun to fear for their long-term futures. The effects of the 2008 financial crisis in the United States were beginning to be felt in Ireland. Staff were aware that their careers at INBS were tied to the longevity of Fingleton; he had no succession plan in place, and the bank was built around him and his reputation for lending. And Olivia Green had given evidence in court about his reckless practices that damaged Fingleton. Paul Moore was likewise openly critiquing a thoroughly systemic problem in his organization—the very culture that pervaded the sales group—and Eileen Foster was speaking up about the normalized corruption that had become integral to Countrywide's business model. Olivia, Paul, and Eileen were each drawing attention to work practices that lay at the very heart of their organizations.

Under this view, the position of the whistleblower represents a distinct threat to the whistleblower's boss and colleagues, which prompts retaliation against the person who occupies the position. This theory moves us toward a deeper understanding—it explains the impulse that might lead to retaliation—but does not account for the extreme nature of the punishment delivered for speaking out. Nor do such theories explain its acceptability—that is, that severe whistleblower retaliation frequently goes unquestioned and is considered almost predictable. This response makes little sense, particularly when whistleblowers such as Olivia are describing aspects of their organization of which everyone is aware and doing so with the apparent motivation of helping a friend and in the ultimate interest of stakeholders. How does this act result in such severe, and yet acceptable, reprisal? What gives rise to this shocking situation, whereby we can almost foretell that harsh and extreme punishment will be meted out to those who speak up?

CENSORSHIP AND IMPOSSIBLE SPEECH

An obvious place to begin is with the idea that whistleblowers go against strong norms within their organizations. In global finance, there are deep-seated reasons for firms' cultures of complicity, and these are supported by the wider institutional, regulatory, and even societal cultures in place, as described in Chapter 3. Whistleblowers like Olivia attempt to resist this culture of silence, and they are penalized. What precisely is it about them that makes this injury possible?

Sociologist Erving Goffman describes how those who deviate from a collective norm can be severely punished as a result. Philosopher and gender theorist Judith Butler sheds light on how deviation specifically relates to speech through her work on censorship.[25] Censorship can be a powerful mechanism of control, determining what can and cannot be said in certain situations. Its real power comes from it in effect operating through the regulation of recognition: it grants or denies subjecthood. This means that boundaries are developed in which some kinds of speech are considered valid in a given setting, and others are ignored. This delineation works because it produces particular kinds of subjects; only certain types of speech are considered "legible as the speech of a subject."[26] Coherent subjects thus emerge as a result of acceptable utterances, whereas others who transgress are excluded from viability. These outsiders have articulated speech that is considered "impossible" in terms of the dominant normative framework. Their impossible statements are destined to remain unheard and demeaned as "precisely the ramblings of the asocial, the rantings of the 'psychotic.'"[27] Those who engage in illegible speech are not even considered to be subjects who must be ignored. Not afforded the status of subject they remain subhuman, incoherent, "psychotic." The point is that censorship effectively regulates speech because it produces categories around subjecthood; subjects come into being, or not, in relation to their adherence to the implicit rules of "speakable discourse."[28] Censorship acts as a powerful matrix of control because it determines who will and will not be recognized as a subject.

In Olivia's recollections in these interviews, examining the subject who speaks and tracing the "I" as it is positioned is very helpful in answering the questions posed earlier. She likens her act of speaking out to "signing her death warrant," describing how, afterward, both work and life itself "became impossible." Once she was known as the INBS whistleblower, Olivia's self, her I, came to be equated with psychotic, illegible utterances. Her very existence in the organization was made untenable. She describes the overt monitoring of her every move: "If I was here, then I should have been there." There was no proper place for Olivia. Her I simply did not belong, she was "stripped of everything . . . stripped of any power." Her presence in the organization was as a hollow entity, not a functioning employee; she existed to simply "turn up and be watched and scrutinized." Many others interviewed for this book described themselves in similar ways. What dynamics were driving this regulation by (denying) recognition?

In each incident of censorship, implicit forces are at work in the background to structure and organize the "conditions of intelligibility" of speech.[29] These forces are already present, compelling certain kinds of statements and certain kinds of subjects to emerge. It is important to examine them; as Butler notes, "The question is not what it is I will be able to say, but what will constitute the domain of the sayable within which I begin to speak at all."[30] For Olivia and other financial services whistleblowers, an interlinked matrix of power operated within their organizations to instill norms of silence and compliance. In Chapter 3, details of the forces contributing to this are described, including a deference to authority, a lax approach to the rules, and a privileging of growth above all else. Here we see how these can manifest at the micro level of the person who attempts to resist them. A "domain of the sayable" was created in this small corner of the financial services sector. This was a productive enactment of power because it enabled certain kinds of subject to emerge, creating categorical boundaries around who was in and who was out, who could speak and who must not. Olivia had stepped outside this norm, and so she was not recognizable in the categories pertaining to her workplace. She had taken on a particular, new position: the source of impossible speech. She was no longer simply a transgressive employee, a colleague who happened to have made some challenging and unsavory comments; as whistleblower she was now a fully impossible being.

This conception helps us see how and why such a stark distance was constructed between Olivia and her colleagues and how, so quickly, she was ostracized simply for what she had said. It also helps in understanding the ambiguity with which whistleblowers are often perceived. Speaking out is a particular and powerful kind of deviance; whistleblowing statements are impossible speech acts and those who engage in them are considered unintelligible. But how to explain the strength of the reactions against her: the extreme nature of the whistleblower retaliation Olivia and others experience?

VIOLENCE AS A RESPONSE TO SPEAKING OUT

First, it is helpful to conceptualize such experiences as more than simply retaliation; they are acts of violence. Violence is more than physical force. The bullying Olivia experienced was physical, as when a door was "accidentally" closed in her face, but it was also emotional; she was humiliated in public when her papers were scattered to the floor at a meeting and she had to bend down and pick them up in front of her seated colleagues. She was accused of bad practice, and her responsibilities at work were gradually removed. These experiences were forms of violence, but not violence as we traditionally assume it to be.

In *Frames of War,* Butler usefully expands our conception of violence, its causes and impacts.[31] In addition to the physical acts that we typically imagine when we think of violence, it can also occur through excluding certain people from categories of personhood that have become dominant. Marking them off in this way can invoke violence on, for example, those who "choose" unusual gender or sexual identifications.[32] Butler's concept of normative violence encapsulates this experience, adding it to more overt, typical forms of violence.[33]

Violence occurs in two phases; first, groups are excluded from the norm and presented as threats to it. This paves the way for violence to be legitimized against them:

> Such populations are "lose-able," or can be forfeited, precisely because they are framed as being already lost or forfeited; they are cast as threats to human life as we know it rather than as living populations in need of protection from illegitimate state violence, famine or pandemics.[34]

Butler develops these ideas in the context of the U.S. military engagements in the Middle East. She describes how both the state and the media play a role in portraying the people of this region as deserving targets of violence. They are carefully framed as not fully human, not vulnerable, and hence not deserving of protection. Considered a threat to U.S. citizens, it is easy to dismiss them. Their deaths are not worth grieving, and so their lives do not demand the same care and protection as would be granted to a citizen of the West. Forfeiting such lives through waging war is therefore justifiable. When violence is exerted against people who are considered to be human, it typically evokes revulsion and efforts to prevent it. But when derealized persons are involved, violence is legitimized because they are not considered to be grievable entities worthy of protection.

This preapproved violence is reflected in Olivia's description of her isolation. She was treated in subtle ways as someone apart from the rest of the firm, such as at the credit committee meetings, where she felt "exposed" because her colleagues were all seated in a group at one end of the table, "ready . . . to pounce" on her, alone at the other side. She was the exception, the black sheep that people were "afraid of even speaking to," which indicates that she was seen as something different, something exceptional and frightening. Moreover, the violence that Olivia's presence appeared to call forth is more than can be represented by the somewhat rational strategic actions implied by the term *retaliation*. Rather, the responses of colleagues and managers were vicious and chaotic, as we saw with grown adults engaging in childish behavior—scattering papers and other acts. These confused and panicked reactions point to a situation in which the retaliating person does not know how to act—a somewhat unintelligible and irrational reaction is evoked. Perhaps this embodied, visceral response also emerged because of a deep-held need to defend the structures of banking that Olivia appeared to threaten, a point I return to later.

Normative violence is violence in its "primary" form because it operates by first creating exclusions and foreclosing subjectivity and then facilitating more typical, overt forms of violence, including physical ones.[35] Considering normative violence in these settings allows us to perceive how it is inherently social—part of normal organizational practice. The bullying Olivia experienced was not just the preserve of her boss but permeated interactions with other senior managers; she felt that the isolation involved all but eight colleagues in a huge organization. Moreover, this violence represented an important symbolic act signaling to coworkers exactly where the boundary around acceptable and impossible speech lay. Scholars have noted that whistleblower retaliations can represent such signals and discourage others from speaking out about wrongdoing, and here we see more clearly how and why this occurs. Normative violence in these events is social, and it is organizational.[36]

Conclusion

Bringing these concepts together helps us see how Olivia and whistleblowers like her are not simply speaking out about wrongdoing in their organizations; they are engaging in impossible, quasi psychotic speech that places them in a new category in which they are excluded and banished and not acceptable to the organization. This primary exclusion then paves the way for a secondary categorization that portrays them as viable candidates for normative violence. From the perspective of colleagues and managers then, violence against whistleblowers like Olivia is not violence, because people like her are not valid. In her case and those of Paul and Eileen, violence was more than just physical; it was also emotional, as a result of their engaging in impossible speech.

It appears that the cruel expulsion of the whistleblower from organizational life, both materially and symbolically, is an important part of business as usual within financial sector organizations. The censorship-driven regulation of subjecthood supports this through granting or denying recognition. Existing research into whistleblower retaliation details the types of reprisal that people experience, the kinds of contexts that can give rise to it, and the reasons that can compel colleagues and managers to act in such ways.[37] Although valuable, these approaches do not allow us to see why violence emerges so quickly and why it involves such extremes. The result is an inherent acceptance of this excessive aggression against whistleblowers. It is important to develop new perspectives on whistleblowing retaliation that overturn the implicit narrative of the whistleblower who is destined to suffer, with society destined to acquiesce. Different concepts are required to break apart these well-worn frames.[38] Only through such rethinking can we begin to understand how and why such extreme—violent—behavior is legitimized in organizations.

6

Speaking Out in Public:
Toward Possible Speech

THE PRECEDING CHAPTERS remained at the level of the organization. The focus was on the reactions of managers and colleagues to people speaking up and how those people in turn responded to these reactions. Desires for recognition, and its refusal, are important dynamics in whistleblowing struggles. In what follows we move outside, beyond the organization. People are sometimes forced or choose to go public with the information they are trying to highlight. They see that the problem is not being dealt with internally, they are concerned that it will continue, and so they decide to speak out to a regulator, a journalist, or the police. In many such instances people become known in public as a whistleblower. No longer private citizens, they come to be associated with the act of speaking up and of going outside the organization to do so. This chapter focuses on how those occupying this public position of whistleblower are perceived. Specifically, it asks whether, when one has been assigned an impossible position within the organization as someone not worth listening to, it is possible to change this situation. Can a whistleblower move from being seen as a source of incoherent illegible speech to a valid and respected person, one who is recognized, valued, and crucially, allowed to speak?

Going outside, or external whistleblowing, is a significant area of research, not least because of the importance of public perceptions of people who speak up. Opinions are often ambivalent; they can shift dramatically on the basis of how, for example, the whistleblower is framed in the media. These public perceptions can make or break a person's campaign. They often determine how the whistleblower will be treated, and whether their claims about wrongdoing will be heeded.

Not Being Heard: Financial Services Norms

Sometimes whistleblowers succeed in gaining public attention for their stories. The most common outcome, however, is to be completely ignored, by the public, media, politicians, and relevant authorities.[1] The majority of whistleblowers are not listened to.

In September 2008, the Irish government learned that many of Ireland's banks did not have the funding, or liquidity, needed for financial stability. In response, the government offered a blanket guarantee on all bank loans, and this partially led to a European Union bailout of €68 billion, a huge sum in a country of four million people.[2] Taxes were raised and severe austerity measures were imposed that continued for years. The government claimed that it could not have known the state the banks were actually in. It claimed that it was taken by surprise; however, Jonathan Sugarman attests he had alerted the regulator to this risk, months before the crash. In May 2007, Sugarman had been headhunted from his German bank to join UniCredit's Irish operation. The move was a promotion: he would be head of risk. As risk manager, he was responsible for ensuring that the bank had adequate liquidity—that is, enough cash and assets at the end of each trading day to reasonably meet its liabilities. This is an essential function in banking. When it breaks down in many institutions at once this can lead to a banking crisis, as indeed happened in Ireland a mere year after Jonathan's resignation. At UniCredit, Jonathan had seen repeated breaches of the regulations regarding liquidity; his bank was engaged in very dangerous practices. Realizing that he was sitting on explosive information, he raised the problem with his boss, but nothing was done. Jonathan then contacted the banking regulator. This was a requirement by law, because of his role as head of risk. He reports that the regulator, the government's ultimate watchdog in Irish financial services and thus the final authority, effectively ignored his claims. He embarked on a long wait, during which he continually tried to raise awareness of what he had witnessed.

Over the next five years, international events were taking place that signaled lax compliance practices at his bank elsewhere; UniCredit came under investigation for problematic business practices by the U.S. Treasury Department and the Department of Justice and was found guilty of tax fraud.[3] And still Jonathan waited. The authorities took no action on this major liquidity breach at the International Financial Services Center. No sanctions or prosecutions were brought forward. Jonathan himself was not contacted. His story was told in media outlets, including Australia's ABC News *Foreign Correspondent* and Belgian and Greek state TV channels, and he was named in the Austrian parliament in debates on the banking crisis. The Irish political magazine *Village* reported extensively on the matter and an article appeared in the national broadsheet the *Irish Times,* with the names and details withheld. Other than that, there was silence in Ireland around Jonathan's allegations.

Why was this? His story appeared to be explosive. In an era when everyone in the country was talking about the banks and the problems they had caused, demanding answers to these questions, Jonathan was a whistleblower with just that: a set of answers. But he was denied an audience in Ireland. Jonathan's attempt to speak up occurred in a particular context. Strong norms were in place that influenced both the ability and the desire of Ireland's political and banking institutions to heed such warnings. The regulator, housed in the Central Bank of Ireland, was no exception. While Jonathan was raising his complaints, Ireland's financial regulator was already in trouble with its European counterparts, and as a number of commentators observed, this meant it was unlikely to welcome information about wrongdoing in the sector.[4] The regulator was charged with overseeing a particularly laissez-faire financial services industry in Dublin, which had been dubbed "the Wild West of European finance" by the *New York Times* in 2005.[5] The German regulator, BaFin, had frowned on Ireland's lax regulation of its international banking sector for years.[6] It had recently issued warnings about the lack of robust financial oversight in Dublin, not least because of the near collapse of the German Landesbank Sachsen due to irregularities that had been traced back to Ireland.[7] There was more history there; in 2008, lack of liquidity at the Dublin Depfa bank, relating to the collapse of Lehman Brothers, had very nearly caused the failure of the entire German banking system, according to the head of Deutsche Bank.[8] So when Jonathan arrived at the offices of the Irish financial regulator on Dame Street waving his smoking gun, it may have been the kind of news that this office did not wish to hear, certainly not to share. For these and other reasons, it is perhaps unsurprising that Jonathan's news was less than welcome. He was seen not as a messenger to be greeted but an irritant to be ignored.

This lack of attention on the part of the regulator was implicitly permitted by wider civil society: the journalists, commentators, mainstream politicians, and their constituents, all of whom effectively supported this silence. Regulatory authorities are not immune to the influence of these parties, and if a sufficient number had supported Jonathan's cause, the financial regulator would have been forced to act. Why the reluctance from people more generally to address this issue? Why was Jonathan destined to remain an impossible, incoherent nonsubject? It is helpful to look at another example in which the opposite happened.

Winning Strategies?

Having previously been in the Swiss army and worked as an accountant, Rudolf Elmer had been with Julius Bär from 1987 to 2003. Julius Bär is one of Switzerland's most respected and oldest private banks, dealing only with wealthy individuals.[9] He first worked as an auditor screening complex transactions at the bank and then was promoted in 1994 to chief operating officer and compliance officer at the Cayman Islands branch. He was tasked with overseeing operations in the Cayman office. By 1998, he had begun to ask questions about certain financial structures that were set up to facilitate tax avoidance or worse in Julius Bär's Cayman branch. He also questioned the clear policy of providing services for tax evasion and excessive secrecy for clients. Among these clients were people with criminal convictions, including drug-related ones. Rudolf reports that he could see that the practices were immoral and also perhaps criminal, particularly after requests for him to authorize certain transactions.

Rudolf had developed a reputation in the Zurich, New York, and finally the Cayman offices of Julius Bär as being a "critical thinker" who often raised problematic issues with his senior managers.[10] When he began to ask questions about dubious transactions, it came to little: "They listened to me but not much changed." He began to try to rectify the problem himself.[11]

> I felt for a long time [that] I can solve the issue myself, that the higher
> up I get on the ladder, the easier it would be to do this. So in the Cay-
> mans I also tried with internal auditors, external auditors, and even
> authorities, but they didn't pick it up or didn't want to pick it up. So
> what can you do?[12]

Rudolf was too worried to raise a formal complaint, because of what he had heard about the Caymans:

> Filing a complaint in the Cayman Islands would have meant the death
> penalty one way or another! In 2008 a Swiss banker, Frederic Bizet, was
> made unconscious and placed in his car, which then was put on fire. I
> played in the soccer team of the police force, and I knew how things
> worked on these pirate islands.[13]

In 2002, documents were leaked that related to the setting up of anonymous trusts in the Caymans. The bank carried out searches of staff members' homes. Rudolf was asked to take a lie detector test, which he failed for not completing, because of back pain.[14] He was fired for this.[15] He announced that he would challenge his firing, stating that it had been a response to his continued attempts to solve problems as he perceived them. Feeling that it was futile to approach the courts in the Caymans, because of the influence of his bank there, he filed a complaint in Switzerland.

At the time of his firing, Rudolf had a backup of the bank's computer data in his possession. As the appointed chief operating officer and hurricane emergencies person, it was his job to take a backup tape home every evening in case of a fire at the bank. The data was in his possession when he was fired because he was legally responsible for it, although Julius Bär would later claim that the episode was theft. It contained the details of trusts, companies, and mutual and hedge funds that were run through the Caymans, along with the names and accounts of many tax cheats from different countries. That the names were tax cheats was clear to Rudolf from the internal memos and notes that accompanied the documents.

He said he was threatened by the head of Human Resources, who told him that if he took action in the courts he would be finished. He describes how he began to use the data he had to build support, to protect himself and his family. After a detailed analysis of internal memos, notes, and procedures, particularly focusing on the bank's Trust Department, he leaked this data to the local tax authorities in Zurich and then to those at the Swiss federal level. Getting no response, he took the evidence to the Swiss federal prosecutor. Nobody wanted to know. Rudolf wanted a public court trial so that he could gain transparency for what was happening. He knew, however, that it would be a difficult task because, as he noted,

> Swiss bank secrecy is a golden calf and needs to be protected at all costs. . . . The interest of the Swiss government is clearly to demonstrate that Swiss bank secrecy is above everything and has a kind of global power. Above everything, it is to send the message to multinational corporations, financial institutions, and high-net-worth individuals, worldwide, that even if you are a criminal, your assets are safe in Switzerland; our privacy laws regarding Swiss bank secrecy will protect you globally![16]

In 2005, the leak of information from Julius Bär was reported in the *Wall Street Journal* and other media, and the bank took action.[17] Rudolf was charged with violating Swiss bank secrecy by releasing data belonging to Julius Bär and Trust Companies, Cayman, despite this entity not being a bank per se.[18] He spent thirty days in custody and was denied legal assistance by the prosecutor in charge.[19] During this time Rudolf's health was suffering; he had a medical diagnosis that showed he was incapable of withstanding the rigors of confinement but was kept in prison regardless.

Rudolf and his family became targets of intimidation and harassment by people he claims were Swiss and German private investigators that the bank had hired. This continued for years. His daughter would later receive an undisclosed settlement from the bank for this harassment.[20] Rudolf's complaints about the hounding were consistently ignored. The law did not provide assistance.[21] He then approached the Swiss media to see whether they would help draw attention to his case. However, he found that the Swiss media appeared to more often favor Julius Bär, presenting Rudolf as either a disgruntled employee or, worse, a person with a mental illness.

> [They] preferred to write about the whistleblower, that is me, as mentally ill and / or out for revenge. The articles did not mention any wrongdoing by the bank in the Cayman Islands, even though the journalists had plenty of evidence.[22]

In the newspapers that did take up his story, the articles negatively portrayed him as an unreliable, suspect banker who was looking for vengeance. They did not focus on the wrongdoing. This media ambivalence can be a common experience for whistleblowers.

With little support available from the Swiss media and with the law appearing unable or unwilling to help, Rudolf turned to civil society. He asked for help from the Swiss Foundation of the International Social Service and their Rights for Children program to see if they could help protect his daughter but to no avail. He contacted a university professor who was known to be active in anti-corruption advocacy. According to Rudolf, this man suggested that if Julius Bär was involved in any activity, it could be assumed that this had been agreed with the tax authority and so was within the law. He did not even look at the facts of Rudolf's case.[23]

RETHINKING THE SUBJECT POSITION

By 2007, it appeared that all avenues had failed Rudolf in Switzerland. Nobody was interested, despite what he saw to be the urgency of the problem. He found himself in a place in which many other whistleblowers end up; he was stuck. Rudolf was suffering extreme forms of retaliation, and he could not get help. Exasperated by the absence of any support from the obvious places, Rudolf began to rethink his position. He approached a former judge in Zurich, known for his integrity:

I said, "You work along with people, leading people in politics and the courts." He replied, "Look, the issue is [that] the state or the government or however you call it has a policy. Supporting the financial industry, and the support *of* the financial industry, is a key thing in a government. It means the well-being of society, or at least that is the way it is presented. . . . So, therefore, you will never have any support in such a secrecy restriction from organizations which are powerful."[24]

This judge was telling him that Switzerland was a country in which bank secrecy was paramount. As a whistleblower, his position in society would always remain completely unsupported by powerful organizations. It was understandable that he would receive little help from Swiss authorities, and in fact it made perfect sense that he had been prosecuted for what he had done. As Rudolf said,

> States have a stake, and prosecutors and judges are part of the state; therefore, they have to do what is in the best interest of the state. Certainly, some prosecutors and even judges are aware that principles of legality become questionable, but the interest of states is superior to any laws. That is one of the key insights I learned.[25]

Large amounts of money were involved. Rudolf said,

> It is not only a political issue, it is also an economic issue in which financial institutions, multinational conglomerates and ultra-high net worth individuals make a lot of money profiting from tax, legal, [and] regulatory loopholes in secrecy jurisdictions.[26]

Rudolf began to query how he was positioned in relation to the politicians, law enforcers, and journalists in his native Switzerland. As a would-be whistleblower in a country where the protection of bank data is a "golden calf," Rudolf would never gain a voice. As someone attempting to speak out about tax issues, he was "seen as a highly political problem."[27]

> In Switzerland, I could have gone to *all* the newspapers and told them the story. And someone would have reported about it. But the ones who would report about it would have reported me as a madman, which actually happened on Swiss TV, the state-sponsored channel.[28]

A conversation helped him think about how his position might be articulated in interesting new ways:

> [A] police officer I talked to said, "Look, you work in the state of Zurich. You can approach every newspaper editor in Zurich; I'm pretty sure they won't support you. You need to go to a newspaper out of the state of Zurich, even outside of Switzerland, and *they* would report about it, and you need to have that opportunity to make that case." [And I realized that] it's a bit of a dirty boys game, [as] we call it in Switzerland.[29]

Rudolf understood that by staying in Switzerland his position as whistleblower would have no legitimacy. It was not that he had not contacted enough people, hired sufficient lawyers, or spent enough time chasing newspapers. It was simply never going to happen. Like Jonathan Sugarman in Ireland, he occupied an impossible position; his warnings were ignored as ramblings, and he was not recognized as a legitimate voice. Exhausted and sick of the long-standing "defamation, criminal charges, blackmail and psycho-terror," he said,

> I searched the Internet and came across Wikileaks' page. I contacted them and discussed the matter at length because I wanted to be assured that they would not abuse the information to make money.[30]

He provided documents on his recent court case that evidenced the harassment he and his family had experienced. He was not sure whether to add his name, having had enough of the pain that can come with being in the public eye. In the end, he explained,

> I put my name on my first whistleblower letter to Wikileaks. It gives more credibility to the fact that falsified data was published. Because it was an act of civil disobedience, my name was necessary.[31]

WikiLeaks published. Rudolf had given a short list of fifteen clients and their tax information to the website, although the names were not made public. The *Guardian* scrutinized the list and concluded that it gave details of "numerous trusts in which wealthy people have placed capital."[32] The trusts were registered in the Cayman Islands and so the beneficiaries paid no taxes on the profits.

What Rudolf's information showed was not only how many wealthy people seemed to be unwilling to pay their taxes to their home countries but also how his and other banks actively promoted this kind of behavior. The issue went far beyond Julius Bär and its clientele; rather, it pointed to a whole system of tax evasion that was supported by many organizations. It was inevitable that assisting in this were bankers in Vaduz, Liechtenstein; Zurich (like Julius Bär); and Frankfurt, Germany. Moreover, *Guardian* reporters connected the data with some names and backgrounds of criminals and drug dealers involved. Despite strict libel laws in the United Kingdom, they published these, giving a context to Rudolf's information.

WikiLeaks wrote and published an article supporting Rudolf's claims.[33] The organization also helped Rudolf translate the documents detailing his complaints about harassment and intimidation and file them with the European Court of Human Rights on behalf of himself and his family.[34] Rudolf was very grateful to the online collective. Now, after six years of trying to be heard, his information was gaining an audience. The situation escalated. Julius Bär's lawyers challenged the publication of the data. In a high-profile trial, the bank procured a court order in California to close down the entire WikiLeaks website. Suddenly WikiLeaks, the site that had published evidence of human rights abuses in China and political corruption in Kenya, was offline. From the *Los Angeles Times* to the American Civil Liberties Union, groups and individuals argued for its reinstatement; the story was followed by millions of Internet observers, many of whom had not previously heard of Rudolf, WikiLeaks, or indeed Julius Bär. Groups cited the First Amendment in defense of the website. Amid huge publicity, WikiLeaks challenged the order, and it was eventually overturned. Rudolf had done well from his engagement with WikiLeaks, albeit it was a stroke of luck:

> I was lucky that the bank tried to close down the server in California, which actually they can't do; the so-called Barbra Streisand effect. [Suddenly] people wanted to see and read about what's on WikiLeaks.[35]

One unforeseen consequence of this was that the U.S. Internal Revenue Service heard about Rudolf and got in touch with him. He cooperated with the IRS and with investigators and others there who monitor tax havens, including U.S. Senator Carl Levin of Michigan. Rudolf supplied information to U.S. tax authorities in early 2009. These documents, according to the *Guardian,* reveal the names of hundreds of companies, funds, trusts, and individuals, along with their transaction details, and run to thousands of pages.[36]

Rudolf's new-found recognition garnered high-profile supporters. Jack Blum, a lawyer in Washington, D.C., well known for speaking out against tax havens and the banks that operate within them, told the *Guardian,*

> What Elmer is doing is extremely valuable in the process of educating people of the need for major reform. This is a system for enabling a certain class of people to avoid their societal duty, which is to pay tax.[37]

Jack Blum was more than a lawyer; he had become a public advocate for Rudolf. Other support organizations included members of French non-profit LiberteInfo, who wrote letters on his behalf to the European Court of Human Rights and to the head of the Swiss Federal Department of Justice and Police and others in 2011. Rudolf was contacted by a documentary team about making a film of his story, entitled *Offshore.* Achieving the status of recognized whistleblower brought him public attention, changed how he was perceived, and drew well-known people to his cause.

Paralleling Rudolf's struggle was that of Bradley Birkenfeld, who spoke out about offshore tax evasion schemes that enabled U.S. residents to hide assets. His claims led to Switzerland being forced to hand over the details of over four thousand accounts to U.S. authorities investigating UBS, a Swiss bank. This drew more attention to Rudolf's story, as did a second release of information via Wikileaks in 2011:

> I have been very, very lucky because of the UBS case, the Birkenfeld case. . . . I was lucky, and I was lucky with WikiLeaks the second time, that I could send the message I wanted to send to society.[38]

He described how, had the UBS investigation and the Wikileaks opportunities not arisen, he would have been in the situation that many find themselves: unheeded and ignored.

He reflected that the vast majority of these new supporters were not Swiss but came from other countries and regions: "Getting support— that's something which is a very interesting thing. The international support is much better than the support I received in Switzerland."[39] The countries from which the majority of assistance came, the United Kingdom and the United States, had vested interests in seeing Swiss tax secrecy being dismantled. As the *Guardian* reports,

> Switzerland is a fortress of banking and financial services, but famously secretive and expert in the concealment of wealth from all over the world for tax evasion and other extra-legal purposes.[40]

Although Switzerland considered such secrecy an essential aspect of its economic makeup, the secrecy represented a significant obstacle for other state governments trying to ensure that their citizens paid their taxes to fund the hospitals and schools in their countries.

At this time, global interest was focused on Switzerland and its secrecy laws. Because of the economic recession that many nations were facing because of the banking crisis, countries needed money. They did not need tax evaders taking the state's rightful property and hiding it away. As the *Economist* phrased it in 2012,

> Governments once turned a blind eye to their wealthy citizens' offshore tax acrobatics. Now they are strapped for cash and hungrily hunt every penny in tax revenue. So a cold war on banking secrecy is turning hot.[41]

During this period, nations were buying databases containing information on tax evaders, such as the one Rudolf held, for cash. Switzerland's next-door neighbor Germany had done such a deal for information on Liechtenstein bank accounts.[42]

By 2011 the European Union was considering sanctions against Switzerland, and the Council of Europe was planning a clampdown on countries considered to be facilitating tax evasion. In addition to a spotlight on Switzerland, the Caymans had become a target for politicians all over. The issue was raised in the UK House of Commons, and when he was still a senator, Barack Obama had specifically mentioned the islands as a "blot on the US fiscal landscape which ought to be investigated."[43]

For all these reasons, it is not altogether surprising that support for Rudolf came from specific geopolitical localities. We can see why media organizations such as the *Guardian* and authorities such as the U.S. Internal Revenue Service showed a keen interest in his story and were prepared to take him very seriously indeed.

Rudolf had gained a valid subject position, and this led to high-profile supporters, particularly in media outlets, whose influence secured his portrayal as someone to be listened to. This also occurred for other whistleblowers featured here; Paul Moore had a connection at the BBC that led him to appear on a TV program *Newsnight,* where he spoke out about the problematic sales culture at HBOS, exposure that gave him a profile and contributed to his evidence presented at the UK Treasury Select Committee being taken so seriously[44].

The journalist Michael Hudson had taken an interest in Eileen Foster's story and her raising the alarm about staff forging customer documents to authorize mortgages. He began to compile a series of articles about her experiences at Countrywide. Eileen was then able to use these in a strategic way. When the court ruled in her favor, as expected, the new owner of Countrywide, Bank of America, launched a smear campaign against her, releasing statements that she had been a "lone wolf," a "bad manager," and so on.[45] Hudson then published all his articles defending her, and in this way she was able to counter the smear attacks.[46] Most importantly, Hudson had spent a year seeking out other people at Countrywide who had had the same experiences of being silenced, victimized, and then fired for speaking up. Incredibly, he found thirty such people, all willing to talk. Hudson assembled their diverse stories into a coherent narrative for the articles, which gave them greater strength and credibility. Strategically, this approach was very effective.

This kind of recognition and support from influential others was vital to Martin Woods of Wachovia, when he found himself at his lowest ebb in 2009. Emerging from a long legal battle against Wachovia, he received a letter from John Dugan, comptroller of the currency for the U.S. Treasury Department. Dugan told Martin,

> [I am] writing to personally recognize and express my appreciation for the role you played in the actions brought against Wachovia Bank for violations of the bank secrecy act. . . . Not only did the information that you provided facilitate our investigation, but you demonstrated great

personal courage and integrity by speaking up. Without the efforts of individuals like you, actions such as the one taken against Wachovia would not be possible.[47]

This public show of support was very helpful for Martin. The *Guardian* went on to call him "one of the most important whistleblowers of our time."[48] When I spoke with him, he told me about dining with Madoff whistleblower Harry Markopolous, who had become an acquaintance; meeting with a movie director who had shown interest in telling his story; getting to know people close to Senator Levin, one of the United States' most vocal politicians supporting whistleblowers; and being able to call on Julian Assange of WikiLeaks.[49] As Woods commented, this all came about because of his profile in the media and his new status as a valuable whistleblower.[50] As lawyer and long-standing advocate of whistleblowers Tom Devine of the U.S. Government Accountability Project points out, securing well-known supporters is key in advancing one's claims as a whistleblower.[51]

When asked how he managed to attain a public voice in the way that he did, Rudolf said he was "lucky." He felt that he was lucky because of the significant international attention given to the WikiLeaks shutdown and because the Birkenfeld scandal broke when it did. The received wisdom is that some whistleblowers, like Rudolf, are simply fortunate and others, like Jonathan, are not. But what really makes the difference: luck or strategic positioning amid wider flows of power?

Censorship versus Truth

The figure of the whistleblower is constructed against a specific geopolitical backdrop; it can be upheld by the support of people influential in this context, or it can be ignored. In Switzerland, Rudolf's statements had the status of impossible speech acts; they were simply outside the domain of what was considered sayable. The kind of censorship that structured Olivia Greene as an invalid entity, less than a subject, was also operating there. The wider political forces at play within Switzerland determined that Rudolf, as whistleblower, was to be ignored. These helped legitimize the retaliation and violence that he and his family experienced and lessen the importance of his appeals to end it. Just as censorship operates within organizations, so also can it effectively regulate subject positions on the outside, in the wider society. In *Excitable Speech* Butler points out that the state can play a central role in the operation of censorship and the regulation of those who remain outside, noting that "the consequences of such an irruption of the unspeakable may range from a sense that one is 'falling apart' to the intervention of the state to secure criminal or psychiatric incarceration."[52] In Rudolf's targeting by state agencies, we see how this can happen.

Rudolf, however, was beginning to realize his predicament and to see how things might be done differently.

> Strategically, I took the position of saying [to myself], "Look, you have got the financial center of Zurich, you have got the financial center of London, you have got the financial center of New York. . . . Switzerland will not report on my case. Go to a place, London or New York or Germany, who have an interest in making it public that the financial center of Zurich is dirty."[53]

He was beginning to understand that the denial of recognition by others that he was experiencing was caught up in the speech acts for which he was now publicly known. He began to think about how this might be altered. Rudolf Elmer, the whistleblower, was perceived entirely differently outside his native Switzerland. Censorship and the subject positions it creates depend on wider discursive flows of power. When these shift, so also do the positions that are produced by them. Rudolf's self, as a whistleblower, became a symbol for transparency in the arguments over WikiLeaks in California. His self became a proxy for a topical public interest issue in the United States and in the United Kingdom, where tax evasion was costing both nations significant sums of money each year. Rather than as an incoherent entity to be ignored and depicted as mad, Rudolf was now recognized as a valid, honorable whistleblower. Again we see the nation-state playing a significant role in influencing who is deemed heroic and who psychotic.

These insights enable us to question the relation of speaker to truth in whistleblowing. In many research studies and also in media accounts, the whistleblower is portrayed as a person in possession of facts; they have the truth about problematic practices, and they are trying to speak about it. The difficulty comes in being able to gain an audience for this truth. Whistleblowing struggles are more complex, however. Truth claims are contingent; they are deemed valid or otherwise depending on the political context. Tax evasion might be wrong to a UK journalist, but to another person, a Swiss prosecutor, for example, it represents an important aspect of the Swiss economy and therefore a political sacred cow that cannot be touched. Instead of being about truth, therefore, the reception of a speech act is inevitably tied to the position occupied by the teller of the truth. It depends upon the position that the would-be whistleblower holds and whether dominant discursive forces legitimize it or render it invisible. Successful whistleblowing, therefore—that is, whistleblowing that manages to gain an audience— becomes about the impossibility or otherwise of the person who speaks. Was Rudolf a bona fide whistleblower reporting on serious systemic wrongdoing, as he claimed, or was he simply a data thief in a jurisdiction that punished this kind of behavior severely, as others portrayed him?[54] The answer depends entirely on the discursive context in which he makes his statements.

It is useful to contrast this with Jonathan Sugarman's case in Ireland, which was ignored by most parties: the regulator, Irish politicians, and civil society. Initially, both Jonathan and Rudolf were dubbed impossible beings for speaking out about a vastly powerful entity that represented a key part of the nation's wealth; they were considered to be unintelligible, they went unheeded, and in Rudolf's case violence against him was legitimized. The subject position of the whistleblower was performed differently by each; for Rudolf it was about constructing and being constructed as someone in tune with the national interest, even if the national interest was not his home country's. Jonathan's struggle in Ireland directly contravened what was seen at the time as the nation's best interests: maintaining a strong economy that was heavily invested in attracting global financial services firms to a lightly regulated region. Whistleblower accounts are complex and multifaceted but this chapter's observations suggest that it may sometimes be possible to move from a position of impossible speaker to a legible one, depending on the wider institutional and cultural settings.

Beyond Censorship? Outcomes of Legitimate Speech

The question remains: does the experience of being recast as a whistle-blower subject who is now recognized and celebrated prevent the negative impacts that are associated with speaking out in public?

Returning to Rudolf, even with all this activity in the foreign press, by 2011 no Swiss investigation or prosecution had taken place regarding the alleged tax evaders he had exposed, and no action had been taken against Julius Bär for its role in the intimidation of Rudolf and his family. The court case was dragging. It had now been in progress for five and a half years; this was extremely long by Swiss standards. In the meantime, changes had been made to Swiss bank secrecy law. In 2009, penalties for violation were increased by five times, meaning imprisonment of up to three years and a fine of up to 250,000 Swiss francs. Moreover, the threats from Julius Bär had begun again in earnest after Rudolf had provided the details to WikiLeaks. In 2011 Rudolf made another disclosure to WikiLeaks: details of 2,000 anonymous accounts.[55] In a press conference, Rudolf told journalists he was releasing this data "in order to educate society":

> [He was] determined the public should know about the tax law-breaking that is going on. "I do think, as a banker, I have the right to stand up if something is wrong," he said. "I am against the system. I know how the system works and I know the day-to-day business. From that point of view, I wanted to let society know what I know. It is damaging our society."[56]

His words were printed in the *Guardian,* the *Telegraph,* the *Irish Times* and reported on CNN online.[57] These sources declared that Rudolf was not objecting to his bank per se but to "a system of structures" that made tax evasion possible.[58] Through these outlets, Rudolf had finally been given a voice: he was legitimate. This stands in stark contrast to his previous portrayals as a mad person who was causing trouble because he had a grudge against his bank. Instead, he was presented in the media as an expert insider in the banking sector, a voice of authority.

On returning to Switzerland, however, he was arrested and charged with violation of bank secrecy law and other crimes.[59] On January 19,

2011, he was declared guilty and given the choice of spending 240 days in prison or paying a fine and being sentenced to two years on probation. Two days later, he was rearrested for the latest delivery of data to WikiLeaks, which was seen as being in contempt of court, given the earlier verdict. He served 187 days in prison. He continued to appeal, and his case was reopened because of "sloppy" evidence being presented in the first trial.[60]

Even as he was celebrated in some countries, Rudolf continued to be treated with suspicion by sectors of the Swiss media, in the country where his family still lived. Despite his case being still unresolved, the Swiss newspaper *Weltwoche* printed an article in 2012 that portrayed him as a thief and a blackmailer. The newspaper did not clarify that the courts had not yet ruled on Julius Bär's charges.[61] This time, however, things were different, not least because such claims were actively countered by articles appearing in well-respected UK newspapers. He was hailed by the *Guardian* as being the "most important and boldest whistleblower in Swiss banking history."[62] His supporters included John Christensen, director of the Tax Justice Network, who spoke to the media on his behalf. In 2012, for the second year in a row, *International Tax Review* chose Rudolf as one of their most influential individuals in tax practice and administration.[63]

When press articles were written about him, rather than being caricatured as the mad and vengeful ex-banker, Rudolf was given a virtual loudspeaker. In the CNN article mentioned earlier, for example, he was given the last word:

> If convicted, the former banker faces up to eight months in prison, but he remains unrepentant, telling CNN: "I'm on the right side." Rudolf says his aim in going public is "to educate society, because the man in the street doesn't really know what is going on."[64]

Rudolf was quoted directly and was able to say what he wanted. In another article, he declared,

> I have worked for major banks other than Julius Bär, and the one thing upon which I am absolutely clear is that the banks know, and the big boys know, that money is being secreted away for tax-evasion purposes.[65]

He was now able to talk about the corruption he had been highlighting. He could turn the media attention away from himself, the individual, and back to the systems and structures that supported these problems. Rudolf's recognition as a valid speaking subject enabled this.

Other whistleblowers who have prevailed in gaining the support of sectors of the media have also been granted the opportunity of speaking openly and frankly about problems in the banking system, whether it be Martin Woods on money laundering and bank settlements; Eugene McErlean, who was often quoted on the topic of whistleblower protection law; or Eileen Foster.[66] For Eileen, only after the court had ruled in her favor and she felt that the bank would be less able to paint her as unreliable would she tell her story to *60 Minutes*. Prior to this she had been wary of the reprisal from her former employer that a public appearance might attract.

What connects Rudolf Elmer, Eugene McErlean, Martin Woods, Eileen Foster and earlier, Paul Moore, on this point is that all had been cited as credible by particular influential authorities.[67] In their study of whistleblowing struggles, academics Martin and Rifkin liken the whistleblower's journey to a strategic dance, or "political ju-jitsu," that is as much about wrong-footing one's opponent [the organization] and the execution of a careful strategy, than about simply coming forth in a public manner to expose a wrongdoing.[68] Public opinion plays a key role in a whistleblower's ability to expose wrongdoing. Moreover, whistleblowing statements do not occur in a vacuum, but their reception is inevitably framed by the wider discursive context.

Happy Ever After?

At last, even in Switzerland public opinion showed signs of thawing. By 2012 for example, Rudolf was interviewed by a Swiss TV channel for a program on Swiss tax evaders.[69] He seemed finally to be gaining a voice at home. Even so, his is not a straightforward story of winning. In 2012, he reflected on his story thus far:

> If you think about, if you really think about my case, I'm having my eighth year of investigation. I have been to prison [for] two hundred and thirty days. As of today no one can prove that I violated Swiss bank secrecy about Cayman data.[70]

In correspondence with a judge, he learned how he was still perceived in his native land. The judge commented,

> You are more dangerous for the system than the Red Army Faction or the Red Brigade were because you do not use violent action, you use figures and facts. And that makes you a dangerous person or even an enemy of the state.[71]

He still felt that in Switzerland "I am an enemy of the state, and my civil disobedience is not liked at all. I am outspoken, and that is something that creates tremendous problems in a secrecy jurisdiction."[72] Although, on the surface, Rudolf's tale might be interpreted as the story of someone who won, it is in fact far more complex than this. It involved and continues to involve pain and stigma. Moving from impossible to possible subject is clearly not an easy path, and achieving this provides little protection against painful retaliations.

Conclusion

The vast majority of whistleblowers never attain a public voice but rather are ignored for years by their organizations, by the media, and by authorities, including regulators. Their impossible speech acts are left unheard and eventually fade away. In examining what moves such speech acts from impossible to possible, from illegible to coherent, it is useful to consider both sides. The dynamics of censorship play a role in determining who is allowed to shift from a position of impossible individual to a recognized and celebrated truth teller. Rather than focusing on the truth, it is helpful to conceptualize the utterances of whistleblowers as speech acts whose reception are caught up in wider flows of power, of which the interests of the nation-state are key. From a practical perspective, it is therefore essential that whistleblowers be strategic and self-aware, conscious of how they are perceived by others and how different this view might be from their self-perception.

Even when a recognized subject position is attained, this does not guarantee immunity from the kinds of violence that whistleblowers typically experience. Public approval does not offer a shield. A residue of toxicity, of being unacceptable, lingers, for people unable to find employment, shunned by friends and family, and caught up in self-doubt and confusion. Even those rare few who are publicly celebrated remain targets of suspicion for years after. Speaking out is a precarious activity. It may be that all whistleblowers can hope for is the opportunity to gain a voice, albeit a temporary one and without the guarantee that this will prevent further retaliations. This theme, the partial victories of some whistleblowers, is returned to in Chapter 10.

7

Media, Recruitment, and Friends: Excluding the Public Whistleblower

THUS FAR, we have seen how the subject position of the whistleblower can operate within organizations, including how it represents a legitimate target of violence. When people then go public with information about wrongdoing, perceptions of what they, as whistleblowers, represent differ depending on the context. The truth that the whistleblower utters is contingent. How does public perception affect the whistleblower who has foregone anonymity and has become recognizable by strangers for their act of speaking out?

This chapter describes one of the most striking things about life as a public whistleblower: being individualized and targeted for scrutiny. For those appearing in this book, becoming known for speaking out placed the spotlight firmly on them as individuals, regardless of whether others had helped them disclose wrongdoing. For Olivia Greene, Paul Moore, Eileen Foster, and Rudolf Elmer this had happened to some extent while they were still working in their organizations; they were isolated and targeted—set apart from their colleagues. Upon going outside the organization to make disclosures, however, they received a different, more intense type of scrutiny and punishment. These dynamics are upheld by different aspects of a person's world: his or her chosen industry, the media and wider society, and friends and colleagues. They have distinct implications for whistleblowers, their lives, and their families. Through our own attachments to powerful norms relating to global financial services, we all help to maintain these exclusions.

The Individual Whistleblower: A Target for Scrutiny

As a senior executive, Paul Moore had repeatedly attempted to let his board know about the toxic sales-driven culture within certain sections of HBOS bank. He feared that this culture put the entire company at risk and threatened its customers, who stood to lose their savings as a result of the frequent mis-selling that was taking place. He was later proved correct when the bank collapsed, when it emerged that the problem Paul had raised—inappropriate culture—was a driving force in the disastrous financial crisis of 2008 and when he was publicly hailed by the UK government's Treasury Select Committee as an important whistleblower. Back in 2004, however, nobody in the bank wanted to hear his warnings, and its chief executive, James Crosby, fired him. Paul determined to challenge the decision. He contacted his solicitor and began to build a case against HBOS. His role as head of Group Regulatory Risk at HBOS meant that he was a Financial Services Authority (FSA) protected person under UK law, free to speak out about perceived misconduct. This implied that the FSA would support his position.

Learning of his dismissal, the FSA began its investigation. It commissioned the well-known audit firm KPMG to carry out an independent investigation into the allegations Paul made. An investigation was standard practice, but what was unusual was that KPMG already was the audit firm for HBOS and had been for years. The eventual report was based on documents provided by the bank and interviews with almost thirty of Paul's former colleagues. Eventually, some four months after Paul had finished with HBOS, it was ready. The audit firm sent a copy to all involved in the investigation. Paul recalls the day that it arrived in the post at his home. He could not bring himself to open the package: "I left it on my doorstep for two days."[1] Eventually he began to read; the report presented a damning description of him: "Numerous negative comments have been made regarding Mr. Moore's performance in the role of Head of GRR [Group Regulatory Risk]." His personality and his behavior were deconstructed and disparaged. A section devoted to Paul's work performance noted,

> Whilst his technical abilities were in general recognised as strong, consistent reference has been made to Mr. Moore: not inspiring confidence in GRR's stakeholders; not having sufficiently strong influencing and relationship skills; being overly verbose and full of self-importance; not being on top of the detail; and over-stating matters in an overly dramatic and theatrical way.[2]

The report went on to describe, in detail, Paul's behavior in specific situations. That he had, for example, criticized the way that a meeting was being chaired in September 2003 was presented as evidence of his disruptive nature. This was because, according to the report, "a number of individuals considered this behavior to be inappropriate." The sources of these opinions were not given nor were the names of those who suggested that, at a meeting in May 2004, "Mr. Moore was perceived as lecturing the committee in a patronizing manner, and offended individuals present with the style."[3] The Group Audit Committee meeting at which Paul had struggled to draw the attention of senior executives to the findings of his review of the sales culture was another focus. At this event, apparently,

> Mr. Moore expressed strong views in an overly aggressive manner, he was emotional and not reasoned, measured or coherent. His behaviour was described in different ways ranging from prickly to ranting to extraordinary to outrageous.[4]

The report concluded that aspects of his personality were difficult, that Paul had had conflicts with senior management, and that the bank had been quite correct to fire him. Few positive aspects of his lengthy career were highlighted. His long service with some of the United Kingdom's most notable institutions, including seven years as a partner with KPMG itself, was ignored. So too were his excellent character references from managers both within and outside HBOS.[5] According to Paul and his legal counsel, the report represented an unfair attack on him at this crucial time in the investigation.[6] His solicitor wrote to HBOS, saying that the investigation was not balanced, had been poorly conducted and could not have been independent.[7]

In 2012, Paul made a formal complaint to the UK regulator against KPMG based on the report's content, just a week after news had broken that the former head of HBOS's corporate bank, Peter Cummings, had been fined over £1 million for his part in the eventual collapse of the bank. Back in 2005, however, the report was presented as a thorough and fair evaluation, provided by an independent and reputable organization, and it stood. That same year Paul pursued his case for unfair dismissal as a whistleblower and accepted a settlement of approximately £700,000.

In the years that followed, the global financial crisis occurred not least because of the risky practices of banks worldwide including those that had been the focus of Paul's disclosure. When eventually the UK government formed a Treasury Select Committee to investigate the causes of the crisis in that country, Paul contacted the chairman to tell his story. Asked to formally contribute, he carefully compiled a five-thousand-word report on everything that had happened to him. He included meeting minutes, emails, and notes from conversations that took place during the period of dispute, 2003–2004. Submitting his evidence, he was called to testify, and UK newspapers took up his story. Politicians spoke up on his behalf. "Paul the whistleblower" had gained a voice, legitimized by powerful supporters. As with Rudolf, Eugene, and Eileen, this endorsement by influential others enabled him to have a public voice, which he then used to draw attention to the problems inherent to the UK banking system. Feeling that he had been undermined and smeared by HBOS bank in the KPMG report, he was now able to make this point clearly, directly informing TV and newspaper journalists and the Select Committee that he had evidence that would prove him to be correct and that the report was little more than a "whitewash." Framing his story as a "public interest," or national, issue, Paul was able to speak freely:

> I believe the public interest demands this conclusion as well as my reputation. I have all the underlying documents, which support the detailed resume of additional evidence if these are required. . . . I believe that my allegations raise important questions of potential wrongdoing / incompetence by the relevant parties which should be followed up.[8]

He continued to submit evidence to the committee for months, making broad statements about the banking crisis more generally, with the encouragement of the assembled politicians. His statements were publicized in newspaper and TV reports:

> I believe that there are important general lessons to be learned from my personal experiences as a risk and compliance Professional at HBOS and elsewhere that could assist the Committee and others in the public policy debate about what needs to be changed in the governance and regulatory system to help to ensure that the same risks are mitigated in the future.[9]

As had Rudolf and others, Paul had found a conduit to make his voice heard.

Of the hundreds of journalists who reported on the case, most were on Paul's side. Even so, there was some ambivalence; the *Telegraph*, for example, wrote that Paul was out to wage a personal vendetta against his former bosses.[10] The chairman of HBOS, Lord Stevenson, publicly refuted Paul's claims in his submission to the committee.[11] His evidence: the KPMG report. HBOS then leaked the report to journalists, who seized on it. Paul was asked to respond to the claims it made about him:

> I got a call from the editor of the *Financial Times*. He said, "We have got the KPMG report. It says you are a lunatic, you are extraordinary, you ranted, you're prickly. . . . What have you got to say about that?" And I said well I *am* probably a bit extraordinary. It *is* extraordinary to challenge the business strategy of somebody like Crosby.[12]

The allegedly independent KPMG report and subsequent media articles focused on analyzing and deconstructing Paul's personality: the spotlight was on him as an individual. The problems he was trying to highlight: the overheated sales culture and lack of regulation at HBOS, were secondary.

Paul Moore was not alone. Most people interviewed for this study found that the media had run articles that promoted the retaliatory organization's point of view over their own account. This occurred both in the initial stages of speaking publicly and even after gaining legitimacy as truth tellers. Most found themselves individualized and scrutinized in the media. In this regard, Paul's story was not unique.[13]

Eugene McErlean, a senior internal auditor at Allied Irish Bank, had spoken up about serious levels of customer overcharging that were so prevalent as to have become systemic within his firm. He was also treated with suspicion, this time by sectors of the Irish media. Ignored within his bank, he approached the regulator as he was obligated to do. He was then implicitly scapegoated by his employer, who attempted to connect him to a completely unrelated scandal that had taken place in the United States. Such was the influence of Allied Irish Bank that this dubious assertion was taken up by leading broadsheet newspapers.[14] The blackening of his name continued for years, even after it became widely known that he had told the truth.[15] He was also treated with disdain by some politicians during a government investigation into his case. A member of Dáil Éireann, the lower house of the Irish parliament for example, described him as a "disaffected employee who is stirring up problems for a bank that is currently in a weakened position."[16] Eugene McErlean, the individual, became the problem rather than the serious issues he was trying to highlight.

Rudolf Elmer found himself the subject of regular smear campaigns in Swiss newspapers after releasing information on his bank's role in facilitating tax evasion and ultimately stealing from nations' treasuries including the U.S. He recalls,

> The bank's tactic of retaliation was clear: Spotlight the whistleblower, not the wrongdoing. Build a damage record against him, threaten him, isolate him, physically and psychologically attack him and his family, and paralyze his career by blacklisting him.[17]

The bank, Julius Bär, was active in promoting a negative image of Rudolf in the press. In 2011, bank representatives issued a statement, just prior to the second WikiLeaks revelations:

> The aim of [Elmer's] activities was, and is, to discredit Julius Bär as well as clients in the eyes of the public. With this goal in mind, Mr. Elmer spread baseless accusations and passed on unlawfully acquired, respectively retained, documents to the media, and later also to WikiLeaks. To back up his campaign, he also used falsified documents.[18]

Even though the Swiss prosecutor would later state that the incident was not one of theft, because you cannot steal something you have been made responsible for, the bank persisted in deeming Rudolf a thief. Well-known newspapers, obliged to report both sides, naturally contacted the bank for comment around the time of the WikiLeaks event and reported accordingly. According to the *Economist*, "Julius Bär said Mr. Elmer was 'trying to make a living' out of his case and had 'lost credibility.'"[19]

CNN reported that

> a spokesman for the company told CNN Elmer was a "disgruntled and frustrated" former employee who had "embarked on a personal intimidation campaign and vendetta against Julius Bär" after he was denied a promotion. The firm claims he stole documents and made death threats against two members of the bank's staff.[20]

As Rudolf concludes in relation to his dealings with the press after he spoke publicly:

> You have to think about it, what you want to disclose and to whom. Because there are journalists out there who, in the end, will make you look bad and mad. I think you can't trust the media, definitely not. That's an approach you have to take.[21]

He went on to discuss how these outlets, although they can be useful, need to be treated with caution. Journalists tend to "spotlight the whistleblower" as Rudolf noted, and the whistleblower becomes a target for scrutiny.[22] We see this clearly in the recent media obsession with well-known whistleblowers such as Edward Snowden, Julian Assange, and Chelsea Manning in which more attention is given to the individuals, their personalities, and their private selves than to the information they report.

This kind of individualization of the person who publicly occupies the category of whistleblower is common, even beyond this study.[23] The internal whistleblower can find herself isolated from others in the organization, portrayed as different from them, and singled out as one to be analyzed. Once she goes public, however, this individualization is heightened and targeted; the whistleblower's personality is forensically deconstructed and presented in a way that disparages the person for all to see. This involves selective categorization of people's traits. Paul Moore's passionate expression of strong views on ethics, and refusal to acquiesce to the status quo could also be regarded as essential attributes of an effective head of regulatory risk, particularly in the context of a boom economy when so many forces are acting against prudence. The KPMG report, however, painted these as egregious flaws. This frequently occurs; after a person has spoken out about the bank, it is common for an investigation to be commissioned, and this often involves investigating the so-called whistleblower as well as, or instead of, the original issue. The overall effect of this singling out is then amplified because of the media attention that can ensue.

SUBJECTION AND EXCLUSION: NORMS OF INDIVIDUALISM

This individualization is complex. Occupying the category of whistleblower causes one pain on a number of levels. It hurts to be in this position, but ironically, once in the public eye, people can feel compelled to stick with it and to defend themselves as a whistleblower. This is often the only way to convince others of their claims.

Philosopher Judith Butler's account of subjectivity and its ethical implications have direct relevance here. The radically social, ek-static self depicted in this theory poses an important challenge to traditional ways of understanding personhood. The conception of the self as an isolated and individualized, "unitary subject" is illusory and hides the ways, beyond our control, that we are embedded in others.[24] In developing these ideas, Butler is inspired by theorist of power Michel Foucault's work on the rise of individualism in today's world. Foucault points out that the solitary "individual", as a way of thinking about persons, is relatively recent. In previous eras the person was considered to be little more than part of a collective—a religious congregation, for example, or a close-knit locality. However, the rise of capitalist forms of production and other influences mean that today we tend to think of the person as an autonomous, free-thinking, and independent individual.[25] Foucault's genealogical work traces this process of individualization as it evolved in the context of the medical profession, prisons, and other institutions particularly relating to the state, in which individual cases were necessary to effectively categorize, and control, the population. He argues that "the measurement of overall phenomena, the description of groups, the characterization of collective facts, the calculation of the gaps between individuals, their distribution in a given 'population'" make possible such control, thus "the power of the state to produce an increasingly totalising web of control is intertwined with and dependent on its ability to produce an increasing specification of individuality."[26] Although "the individual is not the initial, most acute form in which life is presented" and emerged because of particular forces and shifts in history, it remains dominant today in the way we think about people and populations; the individual (perspective) is king.[27] This is further amplified in contemporary Western society because of the rise of therapy culture and the psy sciences (psychology, psychoanalysis, and so on) since the 1960s, which promote an inward focus: an obsession with the individual self.

For Foucault, the increasing domination of individualism as a way of relating to the self is one of the most pressing issues in contemporary life because it has dangers: when people become overly attentive to the individual, including their own selves, they lose an awareness of and an interest in the concerns of others around them.[28] They do not feel responsible for nor do they care about them, and the notion of collective action becomes a thing of the past; it is unthinkable because of the contemporary obsession with being an autonomous individual. A second real danger is that, when such a perspective dominates, its narrow focus can distract from how power is exercised at the macro level.[29] We are too busy examining the individual self, and we ignore the wider flows of power that affect our daily lives.

In the whistleblowing described here, an explicit focus on the person who is speaking up can distract from the wrongdoing that he or she is articulating. Public scrutiny of the whistleblower can also distract our attention from the powerful entity, the financial services institution, engaged in this wrongdoing. We target the self of the whistleblower for analysis; we concern ourselves with his or her personality traits, their biography, and whether we deem the person good or bad. The report on Paul Moore focused on his "relationship skills . . . being overly verbose and . . . dramatic" rather than his bank's gross jeopardizing of its customers' savings and its employees' futures. What Foucault and Butler show us is that our tendency to examine aspects of the social world such as whistleblowing in this way—by focusing immediately on the individuals involved—is not a given but is historically contingent. It is also dangerous.

This is not an easy situation to rectify; various forces operate to maintain our tendency to individualize whistleblowers, with two in particular being influential—one is rather obvious, the second more surprising: the role of the media and the responses of the whistleblowers themselves.

PERFORMING WHISTLEBLOWER: A HURTFUL NORM

Why does media attention amplify isolation for whistleblowers? Many seasoned whistleblowers share the view that, in the main, media outlets are not interested in following the complexity of their stories, particularly in industries like banking in which the details of the wrongdoing, such as complex financial algorithms, are often difficult to understand.[30] It is more entertaining to instead paint a caricature of the individual. Rudolf Elmer understood why this was happening to him; he felt it was easier for newspapers to report in this way:

> It was simple and efficient to focus on the person and the judiciary nightmare [of his ongoing court case], because the facts about malpractice are a bit more complex, and the will was not there to make any statement about "dirty conduct in business."[31]

The reluctance could also be due to detailed reporting taking time and money, and in recent years most mainstream media companies have either reduced or eliminated their investigative reporting functions. In relation to financial sector whistleblowers, many large media organizations have links to major banks through loans they have taken out and a heavy dependence on advertising revenue from them. In a time of dramatically reduced profitability in the newspaper sector, these obligations have particular salience.[32] As shown with Rudolf in Switzerland, media companies are also influenced by the institutions of government and encouraged to echo the views of the state.

As another reason, the whistleblower is not a passive recipient in this process. Becoming known as a whistleblower in public means becoming a target for analysis, but to survive this the person often has to rely on the very forces that contributed to his or her isolation in the first place, including the media. Ironically, therefore, the very parties responsible for the kind of spotlighting that proved so problematic were also an important source of help. Rudolf Elmer found that the UK *Guardian* was a significant source of support:

Some mass media were interested in my concerns. They supported my initiative in one way or another. As a CPA [certified public accountant] I like facts; reporting is based on facts and figures. In my case I do not really mind anymore. I know the game is "If you cannot destroy the evidence, then beat the witness." That is happening with some media; others report facts.[33]

The media that were helpful and supportive to Rudolf were often based overseas, in countries that had an interest in spotlighting and criticizing Swiss bank secrecy.[34] For Paul Moore, Eugene McErlean, and others, some media sources were similarly useful and sometimes essential in their struggles. Before getting involved with the Treasury Select Committee and giving his evidence, Paul had decided to break his silence and his gag order with HBOS and speak to the media. A good friend at the BBC arranged for him to be interviewed on the popular *Money* program.[35] After he was called to testify, he contacted many journalists and TV shows, not least to defend his position given the smearing of his name that was occurring, for example, as a result of the KPMG report being leaked to the media. He quickly responded to this by going to Sky News, Channel 4 News, and the BBC, among other outlets: "In every interview to camera I said pretty much the same thing . . . [that the KPMG report] will not subject itself to proper independent scrutiny without falling down like a house of cards."[36] He told his audience that he had full and detailed evidence to support his claims. His statements were widely reported and brought significant public and political support, which contributed to the politicians at the Treasury Select Committee taking his evidence extremely seriously. Jonathan Sugarman received sporadic attention; media in other nations took up his story of speaking out about repeated liquidity breaches at UniCredit's Irish operation. Meanwhile, the U.S. TV show *60 Minutes* was influential in spreading word of Eileen Foster's and Bradley Birkenfeld's stories. Birkenfeld blew the whistle on his bank UBS's special tax evasion schemes that enabled U.S. citizens to hide assets offshore. He then used the media many times—for example, publicizing his request for clemency from Barack Obama, on U.S. National Tax Day, the day upon which income tax returns are due for many. These stunts were taken up by media outlets across the United States and, according to the *New York Times,* they caused the Internal Revenue Service so much public embarrassment that the organization simply had to intervene.

Although this media attention was helpful for public whistleblowers in gaining support for their causes, there was a trade-off. To persuade journalists and TV reporters to publicize their stories, whistleblowers frequently had to make public their personal histories and family situations: to supply photographs and intimate details. Paul Moore spoke openly about his struggles with alcohol and its effect on his family in his attempts to show the real-life impacts of whistleblowing.[37] Such efforts were essential in his building a public profile in which he could be painted as sympathetic figure deserving of support. This was a common feature across people's stories. It was, in other words, essential for whistleblowers to take an active role in turning the focus onto themselves. Their actions then contributed to the scrutiny they received as public whistleblowers. Thus, although individualization is a problematic aspect of occupying such a position for reasons detailed here, further individualization is, paradoxically, required to overcome the problems it brings, such as smear campaigns. The subject position of public whistleblower therefore enrolls people in an ongoing game of spin, played out in the public media, from which they cannot escape.

As described earlier, people's identifications with particular categories are not static but are performed over a period of time.[38] Occupying the label of whistleblower is a complex process. It is a source of hurt because of the vulnerability resulting from being exposed. But it is also productive, in that this position grants a sense of place in the world. It offers an attachment to an recognized category—that of legitimate whistleblower—albeit this attachment is painful. The alternative is nonexistence. This reflects the push and pull of psychic attachments to normative categories that we all experience. While she is ignored, the whistleblower is nothing, irrelevant and ambivalent because of what she is saying. When the public spotlight arrives, she becomes something, even if this recognition comes with a price. We are frequently compelled into subjectification with categories that ultimately hurt us because we are passionately attached to them. This insight, which represents one of Butler's major contributions to Foucault's work on power and subjectivity, can help us understand the counterintuitive situation in which many whistleblowers found themselves actively contributing to the individualization and scrutinization that accompanied their public whistleblowing. They were compelled, in Butler's words, to "embrace the [very] terms that injure," to subjectify themselves to norms that ultimately stood to cause them pain in order to ensure their own existence in social life.[39] To not do so would have resulted in being "cast outside," becoming other to the norm of what a valid subject is considered to be. In so doing, however, this version of the label whistleblower, as someone isolated and scrutinized, is thus reproduced. It is the practices of subjection of vast networks of people that ensure certain norms remain dominant, and this is no different.[40]

This enables us to see a new aspect of the category of public whistleblower. Specifically, those who find themselves attached to it and hurt by its association with isolation and scrutiny, can nonetheless be compelled to reinforce it. Recognition as the whistleblower involves a bittersweet attachment because, although it grants people a name and a chance to be heard, it represents a source of pain. Returning to Foucault and Butler's concerns with individualization as a growing and problematic norm in contemporary life, we see that sometimes those who suffer most as a result are also complicit in upholding it. In addition to being individualized and targeted, the whistleblower can be excluded in other ways, described next.

Excluded from Employment in the Sector

Jonathan Sugarman continued to wait. He had resigned from his position because he had not been listened to about illegal liquidity breaches in the Dublin branch of UniCredit. He had heard nothing in response to his disclosure to the Central Bank of Ireland, the financial regulator. He needed another job. Jonathan had a strong résumé; he had many positive recommendations from previous employers, and good risk managers were in demand in Dublin and overseas. He had been headhunted to UniCredit and promised a substantial bonus if he stayed. In flagging the illegal breaches, he had obeyed Irish law, in contrast to his colleagues. He hoped to secure another role quite quickly.

Jonathan's applications for a new position were repeatedly turned down. On one occasion he was politely told that his short six months at UniCredit was a slightly suspicious entry on his résumé. In another job interview, his reputation for having too much integrity had preceded him.[41] Jonathan had gotten quite far in the recruitment process for a position at a well-known company that provides information technology services to the banking industry. During a telephone interview with the firm's New York offices, he was informed that a background check had been carried out: "Although they appreciated my expertise and my knowledge, my integrity was a problem," he said.[42] The firm felt that he was qualified and suitable, but as a consulting organization, they were not comfortable in sending him, a whistleblower, to client firms:

> No bank wants anybody with integrity to walk in and look at their books. They actually gave it to me in writing. They said I was a marked man, that "there is no way any client bank would want you to see their figures; the client would be petrified!"[43]

Jonathan was not alone in experiencing this kind of informal black-listing. His understanding of his employment situation may sound like speculation, but it closely reflects the experience of most people interviewed for this book.

For over two years, Eileen Foster could not find work after having been dismissed from Countrywide / Bank of America. After applying unsuccessfully for 145 positions, she was finally appointed to a role that paid only half of what she would have been making at Bank of America.[44] Eileen had received the Ridenhour award, a prestigious honor granted annually to one person in the United States who is deemed to have persevered "in acts of truth-telling that protect the public interest, advance or promote social justice, or illuminate a more just vision of society."[45] Her former Countrywide / Bank of America colleague Michael Winston was in a similar situation. He had held high-level strategy positions at Motorola, McDonnell Douglas, and Lockheed Martin. He had been global head of worldwide leadership and organizational strategy at Merrill Lynch in New York. But after blowing the whistle he found himself unable to secure work that reflected his experience.[46] "I've never in my life not worked, but I'm unemployable now." He worried that "there will be a time when I won't be able to support my family."[47] Olivia Greene tells how she had been turned down for over sixty positions, despite her excellent experience at Irish Nationwide. She was convinced that this was because she was now publicly known as a whistleblower after her court appearances and media mentions. Following foiled attempts in which she was told, for example, that she was "too honest," she asked a sympathetic recruitment agent to temporarily remove her name from her résumé when it was sent for consideration. Olivia was then delighted to learn that she had been proposed for the third round of assessment at a good firm. At this point she would be invited in for an interview and her name would be revealed. When it was, she was again turned down.[48] Because she spoke out as she did, she says, "I am [now] totally unemployable in financial services."[49] Linda Almonte of J. P. Morgan raised the alarm about the selling of $200 million of credit card debt to external debt collection agencies. She claimed that the details provided were false and that her colleagues frequently robo-signed the forms without examining them. Linda was dismissed and filed a whistleblower case against J. P. Morgan. She struggled to find a new position: "You Google me, and my name is everywhere. . . . Any company that would hire me will see that. I can never live that down."[50]

A similar situation befell Rudolf Elmer, who could not find work in his chosen industry. Perhaps the best example of this, because it involves a testing of the law that is supposed to prevent such blacklisting from happening, is Martin Woods.

Martin had blown the whistle while working for Wachovia Bank, had won a settlement, and had been proved right in making public the bank's involvement in money laundering by Mexican drug cartels.[51] He had been publicly recognized and thanked by the comptroller of the currency for the U.S. Treasury Department.[52] In contrast to other whistleblowers, he managed to obtain a new job in his field. Coutts, a leading private bank in London that boasted the Queen of England as one of its clients, invited him for an interview. He was frank about his work and what had happened at Wachovia. This did not seem to faze the interviewer, and he was informed, then and there, that he was hired as an anti-money laundering expert, the role for which he was trained. Woods was delighted and began to plan for his new position. The appointment was approved internally by Coutts, and Martin signed the contract.

Less than two weeks later, the bank withdrew its offer. An internal Coutts email noted that management had "become aware of an incident at Wachovia" and that they were "keen to avoid any risk of reputational damage that might relate to the incident."[53] In Martin's view, this was a reference to his whistleblowing at his former employer: "Coutts decided they didn't want me because they didn't want me doing that sort of thing there."[54] An expert in fraud and an ex-financial regulator commented that

> to be a successful money-laundering reporting officer (MLRO) these days, you have to know which questions not to ask. . . . Banks don't want MLROs with any skills, experience, or the independent knowledge to be able to stand up to the commercial people and say, "You can't do that!"[55]

Martin's experience is interesting because he decided to sue the bank under the UK's Public Interest Disclosure Act and the Employment Act, which detail that whistleblowers must not be discriminated against or suffer detrimental treatment, including in recruitment practices. Coutts argued that because an external recruitment agency had made the offer, Martin could not be considered an employee and therefore did not have a case under either law. The bank also stated that he had been too late in bringing his claim; there is a time limit for doing so. In this, we see a very clear example of how antipathy toward known whistleblowers works in the recruiting arena: Martin was desirable until he became identified as a whistleblower, and then he was not. Certainly Coutts could have used someone like him. Earlier that year, they had been fined almost £9 million because of failures in their compliance department.[56]

These experiences mirror other studies; despite having excellent credentials and a résumé filled with positive evaluations from line managers, whistleblowers often fail to find work in roles similar to those they have left.[57] The years of training, experience, and positive appraisals that they have worked hard to achieve become worthless, and they typically see a significant cut in income. Here we see how the public nature of some whistleblowing cases amplifies the ambivalence of the potential employer toward the seasoned truth teller; Michael Winston worries that he cannot find work because his name is associated with being a whistleblower, and according to Martin Woods, Coutts did not want him and his surplus integrity because it feared the "reputational damage" that might result.

The public whistleblower is excluded from recruitment circles. There is, however, yet another level at which this exclusion operates, involving one's friends and colleagues.

Whistleblower as Outsider and the Role of Colleagues and Friends

Once they moved into the category of public whistleblower, people found themselves being shunned by former colleagues and sometimes friends. For example, after Linda Almonte was fired for speaking up about sales of fraudulent credit card debt, she was told by colleagues that her former line manager and the branch's manager of operations had called staff members together in a conference room to warn them not to communicate with Linda. One of the staff members said, "It was an unusual statement. . . . Other people had left the bank, and we were not told [to cut off contact with them]."[58] Eugene McErlean had felt cut off from colleagues at his bank, having been made redundant for speaking up about the practice of overcharging business customers that had become prevalent inside his Irish bank. He said,

> From an organizational point of view, there's a lot of ostracization [that] goes on. I think that is a common thing; you are made to feel isolated, you are made to feel outside. There's an in-group in the organization and somehow you're outside that and therefore . . . you lose all your credibility by being outside the organization.[59]

We see similar exclusions in Jonathan Sugarman's story. He described the treatment from former colleagues and friends in the finance sector in the months and years after he resigned his position at UniCredit because of his concerns about its illegal liquidity breaches:

> I have been shunned by a good number of people: friends, colleagues, acquaintances. People whom I wined and dined in this city, in the good old days when I was a respectable banker, not the one who broke ranks.[60]

Speaking about why this might be, he said he feels that former friends and colleagues look at him with discomfort because "they don't want to know how calamitous the global banking system is" and because he represents a constant reminder of their acceptance of it. He has become an outcast in these circles, an unbearable presence that people would be happier to be rid of. Martin Woods of Wachovia experienced a similar reaction from some ex-colleagues:

> A part of their protection, defense mechanism, is to accuse me of being flash and cocky and arrogant and full of himself because then that means that protects them and says they are ordinary, [whereas] Martin Woods is flash.[61]

Paul Moore finally prevailed in his mission to make public his claims against HBOS, with the Treasury Select Committee taking his evidence to be a valuable account of the role played by banks in the global financial crisis. This led to a fuller investigation of what had happened. Politicians on the committee interviewed the bosses who sacked him, asking them why they wanted to fire a risk manager who was doing such a good job. Paul's testimony led to some high-ranking members of HBOS resigning, although the bank itself survived, thanks to a government bailout of £20.5 billion in total.[62] Despite all this, his reputation for truth telling remained a part of how he was perceived in the years that followed; his public profile proved a severe obstacle to his professional career. In a submission to the committee, he described the attitude toward him held by people within the British banking system: "I am still toxic waste now for having spoken out all those years ago!"[63] For Paul and those like him, the category whistleblower appeared to influence how others responded to them; they were deemed toxic, shunned and ostracized. This kind of exclusion by one's former colleagues and peers is common among whistleblowers.[64] Therefore, the position in which the public whistleblower finds him- or herself is made very difficult, not merely because of isolation by one's organization, being individualized in the media or being considered unemployable in recruitment circles. These exclusions are intensified by former colleagues who actively shun the person who has spoken out.

Excluding Whistleblowers: Our Passionate Attachments to Global Finance

How to make sense of what happens to whistleblowers who go outside their organization to report and become known for doing so? They are clearly excluded in many ways: individualized and targeted for scrutiny, they are separated from the group. Their undesirability in recruitment circles casts them outside any organization that might potentially hire them and excludes them from participating in the paid economy, and their expulsion from friendship groups both within and outside their previous organization likewise relegates them to an outside position: they have been cut off and shunned. It is nothing new to report that whistle-blowers such as these are stigmatized and excluded from recruitment circles and that they are spurned by former colleagues.[65] It is important, however, to ask why this is happening.

Through these mechanisms of exclusion, it seems that society has taken on the work of excluding the whistleblower, which was previously carried out by the organization. While they were still employed, Paul and Eileen were ostracized because they articulated things that were prohibited under the implicit norms of financial services. Designated as uttering impossible speech, they were therefore legitimate targets of violence. Now, however, the exercise of violence against this group has moved from inside the organization to the world outside.

Why the impulse to exclude? Why do whistleblowers experience rejection in so many different ways, and why does society carry out this work on behalf of the organization? Perhaps they represent something that each of us once held dear and has since lost. On the surface, whistle-blowers appear to be speaking up for what is right, even when the circumstances are difficult. This is, after all, what we are told to do when we are children: tell the truth no matter what. As we get older, we take on the complexities of the world, and things become less black and white. We get pulled in different directions and gain responsibilities. Perhaps we witness things that contradict our childhood sense of right and wrong, but we let them happen because we do not want to jeopardize our jobs, to endanger our mortgages, to risk bankrupting our families. We need to maintain the recognition we enjoy as good and competent citizens who operate within the norms of possible speech. And we do see problematic things; in the financial services sector, for example, more than 25 percent of staff say that they have witnessed wrongdoing, a figure that rises above 30 percent for those with salaries of $500,000 or more.[66]

Butler's analysis of the Freudian idea of melancholia is helpful here.[67] Melancholia connects the subject and the psyche to powerful discourses.

Becoming a subject can involve sacrificing particular aspects of the self that one has once loved but since repressed: the price of attaining recognition under a dominant norm. Butler describes how early attachments to ways of being that are antithetical to the status quo can in later years become subsumed and repressed. Perhaps this explains our aversion to people, including whistleblowers, who appear to embody our childhood sense of right and wrong. After all, we have worked hard to repress this in our own searches for desired recognition, not least in today's world of work, where to be a normal employee often means not speaking out. We must bury our earlier attachments to what is right in order to survive. Perhaps our institutions, including those in global finance, can endure only through this continued repression of an early love for the truth and a desire to be good. This repression must itself be hidden because integrity and honesty are fundamental values within Western society and are valued and celebrated, on the surface at least.

The loss of what is given up does not go away, however. It instills a grief for what has been actively hidden, which engenders a sense of melancholia for what must never be admitted and never be grieved (the wish to do the right thing).[68] Because of this constant presence, a distinct anxiety arises in the melancholic subject: a fear that the boundary holding back the thing that threatens one's existence will somehow shatter, that the subject will be someday be found out. The threat must therefore be kept at bay. This leads to a visceral disavowal of those things that represent what one once was; it is imperative to distance oneself and to maintain the boundary. Constant vigilance is required along with active, ongoing exclusion, because the threat we fear has been incorporated. It remains a constituent part of ourselves.[69] Part of this work, then, involves projecting the loss of a childhood desire for honesty and frank speaking, and the fear that this grief will take over, onto the person who represents this simple and clear attitude to truth: the whistleblower. This suggests that our melancholic attachments are an intrinsic part of the norms that persist; the logic of today's organizations depends on them.

Certainly this appeared to be the situation with Eugene's former colleagues, who left him feeling he had lost "all [his] credibility" because he was outside the "in-group." Jonathan was "shunned" because he "broke ranks" to speak up, and Martin was seen as "flash and cocky and arrogant" for his actions. The person who has spoken up and is now known as whistleblower becomes unbearable as a result of her association with this category. So, therefore, Paul Moore feels that he is considered "toxic waste" in his industry, and Martin Woods senses that he represents to former colleagues something that they must protect themselves against. Previous research highlights how whistleblowers suffer harsher reprisals when they represent a threat to colleagues and managers, but in this study we see the work involved in these reprisals extending out even beyond those whose jobs are threatened by the whistleblower's presence, beyond the organization. More is going on. In recruitment circles too, whistleblowers caused similar offense by their displays of honesty. Olivia Greene notes that she was considered to be "too honest" to be hired, and Jonathan Sugarman reports that he was told he had "too much integrity." Martin Woods feels that he was seen as being too courageous for having stood up to senior management in serious money laundering cases. Again, traits such as honesty, integrity, and effectiveness that are ostensibly considered desirable in a potential employee have become distasteful; whistleblowers are unbearable because they have "too much" of them.

For these reasons, whistleblowers are unacceptable in society, just as they are in organizations. Their presence threatens the norms that hold our world together, including the ongoing charade maintained by financial sector organizations: that honesty is central to their practices and that corruption does not exist within. Perhaps this is how we all work on behalf of exclusionary organizations. This continued repudiation is necessary for the normal citizen to continue to exist in today's world of work. It is not that we do not care but rather that we care too much because this group represents a part of ourselves that we have lost, a loss that we would rather never acknowledge.[70]

Such a view requires that we examine our own subjective attachments to the organizations and institutions that shape our lives. Are we in thrall to these, affectively attached to the degree that we would be complicit in scapegoating and sacrificing those who speak out? It appears so, from the general absence of meaningful support that whistleblowers can attract. This is a suggested theory of the position of the whistleblower within contemporary worlds of work. It helps us see how and why whistleblowers find themselves in such extreme situations of reprisal and not just within their organizations. It also helps us see why severe punishments are generally accepted by society, perceived to be the unfortunate but inevitable fate of the whistleblower.[71] We care little about, and take no responsibility for, the potential for people's lives to be ruined for speaking out. We do not seem to be concerned.

Conclusion

Perhaps the cruel expulsion of the whistleblower from so many different aspects of organizational life is an important aspect of business as usual within financial services. The boundary is tenuous, but it must be vigilantly maintained through excluding persons who fall outside it. Numerous parties work hard at this: financial firms, their human resources departments, recruitment agents, journalists, former colleagues, friends, and even ourselves. For some authors, whistleblower retaliation is an indication of the strength of organizational power.[72] For others, whistleblowers' treatment by organizations shows how they represent fundamental contradictions within organizational structures.[73] These insights need to be extended beyond the organization to wider society. In doing so, the concept of melancholia helps us move beyond simply tagging the whistleblower as scapegoated and stigmatized. It enriches our understanding of how this stigma works in practice, how we all contribute to it, and how we therefore help maintain the status quo within institutions like finance.

8

Turning Inward: Excluding the Self

PEOPLE WHO SPEAK truth and are identified as whistleblowers find themselves excluded both within and outside the organization. These exclusions operate at several levels: the macro level of global finance, including its recruitment practitioners and journalists but also the more local level of friends and colleagues, both current and former. As Chapter 7 shows, although external to the organization, these instruments of exclusion are effectively working on its behalf. Albeit not in any orchestrated way, they nonetheless actively contribute to the isolation and stigmatization of whistleblowers. Is there a further, deeper level of exclusion that relates to an ongoing struggle on the part of the whistleblower herself? In this chapter we explore how the denial of recognition by others can be internalized and amplified by the self, with devastating and often self-defeating consequences.

Auditing in Ireland

Having previously worked as a solicitor, Eugene McErlean spent eleven years with Allied Irish Bank (AIB). For five of those, 1997 to 2002, he occupied the senior role of group internal auditor. This involved leading the team that monitored compliance-related processes within AIB, including risk, governance, and internal controls. One of their projects, running in 2001, culminated in a report titled "Special Investigation Goodbody Stockbrokers Trading in AIB Shares." The report documented concerns about the legality of a special vehicle that was used for trading AIB shares via offshore, blacklisted tax havens such as Nevis and Vanuatu.[1]

As a person whose job involved monitoring risk, Eugene represented an essential function in the bank's system. It was his job to ensure that the organization operated within set limits of safety, as it was for many of the financial sector whistleblowers appearing in this book. However, under the new financial culture sweeping through the banking system, the safety monitor was frequently prevented from doing his or her job. Blocking and paralyzing the person whose role was to say no to excessive and dangerous levels of risk was emerging as a paradoxical feature of this new paradigm. Unbeknownst to him, Eugene was about to be caught up in the inherent contradictions of his chosen profession and would suffer as a result.

Back in 2001, Eugene had become aware of rumors circulating in the office about branch managers illegally overcharging business clients. A diligent audit professional, Eugene decided to look into this and launched a detailed investigation that covered all branches within AIB.[2] It was a challenging project given its scope but he credited his team for producing a thorough analysis regardless. It emerged that stress levels among branch managers had risen significantly in recent years because of new income targets that they had been issued. They were expected to make a set amount of money each year from charging their time to clients and frequently found themselves falling short. Some managers had resorted to padding the bills of their business clients, in small amounts that they hoped would not be noticed. In one example, a customer was billed for three hours of advice from the branch manager after they played a round of golf.[3] Typically customers who were not likely to argue about the charges even if they noticed them were chosen. These included people already in debt to the bank who were therefore in a weak position.

In his report, "Special Issue Audit Report on Fees and Charges," Eugene stressed that not every branch manager was doing this; many were "highly honourable and upright."[4] This group was under similar pressures, however, and sometimes would add a charge when sending the customer's paperwork to head office without deducting the amount from the client's account. This was not typical corruption in Eugene's view, involving one or two greedy individuals, but rather it was systemic; the entire structure was set up to encourage and even coerce bad behavior.[5] In its conclusion, the report estimated that business clients at the bank had been overcharged €65 million.

The Irish banking regulator was not in a position to sanction this because, as in many countries, a light-touch regulation regime was in place; financial institutions were effectively allowed to run themselves so long as they adhered to some broad guidelines about appropriate conduct. Banks had to regularly report whether they were complying and were obliged to come forth if problems had arisen.[6] The onus was therefore on the banks themselves to declare wrongdoing, rather than the regulators to actively police. Regulatory authorities did, of course, have oversight of banking practice and could issue cautions and warnings, but by and large they did not actively intervene. This was the case with the Financial Services Authority banking regulation authority in the United Kingdom, the Securities and Exchange Commission in the United States, and the Central Bank of Ireland.[7]

Eugene provided AIB's senior management with a copy of the report on fees and charges. Another was given to the Central Bank of Ireland, in which the country's financial regulator was housed at the time.[8] Eugene was informed shortly afterward that the head of the bank was taking the report very seriously and that something would be done to rectify the problem. Steps would be taken to stop the discretionary overcharging of business clients, and customers who had been wrongly billed would be reimbursed immediately, in the summer of 2001. It appeared as though things would be changing.

After three months of waiting, a scheduled progress review was carried out into the proposed changes. Nothing had been done. The chief executive's stated plan had not been carried out. Millions of euros had effectively been stolen from people's accounts, and it seemed as though the bank was hoping to ignore it and move on.[9]

Concerned about this apparent cover-up within the bank, Eugene took his findings to the Irish central bank, as he was legally obliged to do. Meanwhile, back in the AIB office, worrisome changes were being made. Eugene and his team had begun to feel increasingly isolated in the bank, and now the report that was based on months of their hard work appeared to have been ignored. Just before Christmas 2001, Eugene's audit department was effectively demoted in a restructuring of the organization. The team's authority within the bank was greatly lessened. This was almost unprecedented in a bank, he later reflected. "I was extremely concerned about that because it broke all sorts of Basel guidelines as to how the audit function should be placed in an organization."[10] Weakening an audit department in such a way threatened the effectiveness of future investigations; it would not have the authority to see these through. Feeling some trepidation about the consequences, Eugene nonetheless wrote to senior management to protest these changes. "I wrote a memo about it, knowing what the reaction would be."[11]

The reaction was that he lost his job shortly after. Months later he was asked to the offices of the financial regulator, where he was invited to withdraw his comments about AIB's wrongdoing. After telling the authorities that he would not retract, he claims he was "out on the streets after five minutes."[12] Moreover, he was implicitly scapegoated; his firing was presented in public as part of a clearing-up exercise after a scandal involving a rogue trader in the bank's U.S. operations. He was painted as a disgruntled ex-employee seeking revenge in newspaper articles and in parliamentary debates in which he was discussed.

Internalizing Exclusion

Stories of the public vilification of a whistleblower are by now familiar. Eugene found himself internalizing his, however. He described the sense of isolation that came with the negative publicity and the response from his colleagues:

> The isolation is the main problem that I experienced. You are on your own against this massive organisation, in fact two organisations—the bank and the regulator. They have lawyers and you are on your own. You are made to feel isolated and somehow you are an outsider and you lose all credibility when you are outside.[13]

Eugene was aghast at how, even though he felt he had done the right thing for the bank, the industry and the country more generally (AIB being one of the two pillar banks in Irish society) he was somehow positioned as an outsider. As his case developed, a number of politicians spoke up on his behalf. When Shane Ross, a senator in Seanad Éireann, the upper house of the Irish parliament, took on his case and talked about him in the Seanad his story gained attention in the press.[14] He was then acknowledged in the Irish parliament and in the media as having been right all along, although suspicion lingered. At this point, Senator Ross stepped in again and insisted that Eugene be given a full and public apology by senior management at AIB, his former employers, and by the head of the Irish regulator.[15] This proved to be very important for Eugene. Even so, for a long time afterward, he struggled to make sense of the smear operation:

> I certainly wasn't prepared for that. But I found that you have to deal with it. And certainly it is very difficult to deal with because— . . . You know at some points, it *does* feel very personal, it does [make you think,] Is it actually true? Am I the one with the problem? And, Have I totally misread this whole situation?[16]

Eugene was continually questioning himself. Olivia Greene found that a similar creeping self-doubt arose from being part of a legal case involving her former employer, after she appeared on a prime-time TV show in Ireland about the corrupt practices at Irish Nationwide. She had been bullied by senior managers and colleagues as a result. It was difficult to prove the extent of the bullying, much of which had been informal and subtle:

> [It's] certainly very hard to prove how badly you have been treated and how it's affecting you mentally, physically, . . . you know, just your whole being. It's like, being bullied is very, very hard to prove.[17]

It was difficult to convince the court of the effect that these experiences of being bullied were having on her, but it was also difficult to convince herself. She began to query her own thought processes:

> Because it's so difficult to prove you are the innocent party, you actually almost feel guilty. And then you start doubting yourself. Once you start doubting yourself, you start asking, Am I right in having taken this case; should I have taken this case?[18]

Despite being certain of what she had experienced, she was beginning to turn the skepticism exuded by others, including many of her colleagues and even neighbors in her local village, onto herself. Jonathan Sugarman experienced this kind of self-doubt and questioning:

> I was saying, "This is unreal." . . . I mean, all I did was obey the law: it does say five years in prison for breaching the law. In the meantime, you know, surely if I have done the right thing here, how come I am the only one taking the brunt?[19]

Jonathan was unsure about his own judgment. How could he be the only person to speak out? As had Olivia and Eugene, he began to turn inward and question himself.

Paul Moore describes his reaction to reading the extensive KPMG report that he knew would be a determining factor in his struggle for a verdict of unfair dismissal, "It was devastating. Can you imagine being described like that . . . ? When you set out to do your job to the best of your ability?"[20] Although he ostensibly knew that he had been fired because he repeatedly called attention to the risky practices taking place in the bank, it was difficult for him to read the document, especially because Paul had worked for KPMG before joining the Halifax. He read and reread the painful words: "It seemed like a disaster—it made me introvert on myself and question myself."[21] He was plagued by a sense of futility in the face of this weighty opposition. Paul began to internalize what he was reading and hearing and to doubt himself. This continued as he pursued his case against the bank, claiming that he was fired for having been a whistleblower: "I cannot tell you how awful it is to be sent to Coventry—not be able to get anywhere. It really is horrendous. Because you lose your entire raison d'être. You lose your soul."[22] Living in a world in which people generally pay attention to the mainstream media, and in which there is an accepted, albeit sometimes grudging, deference to authority, it is not easy to listen to character assassinations and keep your mind free of them. Paul, Eugene, and Olivia were sure of what they had witnessed within their financial institutions; they had proof. They had each convinced themselves that it was wrong and should be highlighted. Even so, the opposition that they experienced from former colleagues, friends, and bosses slowly began to unravel their convictions; a sense of confusion, misplaced guilt, and self-doubt emerged.

They had felt themselves to be in the right, but what was the right thing, really, in their situation? Could it be that they were wrong, especially given that they seemed to be the only ones to speak out? In the unreality of this situation, people frequently experienced a deterioration in their mental well-being. Paul Moore described his health in the aftermath of his firing from HBOS:

> My mental and emotional health was in very bad shape. I was a mess. I could not think straight anymore. My armpits sweated profusely almost all the time. I was drinking like a fish. I was not sleeping. I was a train-crash.[23]

Most of those whose stories appear in this book struggled at some point with mental and emotional problems, due to the difficulty of the struggle, the isolation experienced, and the overwhelming opposition from so many others. Indeed most whistleblowers, even beyond this study, understandably seek counseling at some point.[24] Research into the impacts of whistleblowing finds a sense of isolation and general anxiety, which can manifest in trouble sleeping and, in extreme cases, suicidal feelings.[25]

Researchers point to the majority of such people having been "exemplary" employees before speaking out: the kind of "high-achieving, respected" individuals that we often hear about in relation to whistleblowers.[26] The emotional crisis that results therefore highlights the brutality of some reprisals. Scholars try to make sense of these complex impacts of retaliation, the self-doubt and self-questioning that ensues. Most conclude that whistleblowing can result in severe mental health effects. Using these terms can be problematic, however, because it reinforces the idea that whistleblowers can be mentally unstable, an idea frequently used by retaliating organizations seeking to smear the person speaking out.[27] In other words, academics who draw on discourses of mental health to describe whistleblowing and explain its impacts risk exacerbating the stigma that often accompanies this group.[28] For this reason, it is important to explore new ways of understanding whistleblowers' struggles with stress. To do otherwise risks supporting the aims of retaliatory organizations interested in painting whistleblowers as mad and discrediting their claims.

Recognition, Guilt, and Self-Violence

How else to understand this muddle of guilt and anxiety if not by drawing on the language of mental health that is so widely used today? And what is the nature of the whistleblower subject position that gives rise to these confusing affects? Norms that implicitly repress truth tellers because of the threat they represent operate both outside and inside the organization. Previously we saw how norms of complicity and silence are inherent to financial services organizations; these ensure that transgressing employees are excluded, impossible beings who do not deserve protection from violence because they are not considered to be valid persons.

The people appearing in this study were not always whistleblowers; they had been members of their organizations and their professions for years prior to the actions that led to their occupying the position of whistleblower. They worked as part of systems that upheld these norms. They too are influenced by the pull of a desire to be seen as normal. Why should we assume that they are immune to the very norms that cause them injury now? What effects do these norms have?

It appears that guilt is a feature of occupying a subject position as whistleblower. Drawing on affective recognition and ideas of subjectivity therein is helpful here, specifically the discussion developed by theorist of gender and power Judith Butler on the emergence of "bad conscience" in processes of subjection. As are we all, the whistleblower is dependent for its existence, in part at least, on dominant social norms: "Our lives, our very persistence, depend upon such norms, or, at least, on the possibility that we will be able to negotiate within them, derive our agency from the field of their operation."[29] For the whistleblowers I met, important norms included those characterizing their everyday working environment in the financial services sector. It could be that, even after people leave their organizations, the norms that contribute to the exclusion of the position of the whistleblower are not fully excised. Perhaps they remain, even at the level of the subconscious. Our psychic makeup comprises a "congealment" of layers of past experiences and losses, which color our actions.[30] This is so despite the possibility that these very norms can cast out and reject one's position—the position of the whistleblower—because of the transgression it represents. This suggests that whistleblowers are paradoxically excluded from the very norms they have once desired.[31] They experience the "continuing inadequacy of the self in relation to its transcendent measure," the norms that "call" it into being, and this is painful.[32] More than this, one's very sense of "I" as whistleblower is produced by this process. As the subject turns back on itself, a sense of conscience and a feeling of guilt emerges.[33] The whistleblower therefore polices herself in relation to how she adheres to the norms of the organization, and punishes herself for transgressing. This impulse to punishment, this self-violence, is part of how the whistleblower subject comes into being and is therefore part of its very emergence. What this suggests is that to be a whistleblower—to occupy this position—is to simultaneously feel troubled by, and question, that part of oneself. To be a whistleblower is to be, at least for a while, at odds with oneself: in conflict, uneasy. This is partly because the legacy of having once been a normal employee remains.

What is the impact of this self-questioning? In leading people to second-guess themselves, to feel stress and confusion about what they are doing, it effectively lessens their ability, confidence, and drive to actively pursue their struggle. This means that what Butler terms the "law", in this case organizational norms around complicity, is a central part of the whistleblower subject; she remains tied to power. Her very existence as a whistleblower "can be purchased only through a guilty embrace of the law, where guilt guarantees the intervention of the law and, hence, the continuation of the subject's existence."[34] The result of this "guilty embrace" is a painful struggle with the self that places the norms of the industry at the heart of the subject and that makes speaking out incredibly difficult. In the self-doubt and confusion that emerges from people's understanding of their adopted position as whistleblower, we see the battle that results as whistleblowers themselves take on the labor of exclusion that was begun within the organization.

Perhaps, therefore, an adherence to norms of complicity and silence, and a desire to exclude and punish those who transgress them, is ironically part of the construction of the whistleblower subject position, just as it is for others who are invested in the financial services sector. Perhaps this is the case even as whistleblowers now renounce these very dynamics. For this reason, when people occupy the whistleblower position and experience ostracizing and violence, on some level they play a part by turning this back on themselves—the exclusion of the person who speaks out is a dominant norm within their worlds of banking, and this is not easily shaken off. Rather, it is directed toward the self in confused feelings of self-doubt, guilt, and depression; people berate themselves for transgressing.[35] They police themselves for being impossible. For example, Eugene McErlean appears to internalize the isolation that he experiences from important parties in his world of banking, not just his own "massive organisation, [but] in fact two organisations—the bank and the regulator." He cannot understand how "somehow" he has become an outsider, beginning to question whether it is actually true. "Am I the one with the problem?" he asks. Olivia Greene describes feeling "almost . . . guilty," doubting herself as to what she has done and whether she was right. Jonathan Sugarman sums it up well in describing how obeying the law, reporting the misconduct he had witnessed, and "taking the brunt" had a result that was simply "unreal." Importantly, for each it was whether they had done the "right thing," in the end, that appeared to be in question; that is, the label of whistleblower has been thrown into chaos. Having seen that they are impossible in the eyes of others, they have become impossible to themselves. Guilt constructs the very subject position of the whistleblower.

Other literature describes the effect of the kinds of public exclusions described here on people who speak out. We know that people struggle with self-esteem and that this contributes to difficulty in finding new employment. Retaliation, stigmatization, and the other sources of suffering for those who speak out, are typically exerted by external forces—they act from the outside on the whistleblower. With whistleblowers, however, we see the complex internalization of norms from the outside and a turning against the self. Whistleblowers are not separate from society; they are subject to the same powerful norms surrounding what is acceptable behavior for employees.

Internalizing Exclusion: Complicity in Suffering?

What are the wider effects of this aspect of public whistleblowing? Again, it is useful to return to the broader picture: to understand how the micro level of subjection might intersect with powerful discourses. The disparagement of the position of public whistleblower, felt so painfully by people, had implications for their overall struggle. Specifically, the internalization of exclusions by the whistleblower can lead to a downward spiral that can ultimately be harnessed in the service of a retaliatory organization that wishes to smear an individual. For a company that intends to publicly discredit the person making the claims, the mental and emotional battle described earlier provides a wonderful opportunity—it can be used to further demean them.[36] Many retaliating organizations draw on such experiences to further stigmatize whistleblowers and claim that they are unreliable because they suffer from mental health problems. For example, the KPMG report on Paul Moore raised concerns about his mental health, using phrases like "extra-ordinary" and "ranting."[37] Paul was not alone; implying that someone is not mentally sound is a surprisingly common tactic in retaliations against whistleblowers and appeared in almost every story gathered for this book. A particularly shocking instance of this involves a German banker, Gustl Mollath. He spoke out about money-laundering activities at the Hypo Vereinsbank, some of which involved his wife.[38] He was accused of lying and then was committed to a high-security psychiatric hospital where he remained for seven years. Evidence emerged that there was indeed money laundering taking place and moreover that it had been detailed in an auditors' report; the bank had evidence that Mollath was telling the truth but had not submitted it to the authorities during his trial. Instead, a diagnosis by court experts of paranoid personality disorder caused him to be locked away. A recent study of the impacts of whistleblowing disclosures highlights many further cases of this nature.[39]

Emotion is key here. Even the smallest displays of feeling can appear to an onlooker as though the person is extraordinary and problematic and can fuel accusations of having mental health problems.[40] This places whistleblowers in a difficult situation; it is not easy to remain impassive when being bullied and, as sometimes happens, seeing family suffer too. Rudolf Elmer discussed the challenge in remaining unemotional, especially when his family was being harassed by private detectives hired by his former employer after he had gone public about the bank's role in facilitating tax evasion. "They are going to make you mad [i.e., angry], and you are going to act mad," he said.[41]

You have to think strategically, but they would like that you act emotionally. For instance, we had eleven private detectives following my wife, my daughter, [and] me on certain days. When I noticed them I got emotional about it, and that's normal. . . . That was a mistake. . . . This is a very difficult point for everyone who goes in that direction: emotions. You have to control your emotions, even though you know you are being harassed.[42]

As we saw earlier, his emotional response was exploited by the bank, who referred to it repeatedly when making statements to newspapers. They cited it as evidence that Elmer was unstable.

Paul Moore found himself getting angry and emotional when he was trying to raise awareness of the toxic culture within HBOS bank: "Did I let my anger out? For a period of time, in my soul I had anger. It was anger about people who refused to cooperate. . . . Anger with the cultural indisposition to challenge."[43] We have seen how the KPMG report into his whistleblowing claim made a big deal out of such emotional displays; they were used to disparage his character and his sanity. Paul described how he learned quickly that to be seen as angry, or display any kind of emotion, was a mistake. Similarly, Rudolf Elmer found himself continually trying to control and hide his feelings. He sought help from psychologists to do this. His advice to other whistleblowers, after the fact, was not to "act emotionally" in public, instead find an independent and honest psychologist and work out these impulses in private. On this point, Tom Devine of the U.S. whistleblower advocacy group Government Accountability Project advises would-be whistleblowers that the "calmest person in the room" is often taken to be the most credible.[44] Accusing someone of struggling with mental health is an effective reprisal strategy because it taps into the stigma that prevails in relation to mental health.[45] It is also somewhat self-reinforcing; experiencing rejection by colleagues, powerful industry parties and sometimes oneself, whistleblowers naturally go through a period of internal struggle and turmoil. Emerging as emotional displays, these can be interpreted by others as signaling mental health issues. Whistleblowers are frequently formally encouraged by their organizations to seek help from mental health professionals. Their accessing such services is then painted as evidence of their illness, and this reprisal can lead to an increase in stress and anxiety, which is further exacerbated by the self-doubt and confusion that result from embodying a position that goes against the dominant norms of one's social and occupational world. The whistleblower must continually try to suppress her reaction.

We see that the label of whistleblower causes pain to those affiliated with it but contains the further paradox that to acknowledge or in any way display this pain further intensifies the problem. Once again we have a situation in which whistleblowers are unwittingly, and unfairly, complicit in the difficulties that they experience.

Conclusion

These insights help us understand the apparent dissolution of people's sense of self when speaking out, which tends to be labeled somewhat simplistically as mental health suffering by journalists and academics alike. This perspective enables deeper insight into being publicly known as a whistleblower. It adds yet a further layer to the analysis of whistleblower exclusions presented earlier. These were, first, macro—they operate at the level of society and include processes of individualization involving the media and ostracizing by industry recruiters. Second, they work at an intermediate, more local level, being upheld by former colleagues and friends. In this chapter we see a further, deeper level; exclusions are internalized by people themselves, which can endanger a stable sense of self as whistleblower.

Whistleblowers do not somehow remain immune to the exclusion and character assassinations to which they are exposed. These can lead to a fundamental questioning of the self, a sense of guilt, and self-doubt. People can reject themselves, even as they simultaneously claim to believe that they are correct in their actions and morally right. The very impossibility of the position of whistleblower that they occupy plays out at the level of the person herself. The overall effect of this can include upholding norms that encourage silence in organizations and punishment for those who speak out.

9

Coping with Retaliation: Affective Recognition

THUS FAR, the picture has been somewhat bleak in relation to whistle-blowing. People who speak up are deemed impossible for doing so; they are excluded by organizations within global finance, by friends and colleagues, and even by the self. And yet we know that people do survive the experience, albeit they are often transformed by it. What enables this survival? This chapter, Chapter 10, and the Conclusion explore this question and begin by highlighting the importance of recognition offered by others for developing a subject position of whistleblower that is livable, even as it is impossible. This process has a darker side and can involve excluding others who are deemed less ethical.

Wachovia's Blood Dollars

The carnage wreaked by Mexico's drug wars is well known, with public beheadings almost regular occurrences, teenagers being shot, and rural migrants massacred on ranches.[1] In 2006, Martin Woods found himself in the middle of the flow of money that was the reason for the very existence of drug cartels. He had been with Wachovia bank for a year, working as a senior anti-money laundering officer in the London office. Just a few years previously, Martin had been central in bringing a massive fraud case against Bank of New York for money laundering. He had been praised and gained a reputation for diligence as a result.

An important principle in anti-money laundering work is to always know your client. On arrival, Martin was surprised to see that the information on clients in Wachovia was scant, and he set about gaining a clearer picture. He began to ask why billions of dollars were coming into accounts held at the Miami branch of Wachovia, which originated in currency exchanges in Mexico.[2] The money was coming in travelers' checks, but they were ordered in sequence and for far larger amounts than any tourist would likely need. It was not difficult for Martin to spot that there was something odd going on. "It was basic work" to observe that there was often no identifying information or legible signature on the checks.[3] He began to realize what he was seeing:

> The dollars coming out of Mexico are conflict dollars. They're blood dollars. Many of those dollars are stained with the blood of dead people, because that was the outcome of this whole drug trafficking war that's taking place in Mexico.[4]

Wachovia, his bank, was playing a major role in this. Through filtering the money via Miami

> the money becomes clean—it goes back to Mexico or it goes to other destinations to facilitate further drug dealing. . . . It buys more drugs; it pays for infrastructure, transport, wages; it buys weapons, and those are the same weapons that kill people.[5]

Just as high-end car dealers, property dealers, and solicitors are expected to report suspicious activity that they come across in their work, anti-money laundering officers have a duty to raise attention when they suspect criminal activity.

Martin did his job and routinely filed a number of suspicious activity reports, recommending that the bank block certain parties. These were sent from his office in London to Wachovia headquarters in North Carolina. He also alerted the authorities in the United Kingdom. None of this was well received at Wachovia. In fact a senior Miami manager called his reports "defensive and undeserved." He was told that he didn't really understand Mexico very well and was advised to learn more about practices in that country. He disagreed: "I said, 'I don't need to read up on Mexico. My interests are drug trafficking and money laundering.'"[6] The reprimand and lack of response did not come as a big surprise to Martin. During his first year in the job he had raised questions about money laundering through Wachovia on the part of Hezbollah during the Lebanon war. Following protocol, he had tried to freeze these accounts. He had been reprimanded.

Martin was proved right about his Mexican suspicions when, on April 10, 2006, a plane carrying almost six tons of cocaine was apprehended and found to have been bought with money laundered through Wachovia by the Sinaloa narcotrafficking cartel. Investigators from the Internal Revenue Service, Drug Enforcement Administration, and other U.S. federal agencies began to look into the case. Soon Wachovia was issued subpoenas for information about its connections to Mexico and was being directly investigated for its failure to have an effective anti-money laundering program in place.[7] Wachovia paid one of the largest fines ever levied against a bank for facilitating money laundering, and Martin was praised by senior law enforcement officials for his central role. However, life inside the bank was becoming increasingly difficult for him.

In 2007, Wachovia began to break contact with some of the currency exchanges in Mexico. It responded internally, too, but not by looking into its own practices. Instead, senior management began singling out people like Martin.

First, a superior at the bank told him that he had no business investigating overseas accounts—it was not his remit. Nor did he have a right to ask for overseas documents, given his location in Britain. The bank served him with disciplinary proceedings for his activity, and a hearing was arranged to investigate what was called his professional misconduct. He recalled,

One of my offenses, and I quote, was that I fielded calls from the [London] Metropolitan Police. And, just for clarification, [I said,] "You're saying they rang up and I answered the phone?" and [the investigator] said yes.[8]

According to Martin, the accusation was "nonsense" because the alleged offense involved helping the police:

> I said, "How on earth is that a discipline offense?" He said, "They were about U.S. dollar accounts; they had nothing to do with you, you shouldn't have got involved, and you should have handed it over to the U.S." And then I argued my corner. I said, "They phoned from Mauritius into London a.m., . . . when New York and U.S. aren't even out of bed! And they were on the ground in Mauritius, and they are saying, 'Can we help?' Are you saying I don't help?"[9]

It turned out that the phone call related to a corrupt politician in Africa who had indeed funneled up to $125 million through Wachovia. In addition, Martin was disciplined for filing a suspicious activity report without the permission of his boss, even though the rules state that, as an anti-money laundering compliance officer, he is supposed to act independently. Under the UK Financial Services Authority rules, to put pressure on such a person is unlawful. Martin found his compliance bosses' attitudes to be strange:

> They did not want to know. Their attitude was, "Why are you doing this?" They should have been on my side, because they were compliance people, not commercial people. But really they were commercial people all along.[10]

He describes his frustration at these petty reprisals, noting that Wachovia "had my résumé, they knew who I was!" before he joined; that is, his commitment to the practice of fraud detection should have been clear to them.[11] In the end, Martin was accused of acting in a way that could leave the bank open to potential regulatory jeopardy and even large fines.[12] In the summer, he entered a hospital with a prolapsed disk. Again this senior executive was formally reprimanded: this time for not reporting sick in the correct manner as detailed in his employee handbook.

Returning to work in August 2007, he was welcomed with a warning letter from a senior manager that detailed "specific examples of [his] failure to perform at an acceptable standard."[13] The stress was mounting. Martin suffered a near breakdown, was prescribed medication, and was given psychiatric help.

Surviving Retaliation

We see echoes of other whistleblowers' experiences; Martin espoused a subject position of clear-sighted professionalism in accounting for what he had done, after the event. He portrays himself as continually upholding his professional standards even as he was repeatedly reprimanded for filing reports on his suspicions about the drug money laundering, insisting again and again that his "interests [were] drug trafficking and money laundering."[14] He also experienced some of the same kinds of retaliation tactics as others in this study, including being the target of an investigation that focused on him rather than the wrongdoing, as happened with Paul Moore and Eileen Foster, and being chided for very minor infringements of company policy, as happened to Olivia Greene, for example.

How did Martin, and others like him, cope under such extreme pressure? Finding that he was increasingly isolated in Wachovia bank as he waited for disciplinary action to be taken against him, he describes how he leaned on his old friends from the police force for support. Before becoming a bank employee, Martin had been with the police for eighteen years, first as an officer and then as a drug squad detective in the London Metropolitan Police. He later moved to the National Crime Squad (similar to the U.S. Federal Bureau of Investigation), where he worked as a fraud expert. When asked what he considered his most important source of support during the difficult months at Wachovia, he responded, "Primarily it was cops and ex-cops. I mean massively. . . . It must be that that's my family; that's my brotherhood, you know? Mainly in the UK but some in the U.S. as well."[15] The support he got from this group was of the kind that

> everybody believes [you]. It was, and it is now, [sometimes] just a sound bite. . . . A pat on the back, or a phone call, or an email to say, "How are you?" It's that kind of . . . that comradeship, that friendship that— . . . What happened with the bank is . . . it's a very isolating experience.[16]

For others, the presence of old friends was vital, because friendship can become a rare commodity when one is speaking out. Reflecting on his struggles to highlight his bank's role in tax evasion, Rudolf Elmer noted,

You need to know the right people because you are going to lose a lot of friends. And you are going to lose a lot of people who you believed you could trust, but you will learn you can't.[17]

In addition to old friends, families formed a vital locus of support. Rudolf described the importance of his spouse in helping him through the years of intimidation and threats from his bank in Switzerland:

I was lucky. I have a wonderful wife and a wonderful daughter. My wife actually is the hero; I'm only the one who is the messenger. I couldn't have handled the case without my wife, to be honest.[18]

For yet others, certain coworkers offered vital help during their attempts to speak out. Whereas, thus far, we have seen how whistleblowers can find themselves isolated in their organization, ostracized by others who work there, this is not always so. Many reported support from other colleagues, some of whom had spoken out about the wrongdoing themselves or would have liked to see remedies. Martin said,

Don't forget as well, there are other great people in Wachovia bank; it wasn't "the Martin Woods show." I didn't go in there to get a Purple Heart. I didn't want to get the sack either, you know, but that kind of happened. And there are other great people doing great things.[19]

People described pairing up to form mutual-support partnerships with some of these "other great people." Often a person discovered someone else in the organization who was attempting to raise awareness about the same issue, and they got in touch. When other colleagues do not know or do not wish to know about the wrongdoing, such partnerships represent a significant source of encouragement and help.[20] Olivia Greene at Irish Nationwide and Brian Fitzgibbon, the person whom she helped in fighting his unfair dismissal, are examples. Eileen Foster paired up with her senior colleague Michael Winston whose whistleblowing actions at Countrywide became known to her through a mutual journalist contact. People describe the strong bonds of friendship that can develop under such adverse circumstances. When a person wishes to dissent, the presence of another like-minded individual can be very powerful indeed. As Stanley Milgram notes, "The mutual support provided by [people] for each other is the strongest bulwark we have against the excesses of authority."[21] Such mutual support can be a powerful influence.

Martin Woods also found fellow whistleblowers outside the organization to be very helpful. He met people who had gone through similar experiences at a recently formed whistleblower support group. He said,

> In that room, for those meetings, honestly you think, Any surviving whistleblower of that caliber or of that kind of whistleblowing engagement, at a very high level, they have to be strong to survive. So you are in this room full of these very, very strong-minded people and very, very committed people, you think this is, this is— . . . If you become the sum of the people you hang around with, then my count is going up a gauge just by being in this room.[22]

The strength and courage of other whistleblowers are a source of inspiration for him. There is a privilege that comes with being in this group:

> I'm allowed to move in those circles; it's a nice place to be. It's a privileged place to be, with some of the people you are engaged with, who have this attitude and this mind-set and have contributed so much and made such a difference for different people in different walks of life or are trying to. And are prepared to put themselves in harm's way to try to bring about change or to bring attention to wrongdoing, to pursue justice or to protect other people. There is a set of characteristics and people with profiles that you think, Wow, and I'm in amongst these people?[23]

A number of whistleblower support organizations exist across the world. Such groups typically provide one-on-one help for people considering speaking out, including legal advice and mental health support. Many are staffed by ex-whistleblowers. Despite providing a valuable service as Martin indicates, whistleblower support organizations can find themselves under-resourced. For this reason the number of people they can reach, and the time they can spend on individual cases, tends to be limited. Overall, people found that support from friends, family, and other whistleblowers helped them survive a very difficult process.

RECOGNITION AND A LIVABLE WHISTLEBLOWER POSITION

We have seen how chaotic the whistleblower subject position is. It is precarious and dependent on other forces. It is vulnerable to being enrolled in networks of power that can render it impossible, incoherent, and re-pulsive to some, even sometimes to the whistleblower herself. When a person suffers in this way, reinforcing their status as a professional helps them cope with what they are experiencing, as we have seen in Chapter 4. But constructing oneself as a whistleblower-professional goes only so far to provide a buffer against obstacles to survival. Despite a robust sense of self as an anti-money laundering professional, Martin still struggled with isolation and its impacts, culminating in a breakdown. The same happened to Paul Moore, Rudolf Elmer, and many others. As we saw with Rudolf, moving from a position of impossible to possible whistleblower has many advantages, including providing one with a public voice. It does not, however, protect from the exclusions and rejections that con-tinue to haunt the person occupying the label of whistleblower. What else can assist?

Examining people's accounts in depth, we find other factors that help reconstruct a sense of the livable even amid such painful exclusions. Beginning with Martin, it seems as though an alternative version of his whistleblower self, one that he could live with, was on offer from "cops and ex-cops": his friends and former colleagues in the police force. He perceived them as sharing his commitment to doing the right thing regardless of the circumstances: "everyone believes."[24] These people con-trast starkly with Martin's colleagues and bosses at Wachovia who seemed determined to silence him. The interpretation of his whistleblower-self that is offered by the cops negates the exclusions to which he is sub-jected by his current colleagues. Martin finds a further source of valida-tion for his newly adopted subject position when he meets similarly committed people at the whistleblower support group, who have "contributed so much" to society, putting themselves "in harm's way" to do so. Individuals of "that caliber" offer him a further bolstering. Af-firmation as an acceptable and even esteemed person is offered from important others, despite having previously been refused.

To construct ourselves as valid and deserving of a position in the world that is livable, we seek confirmation of our existence through drawing on particular norms. For Martin, it was an attempt to engage with the norm of whistleblower but in a new and different way. What was driving this? Here it is helpful to return to Judith Butler's work on the Foucaul-dian idea of subjectification. As Michel Foucault notes, discursive power can only be said to emanate through the cumulative actions of a vast network of subjects; it has no central locus. Norms are upheld through complex networks of power that shape the practices of ordinary people, day to day. This means that our accessing of norms and subject positions takes place via the others we encounter; we seek confirmation of our selves and our place in the world through them. Occasionally, when recognition is denied, we are negated, undone, and rendered impossible. In other instances, we find reflections of our selves in others that affirm us as valid, providing us with subject positions we can live with rather than ones that cast us out. Such recognition by others grants us a legitimate place in the symbolic, affirming our sense of self.

Intersubjective recognition augments a whistleblower's sense of self in this way, for Martin and others. Analyzing the position of the whistleblower through this lens is helpful here because it emphasizes the role of power; "we are vulnerable to processes of subjection because they offer confirmation of our existence."[25] Foucault shows how power and subjection are interlinked, and Butler introduces the idea that psychic needs for recognition are met or denied via our encounters with others. Subjection and recognition are intersubjective—they occur between subjects. Self-preservation is almost always interlinked with the giving and receiving of recognition. Intersubjective recognition is what connects us to the norms that allow us to survive. For a whistleblower like Martin, self-preservation was caught up in those others who provided him with a version of the label whistleblower that he could live with. This does not imply that the whistleblower subject position preexists the search for recognition to validate its place. Rather, as Butler notes, the subject is always in process: continually constituted through the process of attaining future subjectivity.

For these whistleblowers, affect and feeling appear to be key in fueling their struggles for recognition. Martin's account, for example, is suffused with admiration. He draws on the "other great people doing great things" at Wachovia, noting that he is not alone in trying to speak out about wrongdoing there. His feelings for others at the whistleblower support group are clear: "They have to be strong to survive." Rudolf Elmer cites his admiration for his wife, the one who is "actually . . . the hero," without whom it would have been impossible for him to maintain his whistleblowing struggle. "I couldn't have handled the case" without her, he said. These affects point to the dynamics of mutual recognition; their display signals that important others concur with the whistleblower's self-construction. Martin Woods's ex-cops, for example, used to offer small affective gestures like "a pat on the back, or a phone call, or an email to say, 'How are you?'" He is invited "in amongst" the other high-profile whistleblowers he so admires, "allowed" to engage with them and "move in those circles." Butler describes how the desires that make us vulnerable to subjection can be understood as "passionate attachments": "we are bound to each other in passionate ways."[26] This is because the reflection of ourselves that we receive from important others, in their offering or denial of recognition, can "[signify] a diminution or augmentation of [the subject's] own possibility of future persistence and life."[27] The dynamics that fuel these psychic binds of attachment are affective. To understand processes of subjection and how these relate to wider flows of power, the emotional means by which people engage in dynamics of recognition are important to examine.

AFFECTIVE RECOGNITION ACROSS TIME AND SPACE

What kinds of others are involved in such passionate attachments to a sense of mutual recognition? Although these attachments often involved people with whom whistleblowers had face-to-face contact, including colleagues, family, and friends, this was not always the case. They also encompassed those far away and even others who are not alive today. Virtual and sometimes anonymous supporters proved vital for many. Paul Moore describes how the general public stepped in as a great source of help and encouragement when he was being featured in newspapers in a less-than-favorable light. One person sent him a silver whistle in the post, which, he notes, he still treasures. According to Jonathan Sugarman, he receives significant support from strangers, and the Internet is key to this. He describes how, once he developed his website and began to use email and Twitter to let people know about his experiences of blowing the whistle on UniCredit Ireland's repeated breaches of legal liquidity requirements, he was followed by people who are active in other anticorruption campaigns. They provided encouragement and praise even while he was struggling to gain the attention of journalists and politicians for his claims. Ian Taplin, the ex–Lloyds Bank employee, similarly found the Internet to be a vital source of support because people got in touch through his website and worked with him to begin a whistle-blower support group. The all-important affective dynamics of mutual recognition operated virtually in such cases.

Faith represented another important, "virtual" lifeline according to some whistleblowers. Paul Moore found great comfort in his religious beliefs and talks about this regularly when he is asked what got him through the more difficult times. Pondering whether to break his confidentiality agreement with HBOS and speak out about the problematic sales culture at the British bank, on TV and before the Treasury Select Committee, he says self-examination through prayer helped him make the decision.[28] This religious faith had more than internal spiritual advantages, however. When Paul made his decision, during the height of the banking crisis, it was a fellow Catholic who worked at the BBC to whom he turned.[29]

In addition to virtual dynamics of recognition, temporally stretched affective connections were important. Many described how an important aspect of understanding themselves as whistleblower involved a strong sense that they were carrying on some kind of family tradition of truth telling or initiating one for future generations. For Graham Senior Milne, who spoke out about both staff and auditors at Lloyds Bank allowing life insurance policyholders to be deprived of their entitlements, this legacy had its roots in the past. On his website, he features quotations from historical figures well known for their bravery in pursuing the truth:

> The search for truth implies a duty. One must not conceal any part of what one has recognized to be true.
> —Albert Einstein

> The truth is incontrovertible, malice may attack it, ignorance may deride it, but in the end there it is.
> —Winston Churchill[30]

Graham also describes how his family has a long history of activism in the face of difficult circumstances that goes back for generations. Ancestors were social reformers and philanthropists, often challenging powerful interest groups in their work. So, for him, a strong tradition of speaking up for what is right exists in his family, and this reflects a version of the whistleblower self that he can live with. Others believe they represent, rather than the last link in a long ancestral chain, the beginning of a future legacy of doing the right thing. They aim to inspire generations to come and hope that their present-day struggle will be remembered and treasured. Envisaging a positive impact on one's descendants is an important aspect. As Martin Woods noted, whistleblowing is full of strife: "At the end of the day, though, when your grandkids Google you, what do you want them to find out about you?"[31] Rudolf Elmer said, when he was offered a settlement with his bank in which his silence was requested, he was unable to take it. Part of this was the thought of the younger generation and his daughter:

> I turn down all offers not only as a matter of principle, but also due to the fact that my daughter and her generation will suffer from what is going on. . . . My daughter needs to learn values and one of the values is integrity and to stand up if something is not right. I understand what I'm doing now. It's not about me, it's about the next generation, what I'm doing. And that makes sense to me, and it is worthwhile going through that struggle and it's worthwhile to continue, and worthwhile not to give up.[32]

For Graham, Martin, and Rudolf therefore, they are connected to others in ways that provide them with a sense of support and strength to continue. Some of these others, however, are not even alive today; they are either past ancestors or future generations of children and grandchildren. Regardless, being part of a wider collective of people who value doing the right thing is central, whether this involves continuing on a trajectory of truth telling that others began before and that is meaningful to them, leaving a strong legacy for those who follow, or indeed inspiring online supporters in distant locations. When the others whom they encounter in day-to-day life—including bosses who retaliate, colleagues who isolate, and journalists who accuse—might be denying these whistleblowers any sense of validity, sources of support emerge that are both atemporal and virtual, transcending time and space. Temporally stretched sources of recognition prove vital. They enable a rewriting of what it means to occupy the position of whistleblower: a new version of the label.

Ek-static Recognition and Survival

In the above accounts, the idea of whistleblowers as being more than themselves and part of a wider plurality emerges again and again. The concept of the affective subject as ek-static helps make sense of this. It refers to the idea that one's self is constituted in and through elements that are commonly thought to be outside the self, including social norms; the self is radically external. This is more complex than simply connecting to others. For sure whistleblowers often formed pair partnerships or groups with other internal dissenters to take on their organization, and from a practical perspective, this was helpful. People frequently described their experiences as involving something more than this, however, as a transcendence of the self: becoming part of something else. Martin speaks about how he feels at whistleblower support group meetings: if you become "the sum of the people you hang around with," he says, "then my count is going up a gauge," just by being in their presence. He feels privileged to move in these circles: "Wow, and I'm in amongst these people?" Rudolf's identifications moved him beyond himself and into a couple in which the boundary between himself and his wife was blurred: "My wife actually is the hero; I'm only the one who is the messenger." He also accounts for his position as whistleblower by being caught up in a longer family legacy that encompasses his daughter, as do others. Butler's account of subject formation emphasizes the "fundamental sociality of embodied life," noting that our psychic attachments to others mean that we "are, from the start, already given over, beyond ourselves, implicated in lives that are not our own."[33] Beginning with her work on gender, the entity occupying the subject position she describes is inescapably outside itself from the start; the norms to which we subject ourselves are not ours, nor is there a preexisting subject that engages in such processes.[34] "The terms that make up one's own gender are, from the start, outside oneself, beyond oneself in a sociality that has no single author."[35] As ek-static subjects, we are therefore constructed by terms, or norms, that are radically external to ourselves.[36] To attempt to become a subject and to gain attendant recognition is "to be at a distance from who one is, not to enjoy the prerogative of self-identity . . . but to be cast, always, outside oneself, Other to oneself," through psychic processes of desire.[37] Although this ek-stasis can lead to our undoing at the hands of others when we are denied recognition, as seen earlier, it is likewise essential for our survival.

Many theories of recognition have been developed.[38] But these tend to assume an autonomous individual who is separated from those others around them and somewhat independent from outside influences, whereas Butler's account views the self as integrally bound up in others, and in forms of power. For her the "passion and grief and rage we feel . . . tear us from ourselves, bind us to others, transport us, undo us, and implicate us in lives that are not our own, sometimes fatally, irreversibly."[39] Drawing on these ideas enables a redefinition of the whistleblower subject as an entity whose boundary is porous and who is radically implicated in others. For the whistleblowers, relinquishing the notion of autonomy and independence and giving themselves up to their inevitable attachments seems to be a vital step in surviving.

Once again, the widely held concept of whistleblowers as rugged individuals who act alone in pursuing what they believe to be correct, unfettered by the influence of others, appears to be problematic.[40] As we have seen, this is a view held by many, including whistleblowers themselves. It leads to an individualizing discourse around speaking up, in which people are framed as lone operators and encouraged to see themselves as such. This perspective intensifies the loneliness of the struggle and the suffering caused by isolation. To rethink the whistleblower as a collective rather than individual entity might helpfully trouble this assumption and enroll others in attempts to speak up, not least because they perceive themselves to be both embedded in them and also in part responsible.

Defending the Self: Subjection and Exclusion

There was, however, a more complex side to the intersubjective attachments that feature in people's accounts of themselves as whistleblowers. Adopting the various subject positions outlined thus far was productive for people. The committed (albeit naïve) professional, the legitimate speaker in the eyes of far-flung geopolitical interest groups, and the valued member of a supportive and like-minded collective were all productive positions to adopt. They enhanced a sense of self, allowing people to bolster their status as a valid speaking subject within financial services. Adopting such positions enabled people to continue with their whistleblowing struggles—to speak out about problems inherent in their organizations and the industry more generally, and about the suffering they had themselves experienced.

In addition to the productive aspect of this subjection, however, there was a more complex side. When experiencing harsh forms of persecution for doing the right thing, it is not at all easy to look at other people—for example, ex-colleagues—and not resent them for remaining quiet while so much aggression is aimed at you. People in this study often constructed their positions of valid whistleblower in contrast to complicit others with whom they had worked. They found themselves actively excluding those who remained silent, just as they themselves had been excluded for speaking up.[41]

In describing his professional role, Paul Moore made the point that his colleagues at Halifax and HBOS must have been aware of the problems:

> If you lend that money to buy an asset which is worth the same or even less than the amount of the loan, and secure that loan on the value of that asset purchased and, then, assume that asset will always to rise in value, you must be pretty much close to delusional? You simply don't need to be an economic rocket scientist or mathematical financial risk management specialist to know this. You just need common sense.[42]

He describes those he had worked with, who did not speak out, as "delusional." It was obvious to all that there were problems in the bank. As he noted in his evidence to the Treasury Select Committee,

> Even non-bankers with no "credit risk management" expertise, if asked (and I have asked a few myself), would have known that there must have been a very high risk if you lend money to people who have no jobs, no provable income and no assets.[43]

Paul mentioned colleagues who said nothing about the overheated sales culture and breaches of FSA guidelines that he was continuously highlighting. Anyone working at the bank must have been aware of the corruption and thus were complicit because they remained silent.

To mix a few well-known similes/metaphors/stories, the current financial crisis is a bit like the story of the Emperor's new clothes. Anyone whose eyes were not blinded by money, power and pride (hubris), who really looked carefully, knew there was something . . . [44]

In other words, it was clear to anyone involved who was paying attention that there were problems.

But sadly, no-one wanted or felt able to speak up for fear of stepping out of line with the rest of the lemmings who were busy organising themselves to run over the edge of the cliff behind the pied piper CEOs and executive teams that were being paid so much to play that tune and take them in that direction.[45]

Paul defends himself as an ethical professional in contrast to these complicit and greedy individuals. In an interview with *Positive Money,* he further distanced himself from the banking orthodoxy in which crooked dealings have replaced the integrity that he deems to be a cornerstone of banking:

An economy without ethics ultimately destroys wealth and creates poverty. The banking crisis drove more than 100 [million] people back into poverty. . . . Mortality statistics of people in poverty [have risen] hugely . . . so the banking crisis was about killing people as well [as other aspects].[46]

Again drawing on his position of knowledgeable professional, he invokes a clear line between this lack of ethics and his contrasting views of banking described in Chapter 4.

Prior to joining Wachovia bank, Martin Woods had been a police officer for years. The difference in standing between compliance people in the two industries struck him powerfully:

Ordinarily in banks, the compliance officers—and it's a standing joke—are seen as the business prevention officers.[47]

He explained that, when the opportunity arises to make money from questionable practices:

. . . there are bankers queuing up to take that money. And what, therefore, they want is a compliance officer who will facilitate that business. What they don't want is a compliance officer who gets in the way of that business.[48]

Martin was a compliance officer who "[got] in the way of . . . business" because this was his job, even though he was not popular for doing it. Describing himself in this way, he positioned himself as different from those others. At the start of his interview he said he would not blame colleagues for not coming forward as he had done: "Banks are pure commercial organizations. And I don't condemn people who don't blow the whistle; I'm not one of those people. I don't judge people for not doing it."[49] He could not help but feel aggrieved, however, by those who do not, especially those who are hypocritical about it. He noted, earlier, that colleagues who do not understand the connection between money laundering and the deaths of thousands of people are simply "missing the point."

> Some people say, you know, "Martin, well done, you. But by the way, I let the money laundering go on at my bank because I want to keep my job, and therefore I'm not bothered about fifty thousand dead people in Mexico. It's nothing to do with me." And I think, Well, you are not an anti-money laundering officer; you are a salary collector. All you do is you go to work every month and collect your salary. That's what you do.[50]

Reinforcing his status of professional, he presents himself as having clear oversight of the wider impact of the activities he was reporting, as opposed to his colleagues who were not compliance people really but rather "commercial people."[51] To uphold his position as truth teller, Martin constructs himself in opposition to those in his organization who witness what he has but say nothing. This perception of an other—the silent, cowardly colleague—was evident across people's accounts.

Prior to speaking out about frequent, illegal breaching of liquidity levels at UniCredit, a foreign-owned subsidiary bank in Ireland, Jonathan Sugarman occupied the same open-plan space as the people working on the trading floor, whose risk levels he was monitoring. Jonathan noted,

> I was soon enough perceived to be the person who was going to interrupt everybody's party, because everybody was in the game of making it look okay. And because I am who I am, and I was hired [as risk manager] to do a job. Especially when Irish law imposes prison sentences for failing to do the job.[52]

Jonathan persisted in doing his job simply because, he said, "[I] was hired to do [it]" and because "I am who I am." It was his commitment to his position that he cited as the reason for speaking up, even though he was seen as the individual who was going to spoil the party. He was a true professional. In positioning himself as such, however, he drew a stark distinction between himself and those others who had not listened to him:

> We are reaching a point where we cannot all be right. . . . At this stage, reality has corroborated my story, in that there was no regulation being enforced—otherwise why were all our banks nationalized? So either I did my job [or] other risk managers and other board members and risk managers didn't.[53]

The apparent legitimacy of these others was eroding: "We can't *all* be right. The fact that our [Ireland's] entire banking system has collapsed probably testifies to a certain conclusion." He takes personal pride in being correct, even though he recognizes the difficulty in obtaining recognition for this.

To construct a position as defender of the truth, many whistleblowers I interviewed articulated a set of others who represented the opposite. This mirrors other studies; it is both helpful and perhaps necessary to create a distance between oneself and all those others who stay silent.[54] A very clear boundary was drawn around what Paul refers to as the "essence of a bank", and around people who act in accordance with this essence. In Paul's words, some people—whistleblowers like him—were adhering to their proper "fiduciary duty," whereas others were simply not. This distancing took place in relation to a number of aspects; people who did not speak out were too greedy, part of the "pure commercial" character of banks described by Martin, and happy to act as simple "salary collector[s]." Or they were fearful of breaking strong norms of silence. They were also painted as mindless bureaucrats, as with Paul's "lemmings" who blindly followed the executive teams. All three characteristics of complicit colleagues were presented as being in contrast to those of a proper professional. They stand in opposition to the very "definition of banking," as Paul notes, and Jonathan points out that it cannot be both ways: either he did his job correctly or they did theirs correctly. He argues that "reality"—the subsequent crisis that unfolded—has revealed him to be the true professional.

This reflects a common feature of social life; our tendency to construct our selves in opposition to those others who are not like us. Subjection can be an exclusionary process.[55] In claiming a stable position for the I, it is tempting to distance oneself from those outside it—an other who is not me.[56] It is a feature of being human that, in the construction of subject positions, boundaries can be drawn around what limits the I, rejecting what is outside. A traumatic rupture has occurred for the whistleblowers described here. They were once deeply attached to their organizations and professions and being cast outside them is not easy. Destabilizing one's sense of self forces an emergency redrawing of the parameters of what is considered to be an acceptable professional. Here we see how the stark exclusion of others can be part of this. All those who do not come up to scratch remain outside, mere "lemmings," as Paul Moore says. "Blinded by money, power and pride," they are the kinds of salary collectors that Martin Woods describes who remain uninterested in the thousands of deaths that their actions cause.

Authors have described how whistleblowers in post-disclosure interviews often work hard to construct and defend an idealized ethical self. This self is exceptionally principled in comparison with those others who did not speak up. As Rothschild and Miethe note in their widely-cited study of whistleblower experiences,

> Through the suffering they have endured—but never anticipated before their disclosure—they have come to see themselves as exceedingly moral. They have distanced themselves from what they now see as the corruption of their former employer, and many begin to see themselves as possessing extraordinary integrity that they now bring to their endeavors.[57]

The preceding analysis explains some of the mechanisms by which this distancing can occur. Specifically, an affective recognition lens shows this to be a tendency that we all share rather than a feature that only whistleblowers possess. Exclusion is a common aspect of subject formation, albeit it can be aggravated by the extreme situations in which whistleblowers find themselves.

This assertion does not therefore denigrate or lessen those who speak out, whose utterances can save lives and avoid disasters. It is clear that many were indeed committed to their role, their organizations and their colleagues. However a deeper understanding of the necessity of adopting and reinforcing a legitimate position in the eyes of others, for those who speak out, moves us toward a more nuanced appreciation of what it is to be a whistleblower. Descriptions of whistleblowers in public discourse and academic debates tend to waver between simplifying them as heroes or traitors or, if they have experienced particularly harsh retaliation, as passive victims.[58] They are assumed to be superhuman champions, tragic sufferers, or devious plotters; there is no room for complexity. These different perspectives have one thing in common: they are all stereotypes— extreme and exaggerated versions of personhood. They do not show the light and dark that we all embody. They prevent us moving toward a more nuanced understanding, one that might generate empathy for whistleblowers.

This is important because, currently, society does not support this group in any meaningful way. The response to stories of whistleblowers losing their livelihoods, bankrupting themselves, and experiencing severe health effects is mostly complacency. And yet we depend on these people to keep coming forward if we want the world to be safer. Perhaps the complacency relates to a lack of compassion for people who speak out, because we do not see that they have anything in common with ourselves. So long as we see them as little more than caricatures, either extremely good or extremely bad but definitely extraordinary, we cannot empathize. Understanding individuals who speak out as having a tendency to construct and reinforce boundaries in opposition to other people, just as we all do, could move us toward a stronger sense of connection with those who find themselves in such positions. To avoid doing so, to deny their fallibility, would exacerbate the problem of simplistic characterizations and further dehumanize this group of people.

Conclusion

For those who speak up, the recognition offered by important others is vital. It can offer comfort, helping one construct a subject position that is somewhat livable, in contrast to the impossible status described earlier. Empirical studies suggest that other people are typically involved in the process of speaking up, but the nature of such attachments and their influence on the whistleblower are rarely discussed. The concept of affective recognition illuminates these issues.

This suggests that whistleblowing research ought to be more sensitive to the display of affects and emotions. Such displays can shed light on the various, vital attachments that people develop to survive. Recalling Milgram, the "mutual support" of fellow dissenters indeed offers the strongest source of resistance to excesses of power and domination. In constructing a sense of self as whistleblower, specifically a livable version of this label, the influence of others is vital. Friends, family, online supporters, and advocacy group members offer recognition, and this is experienced affectively. What this analysis helps us see is the radical externality of the subject availing of this support. This self is ek-static, inescapably embedded in others, and so the subject position of whistleblower is inherently social. This offers an interesting development to existing literature on whistleblowing. In contrast to typical accounts of whistleblower support, the sources of help detailed here are shown to be neither outside the whistleblower, as separate entities, nor inside as, for example, an inner well of strength. Rather, the whistleblower as subject is porous at the boundary, coming into being as already-attached to multiple others.

We see however that such efforts to articulate the self were more complex than might be assumed and can involve people distancing themselves from others, including former colleagues and peers, who were seen as too concerned with money or too embedded in the bureaucratic system in which they worked to speak out. Finally those who engage in whistleblowing are typically seen as excessively good or bad—as stereotypes. It is instead more helpful to think of them as complex selves engaged in struggles for recognition. This emphasizes the humanness of whistleblowing; whistleblowers are just as prone to defending the self to secure their identity as are the rest of us.

From a practical perspective, the question of how to provide effective assistance to people who speak up is currently being debated in a number of countries. Society typically provides little or no assistance, financially or symbolically. If, as appears here, whistleblower survival entails forming and maintaining attachments to important others, such efforts would benefit from considering this dynamic. Attachments, including less obvious ones that are mediated across time and space, are essential in the reconstruction of a livable life. Attachments are essential for the protection and survival of those speaking out now, and for those considering doing so in the future. It is vital for would-be whistleblowers to see that a livable life is attainable, in contrast to the current prevailing attitude that represents whistleblowing as akin to professional and financial suicide. Reconceptualizing the label of whistleblower as radically social might provide a useful first step.

10

Small Victories and Making Fun: Performing the Whistleblower

THE POSITION of the whistleblower is complex and multifaceted. Being labeled as such can involve strong responses by others as the whistleblower becomes an impossible subject: targeted for violence and exclusion both inside and outside one's organization and by oneself. However, people find ways to survive: constructing an account of oneself as naïve professional, as Paul Moore did; presenting one's whistleblower self to a new audience in order to gain a voice, as Rudolf Elmer attempted when he left Switzerland for the United Kingdom; and finding solace and validation from important others, as did Martin Woods. Here we further explore this idea of whistleblower survival.

In Chapter 9, the whistleblower was reconceptualized as a collective self, embedded in and constructed through multiple others. Taking this further, can this label be actively reworked, rethought, and re-cited in ways that might actually effect a change in how it is perceived? Two ways that the category of whistleblower was reinvented by those taking part in this study are explored: the whistleblower as a winner of small, rather than large, victories, and the whistleblower label as a joke. This reinvention provides whistleblowers with a breathing space that helps them to survive difficult challenges. The idea that norms are inherently contingent and thus can be performed in different ways is helpful here. Such performances require relinquishing powerful fantasies, however, and this is not always easy.

Performing the Whistleblower: A Winner of Small Victories

After a series of outlandish reprimands by Wachovia, Martin Woods filed against the organization with the London Employment Tribunal for bullying, harassment, and detrimental treatment. The bank denied these claims but offered an undisclosed settlement, which Martin accepted in May 2009. By this time, he notes, he had become "the most toxic person in the bank," and so he left under the terms of his settlement.[1]

Martin describes feeling frustrated because the bank appeared to have won. On the one hand, his work had been taken up by U.S. officials in the Internal Revenue Service and Drug Enforcement Administration who eventually found Wachovia guilty of funneling over $350 billion in total from Mexican drug dealers between 2004 and 2007, along with ignoring "readily identifiable evidence of red flags of large scale money laundering."[2] Despite the federal prosecutor's claims that the bank would be punished, however, Wachovia (now part of Wells Fargo) settled out of court and paid a fine of $160 million, a tiny amount compared with the bank's annual profits.[3] The deal was based on a deferred prosecution, whereby if the bank cooperated and abided by the law, charges would be dropped after a year. The prosecutors made the point that Wells Fargo had fully cooperated with the investigation and had not been involved in Wachovia's misdeeds.

Martin reported feeling deflated; this was the biggest suit brought under the U.S. Bank Secrecy Act to date, and not one person would be held responsible. He said, "All the law enforcement people wanted to see this come to trial. . . . But no one goes to jail. In fact, everyone involved has either been promoted or gone to a better job at other banks."[4] He had suffered hugely as a result of his work, and yet nothing had come of it:

> What kind of message does this give to the cartels and launderers? What does the settlement do to fight the cartels? Nothing. . . . Where's the risk [for the bank]? There is none—there is only an upside.[5]

His work as an anti-money laundering officer and the painful struggle he had undergone as a whistleblower was ostensibly in vain. In addition, Martin felt frustrated that the regulators who had clearly overlooked the signs of money laundering were not reprimanded. In fact, this organization, the Office of the Comptroller of the Currency in the Treasury Department, received $50 million of Wachovia's fine and formally thanked Martin for his work. Moreover, Wachovia / Wells Fargo was doing fine; its stock price was barely affected.[6]

Martin described feeling disappointed and frustrated, an experience shared by many others who have tried to speak out about wrongdoing. The larger battle appeared to have been lost; the bank had prevailed and he, the whistleblower, had failed. One of the things that seemed to help him cope in the years that followed was his apparent ability to rework this label that he had taken on.

An example of this redefinition relates to Martin's securing of a new position at Coutts private bank. His offer was retracted after he was identified as the (now public) Wachovia whistleblower, despite his stellar references and an endorsement from a headhunter.[7] By this stage, his experience at Wachovia had taught him that, although one does not take down a large banking institution very easily, it is possible to chip away at its reputation and highlight, in small ways, wrongful acts. He thus decided to take Coutts to court for breaking its promise to hire him, a promise enshrined in the contract that he had signed in July 2009. On moral grounds, he felt that his was a strong suit; it was worth a try. He said, "The case against the bank is a pretty tight one and therefore their only option is to win on a technical knock-out, which is to say 'You can't bring the case,' Fine."[8] His argument had weaknesses: a recruitment agent had been involved in the hire, and he had exceeded the time limit allowed for filing. He acknowledged that there was a danger in losing but accepted this, feeling that the risk was worth it.

> But if I'm going to get in that witness box to argue my case, that's when I'll do . . . the maximum amount of damage. . . . I only need ten minutes, but if you give me an hour, blimey, I can do a lot of damage in an hour.[9]

So for Martin, this was not about winning the case as much as it was about making his voice heard about the injustices within this law:

If I don't win this case, *I'm not going to lose*. I might not win, but that doesn't mean I'll lose, if you see the logic in that. While senior managers have determined [that my employment with Coutts] is not in the interest of the shareholders, which is the public and the customers that I work for, that's based on one single fact; I'm too honest to work for you. You can see the *Sun*'s headline, can't you? "This man's too honest to work for our bank!"[10]

For Martin, even if he did not win, he would bring public attention to what he saw as discrimination against a whistleblower in recruitment processes, to the weakness in the law that leaves one vulnerable, and to the overall unfairness of the situation:

Forget legal semantics. They might have a point on the legal case, but on common sense— . . . Basically, once again, what we will be watching in the court is the confidence tricksters that are the bankers. . . . The room will be full of journalists, . . . and they are not going to have to write an interpretation. You don't have to put your slant on it, or spin, you just go with what I say.[11]

Even losing a lawsuit can be a minor "win"—in that the bank's reputation is damaged as a result.

Martin's first small victory therefore is the public exposure for his case that he hopes to gain and the damage that it stands to do to the bank that refused to hire a whistleblower. A second small victory arises from an inherent irony in the situation:

I am insured for all legal costs, for employment matters. Guess who my insurer is? Direct Line. So who owns Coutts? RBS [Royal Bank of Scotland]! And who owns Direct Line? So they are paying for me to sue them! So I'm on a win-win, and plus I was mentioned in Parliament last week.[12]

Martin describes himself in a different way: as one who is savvy about the media interest in simple stories of ordinary people battling the bank. He has become self-aware about his position as a whistleblower and its extreme limitations but also about the strategic advantages that it offers. The newsworthiness of his story gives him the ability to chip away at Coutts's armor and achieve a small victory in doing so. This is resonant of Rudolf Elmer's attitude toward his court case after he spoke out about tax evasion in Switzerland. He requested a public trial, even though he knew he would probably lose, because it meant that the names of 95 percent of tax evaders who had remained secret would become known. Foreign tax authorities would then be able to pursue the issue and request further details from Zurich's prosecution office: "The can of worms will be opened even more."[13] Despite being unlikely to prevail in court, it was enough for Rudolf that he could intervene in the public debate and be able to make small changes in this way:

> Since it has become a public issue and society thinks and talks about it, that is what I wanted to achieve. I have a positive nature and think the truth will surface; that is my contribution to a better world.[14]

He had refused the offer of a settlement from the bank, preferring to go to trial:

> Taking the money would have meant again being part of the "pack of wolves." At that point in time I personally was already in a position where I felt, I want to go through that. [I said,] "I'm not afraid of any court trial; on the contrary, it will make visible to society what is happening. I can use the courtroom to show what is really going on."[15]

Both Rudolf and Martin began with the aim of taking on their banks and publicly exposing the corruption they had witnessed. Their understanding of what it is to be a whistleblower had been shaped by this early goal. Months of difficult struggle, however, seemed to have caused a shift in their positions and their self-perceptions. To defeat a large international bank is a mammoth undertaking, perhaps even an impossible task. Rather than give up, each began to think differently about their position.

Over time, it emerged that smaller and less-obvious wins were possible and that these were important to pursue and to recognize as achievements. Rudolf and Martin were no longer aiming for the grand victory. Understanding themselves in this new way, they each seem to be problematizing, or "troubling" the meaning of what a whistleblower ought to be.[16] Both embody a new version of this subject position: one who battles for, and celebrates, smaller-scale victories in the wider struggle against corruption at his organization. These smaller victories tended to involve opportunities to be heard, to intervene in debates around corruption, and in these ways, to make a difference.

Whistleblower as a Joke

People's performances had the effect of reworking the label of whistleblower as absurd. Realizing that others see oneself, the whistleblower, as different, at times as mentally unstable, and then being able to laugh at this image was a common source of strength among those I interviewed. This is surprising, given the seriousness of the situations in which they often found themselves.

Many described becoming aware that they were seen by others as somewhat crazy. Martin Woods often referred to himself in the third person, as "mad Martin Woods," suggesting that he knew quite well how others perceive him. For him, *mad* meant something else too:

> I call *myself* mad! But they are three initials; they [stand for] "making a difference." I'm happy with that, but you got to understand what it means: it means "I make a difference; what do you do?" That's what I say, "All whistleblowers are mad; they make a difference."[17]

Martin understands that most people would not do what he has done and speak out. He knows that he might appear to others to be unhinged. Rather than giving in to the hurt that this insulting label of mad might bring, he has taken ownership of it, turning it into something of which he is proud. Most importantly, he is making fun of the situation.

Some were quite philosophical about their mad status. Paul Moore of HBOS noted the historical function of fools and clowns in society, back to medieval times.[18] Their job was to speak the truth in a fearless manner, and they were laughed at for doing so:

> Why was it [that] there was a court jester? Because the only way to speak truth to the king was to dress up like a lunatic. Well, *of course* I was presented as if I was a lunatic after I did speak truth to power. And I probably was, really, but there we go.[19]

He had come to accept that he was seen as unusual, reflecting that he had always been something of an outsider:

I never really fitted in! [*laughs*] Because I was speaking truth to power all the time. I was a lot more interested in the truth than the money or anything. I always felt uncomfortable in my own skin, because I kept doing my job [as head of Group Regulatory Risk] really well, and people didn't really like me. I felt very, very uncomfortable about it.[20]

Paul's sense of discomfort relates to his commitment to the subject position of professional, which was dear to him and to which he attempted to adhere even in the face of severe opposition. This commitment made him feel uneasy while working for HBOS when so many others were trying to overturn his work in Regulatory Risk. Having spent a lot of time reflecting on this, he reported that he now felt secure in his difference from some colleagues:

I'm *ab-normal;* that is, I don't seem to follow the standard norms that everybody else does. For a long time I felt very uncomfortable about this. But now I am very comfortable about it: I am glad I'm not normal![21]

For others, making fun of their status as whistleblower emerged as important again and again. After Olivia Greene had spoken publicly about the problems in mortgage lending at Irish Nationwide, she was regularly bullied by senior staff, supporters of her boss whom she had criticized. In one instance, an older colleague phoned her in the office and began to call her names and detail her failings, trying to upset her. Olivia wondered how this man, whom she knew to be quite unsophisticated in his use of vocabulary, had found such impressive words with which to abuse her. Suddenly she realized that she could hear, faintly, a second voice in the background. He was being coached. "Is somebody there and telling you what to say?" she asked her bully. He was so embarrassed that he slammed down the phone. Laughing as she recalled this incident, Olivia noted that it was moments like this that kept her going.

Martin Woods described being very amused that his insurer for all legal costs in his long and difficult case against Coutts, which had overturned his employment contract, turned out to be a subsidiary of that very firm. "They are paying me for me to sue them!" he laughed. Eileen Foster, from Countrywide, recalled how she would get together with other whistleblowers from her firm who had similarly been victimized and then fired for speaking up. After meeting a couple of times, some dark humor emerged in how they spoke to each other:

> It's funny because we all do the same thing now. We will be sitting there talking, and we will say something that is a fact, but we will follow with, "But I can show you the documentation . . . and I can send you a copy of an email!"[22]

Years of being disbelieved, and the resulting diligence with information that they have each come to develop, is now a source of laughter. These dark in-jokes bring the group closer together and come directly from the difficult experiences they have shared.

Rudolf Elmer's eight years of struggle during his battle with Swiss bank Julius Bär saw him spend over two hundred days in jail, his family threatened, and him slandered in the media. We might expect to meet a broken, bitter man. However, when I spoke with him he seemed to have developed a wry sense of humor, along with a fearless *What else can they do?* kind of attitude:

> My lawyer says [she] doesn't know what I'm afraid of. They come . . . [these] threats against me. They don't work anymore because I have too many friends; I can't take them seriously. . . . And if someone sends me an email—"I'm going to kill you," whatever, "going to kill your child and . . ." Who cares! I can't take that seriously, even [though] it's very disturbing to certain extent, particularly when you learn that police are not even interested in it, because the police is a part of the "pack of wolves." But I can smile about it. These are things which I just can smile about; it's so ridiculous. If an average person looks at it and they read what *they* [the bank] wrote and the conclusion *they* drew, [it] just sounds very ridiculous. Or better, they get suspicious und understand the systemic corruption that protects the interest of the bank as well as the state.[23]

Although his case is still being investigated and the bank continues to call him a liar, he now finds this funny because it has become absurd; the bank has lost all credibility. Whistleblowers engage in a kind of self-parody, able to see themselves as they believe others do and ultimately mocking the whole spectacle.

Making fun of the label whistleblower, even as one occupies it, lessens its power to hurt. Thus far, we have seen that the category can cause people extreme injury because of the exclusions associated with it: injuries that can at times be self-inflicted. This hurt gives rise to a powerful temptation to quit one's whistleblowing struggle. What is it about humor that lessens the intensity of the pain that comes with the whistleblower label? In Judith Butler's well-known book *Gender Trouble,* she describes how parody essentially problematizes the "given-ness" of a dominant norm and its effects; it troubles and destabilizes them. To illustrate she shows how humorous and parodic drag performances can diffuse the power of prescriptive discourses around gender and sexuality, particularly around how these should be embodied. There is something about the momentary confusion to which parody gives rise that enables this. One expects to see one kind of identity performance (a woman) and then is confronted with another (a man), and this suddenly throws our acceptance of each category into question. By juxtaposing them, it highlights their contingency, shows that they are neither natural nor essential. It diffuses the power of the label. "If you examine what knowledges we are drawing upon when we make this observation, regarding anatomy of the person, or the way the clothes are worn," then it becomes apparent that this is all knowledge that has been naturalized through a process of normalization.[24] Moments of parodic laughter show that things we had previously taken for granted are in fact fantasies. This then prompts a questioning of our own frameworks, forcing the viewer to query, "What are the categories through which one sees?"[25] If rethinking the label is the outcome, then the humor is the engine of the process; it is the "pleasure, the giddiness of the performance" that instigates our questioning of the "radical contingency" of categories such as sex and gender.[26] Other scholars have pointed out that laughing at power and making fun of the oppressive forces that attempt to control us can loosen their hold on us. Seeing the absurdity of a scene, the person who laughs at it steps outside and perceives it differently.[27]

For those described previously, we see in some detail how this operates. Both the whistleblower and the observer might expect to see one thing: a broken, depressed victim of suffering and retaliation. They are then confronted with something quite different, something ridiculous.

Rather than (or in addition to) being upset about their categorization by their organizations as mentally ill former employees, Paul and Martin laugh at this and use it in their own way. Olivia's sad tale of bullying features a comedic sketch of an incompetent senior colleague mindlessly doing the bidding of his friend and failing to even bully effectively. In the laughter that results, the category of whistleblower is thrown into question. And this helps people to persist.

Subverting the Norm: Giving Up on the Fantasy Whistleblower?

What are the wider implications of these two examples of rethinking the label whistleblower: seeing it as representing a winner of small victories and as a joke? The ways that categories such as whistleblower operate in society are important, as we have seen, because they delineate what can and cannot be thought of as a valid speaker and punish those who fall outside. They give rise to exclusions that are felt painfully and that encourage people to quit their battles. These categories are not, however, "foundational" but are contingent "effect(s) of a specific formation of power."[28] Moreover, subject positions like whistleblower are performative; they represent the culmination of repeated iterations on the part of those who take them up. In each iteration, the norm itself can shift and alter, albeit slightly.[29] To become a subject in the terms of a particular category is necessarily an unstable process because of this ongoing potential for norms to be subverted in their performance and reperformance by those adopting them.

We saw this earlier, as people made fun of the label whistleblower but also in their reworking of it as representing a winner of small victories. For Martin, whistleblower becomes an entity that can successfully intervene in the discourse through the smaller, less obvious practices of subversion that present themselves. These include "[getting] in that witness box" to "do a lot of damage." This reworking involves moving the concept of whistleblower away from some aspects that it had previously depended on, including the legal frameworks in place to ensure justice. "Forget legal semantics," declared Martin. Perceptions of whistleblowing, he declares, now depend on the observer applying "common sense." Others described similar scenes of smaller victories, including sessions in court, mentions in national parliaments, and meetings with the regulator. The whistleblower is no longer an entity whose success or failure hinges on whether he or she is successful in legally overturning the wrongdoing witnessed and bringing the culprit to justice. Rather, the whistleblower is one whose role involves picking away at the reputation of the organization: a thorn in the side of this powerful entity and an essential part of a wider struggle.

Here we see how the norm of public whistleblower is performed in different ways by people who find themselves interpellated by it, defined in its terms. Although, in the main, it is maintained and upheld as it has traditionally been—a source of oppression—in some small instances its performances run off track. Certain kinds of practices spur on this subversion, which can potentially trouble norms.[30] Such practices, including making fun of the whistleblower self and reconceptualizing it as a winner of small victories, represent a new kind of doing of this position.

For this to be possible, people need to question aspects of their self-perception as a whistleblower. Among this study's participants, forging a new position seemed to require a heightened sense of self-awareness and a clearer understanding of their part in the wider picture, albeit this was a small part. It involved relinquishing the earlier conviction that the only definition of success is to see the enemy, the organization, finally defeated and the systemic wrongdoing stopped forever. While this does not mean giving up on the dream of succeeding in the larger struggle, it compels alternative interpretations of this dream. It requires viewing minor achievements as worthwhile goals.

With respect to laughing at oneself, again we see the necessity of problematizing a previously held idea of what a whistleblower is and how she should be perceived. These individuals release their grip on the fantasy that the person who speaks will be taken seriously by all who listen. The dream of an attentive and responsive audience is reworked. Paul and Martin have become aware of how they are perceived by others. This enables them to somewhat stand apart from their fantasmatic attachments to how a whistleblower would ideally be received by others, and perceive the situation anew. In doing so, both laugh at what they have gone through. Martin Woods takes back ownership of the public whistleblower label. It has been used by others against him, but he now reclaims it: "I call *myself* mad." Paul describes it as almost inevitable: "Well, *of course* I was presented as if I was a lunatic after I did speak truth to power." Upon reaching this realization—that they are seen as impossible and nonsensical—whistleblowers then use it, parodying the entire subject position and the exclusions that accompany it. As Paul says, jokingly, "I probably was [a lunatic], really, but there we go." Both Olivia and Eileen understood that their status as whistleblower led to their exclusion by others in the organization, and this resulted in upsetting incidents including telephone bullying in Olivia's experience and being ignored in Eileen's. Instead of accepting and internalizing these exclusions (or in addition to this), they turned them around and made fun of them. Troubling the effects of these norms, through parody, opens them up to subversion. The humor emerges from the incongruity between what they had believed themselves to be as whistleblowers, serious and well-meaning truth tellers, and what they then realized they represented to others: absurd oddities. They play on the juxtaposition of these positions, and this offers a buffer against the hurt that otherwise accompanies the status of impossible speaker.

Disengaging from these imaginary notions means accepting *whistleblower* as essentially a complex and contradictory label, holding vastly different meanings for different people. It may never be accepted as serious or represent a winner of large-scale struggles against organizations; albeit that one continues to hope it will. Early dreams of public recognition as a whistleblower—that one's "I" might attain a status of total and unqualified legitimacy, both celebrated and taken seriously, must be acknowledged as fantasmatic.[31] For Butler, the ability to subvert the norms that interpellate us lies in whether we can relinquish our dependency on notions of coherence and stability; this enables us to usefully misrecognize the terms to which we are subjected.[32] This suggests that those who find themselves associated with categories such as whistleblower might potentially go beyond the continued cycle of failed and painful subjections to norms that injure—they might begin to craft a more livable life.

Is subverting the label of whistleblower really an effective way to change the situation for others? It is clear that it offers something of a breathing space for those compelled into taking on this position. It can also lead us to think about the category differently and to question how it is typically used in society. We know from critical social theorist Michel Foucault, however, that critique is not always effective in overturning that to which it responds. Sometimes apparent subversion can represent "a more devious and discreet form of power," not least because it leads us to believe that we are challenging power when we critique.[33] Studies of critical humor and parody in contemporary workplaces show that, although these practices can form a part of employee resistance to management oppression, they can also ensure that routine and order are maintained because they provide a safety valve for employees to express their discontent but in a safe and forgivable way.[34] Humor contributes to maintaining the existing power structures and it stymies resistance to them. A second point relates to potentially subversive practices like parody always involving dependency on the entity that they make fun of, and this can be dangerous.[35] Acts of parody take place from *within* a particular normative framework, even as they mock and subvert those very norms. That parody will trouble such norms is not a given; rather, only "certain kinds of parodic repetitions [are] effectively disruptive, truly troubling." Other jokish attempts to mock an original will simply become "domesticated and recirculated as instruments of cultural hegemony."[36] The acts described here draw on existing discourses, including those of global finance and social norms around whistleblowing. It might be that the joking and laughter simply lead people to feel they have "escaped" the more painful aspects of these, when in fact they have become "an instrument" of "the power one opposes."[37] Rethinking the label of whistleblower is not straightforward.

Conclusion

What would happen if, through the repeated performance of the label public whistleblower, it evolved into something different? The accounts described here feature stories of subtle acts of low-level subversion. New ways of doing this norm emerged again and again. The whistleblower category became something involving smaller victories rather than large-scale failures to right a major wrongdoing. It also became a joke. These performances offered people a breathing space amid difficult struggles.

Beyond this, failures of interpellation and moments of subversion suggest that we might usefully rethink how we see and do the label of whistleblower. It must, therefore, continue to be problematized—seen as a living, emergent category that, although powerful and oppressive, holds the potential to be re-cited in new ways. It is always contested and will always be thus.

Conclusion

RETURNING to the fairy tale that opened the book, the whistleblower whose journey is replete with obstacles to speaking up is no mythical figure. The stories presented here show how easily a person can move from doing her job correctly and raising an issue to finding herself black-listed and broke. Worse still, the tale of the isolated, struggling whistle-blower is generally accepted; it provokes neither surprise nor incredulity in those who hear it. Certainly, we admire whistleblowers and what they do, and we feel bad that they are made to suffer. But as a society we are complacent about their likely ruin. This has implications for whistle-blowers themselves and for the institutions of global finance that they attempt to critique.

Affective Recognition: A New Perspective on Whistleblowing

New perspectives help us see things differently. Rather than attempting to define who or what a whistleblower is, this book examines what happens to people when they take on this label, whether by choice or otherwise. After all, whistleblowers do not typically decide to be whistleblowers when they first raise the alarm; instead they are often placed in this position post hoc, by a lawyer, as happened Paul Moore, or a journalist, as with Olivia Greene and Eugene McErlean.

This book followed the general trajectory of whistleblowing disclosures from initial awareness of the wrongdoing to the experience of going public. Affective recognition helpfully sheds light on many aspects of this journey, including what helps people speak out, why others do not and how those who do survive. This lens offers insights into why whistleblowers are so violently excluded, both within and outside the organization, and why the retaliations they experience can be so brutal. Affective recognition helps us understand how whistleblowers themselves can, unwittingly and unfairly, play a part in this. Whether through turning a felt abjection inward in a chaos of self-doubt and confusion or complying with audience demands to put themselves in the public eye to gain credibility, their struggles can paradoxically strengthen the position of those against whom they struggle. Reprisals are not simply done to them but are caught up in people's complex desires for a sense of legitimacy. These scenes see people affectively attached to a category of person, in this case whistleblower, that ultimately causes them pain. But later on it is attachments to different versions of this category that enable survival in the face of suffering, through being part of a wider collective and through performing new versions of the whistleblower position.

Being attentive to the affective desires inherent to subjection shows us how macro level forces can influence and affect the local level of the self. A diverse network of people working within the milieu of global finance, including regulators, recruitment agents, and journalists, help maintain norms that effectively censor who can and who cannot speak up in this sector. Affective recognition highlights the involvement of whistleblowers in this censorship, but it also, crucially, illuminates our own role: our felt investments in the discourses of finance, our ambivalence toward those who represent a truth that we have long learned to repress, and our overall complicity in the mistreatment of those who speak out about wrongdoing. We have deep-seated connections to the banks that house our finances because of our need to trust them. Whistleblowers fundamentally challenge this long-held attachment because they highlight its folly. They show us how our trust might in fact be misplaced. Perhaps this means that our own affective desires to consider ourselves customers of safe institutions contribute to our implicit acceptance of violence against the whistleblower that threatens these fantasies. The whistleblower reminds those with even a vague connection to the financial system of its hidden flaws, its somewhat detestable side. Thus, we react to whistleblowers in the volatile, anxious, and affective ways described earlier, because they prompt an urgent need to separate ourselves from these entities that represent a contamination of the self. The abject whistleblower is a threat, and it must be forcefully expelled.

Finally, this new perspective highlights how the norms that so strongly influence people invested in global finance are neither final nor predetermined but may be open for re-performance and sometimes subversion. Just as Paul Moore draws on discourses of professionalism within financial services to defend his whistleblowing practices to himself and to others, so also might his performance change what it means to be a professional in this world. It might subvert taken-for-granted norms about what a banker is, re-citing this category as someone who cares enough about his or her organization, colleagues, and customers to speak out about wrongdoing. The stories of Rudolf Elmer and Jonathan Sugarman exemplify the contingency of other powerful norms within financial services related to speaking out. Each is embedded in a particular geopolitical context that inescapably shifts over time, and in the short term the strategic whistleblower might opt for another country context in which to make his or her disclosures. Overall, therefore, an attentiveness to recognition, or its absence, is helpful in understanding how whistleblower, organization and institution are linked within but also beyond financial services. It is our affective desire for attachments that provides the fuel.

What are the implications of this? This framing suggests a new theory of whistleblowing and a new ontology of the subject engaged in it. Whistleblowing is commonly assumed to be a practice carried out by an autonomous individual acting alone. It is no such thing. Through striving for recognition, the whistleblower finds herself outside herself, caught up in the reflections granted by other people and by wider societal norms. She is not a bounded entity but rather a porous, radically social self. One person may happen to blow the whistle, but this is frequently the result of a series of dialogues both internal and external with communities of other people. Whistleblowing is not the act of an individual; it is an intrinsically collective phenomenon, even when it appears as though only one person is speaking out.

Exploring whistleblowing through an affective recognition lens highlights important aspects that are rarely described in research studies or commentaries on the topic. This suggests a range of avenues for further scholarly research, including the complexity of speaking up as people construct a sense of self in opposition to unethical others, the deep and insidious ways that institutions can shape our selves as well as our behaviors, how this affects our ability to critique them, and finally, how well-worn stereotypes of the suffering whistleblower might be rethought, rewritten, and re-created.

It also suggests some practical implications. Whistleblowers are famously left to suffer the consequences of speaking out, with few supports. This of course deters others from following them, which reinforces cultures of complicity and silence that characterize today's organizations. Viewing whistleblowing as an inherently social act in which we are all involved compels us as members of society to accept responsibility for what happens to these people. Whistleblowers provide us with a valuable service and yet our complicity plays a part in the reprisals they can suffer. An affective recognition lens also helps us rethink existing perceptions that see whistleblowers as separate from ourselves: unusual and heroic others who can be assumed to have extraordinary levels of resilience in the face of suffering, an assumption that is clearly flawed. Under current conditions, whistleblowers are effectively abandoned. In some countries, legislation grants compensation to people who can prove in court that they were dismissed or mistreated because they spoke out. Success in such cases is not common, and the process is expensive. Even when claimants prevail, it is often the case that the original wrongdoing is not addressed. Rare compensation awards are typically based on a multiple of the whistleblower's annual salary: three years for some, five for others. This comes nowhere near alleviating the financial impact of being blacklisted in the industry in which one has trained and worked for years. Various groups have called for support funds for whistleblowers to be set up, administered by independent bodies and funded by fines collected from organizations that have been prosecuted for misconduct. Other potential sources of support include extending the current bounty system in the United States, in which whistleblowers who fulfill certain criteria can directly receive a percentage of the monies recouped by the state as a result of their disclosures.[1] Currently, assistance for whistleblowers tends to be pitiful.

Without meaningful support, those engaged in struggles cannot continue, and for others the idea of speaking out will remain abhorrent. For this reason, to enable whistleblowers to feel safe in coming forward, a collective conception of whistleblowing is needed, one that compels an acknowledgment of responsibility on the part of regular people and those in power that represent them. Finally, without an understanding of the intrinsically social nature of the self, it is difficult to appreciate just how deeply we are influenced by the institutions we work for, upon many of which our well-being depends.

Recognition, Whistleblowing, and Global Finance

Global finance is a system in which power is concentrated among a privileged few and that holds unprecedented levels of influence over the world's economy and nation-states. It lurches from crisis to crisis in ever-shortening cycles and has done so for a long time.[2] For some, this is a weakness of the system, whereas others argue that it reflects the inherent logic of capitalism: itself an arrangement in which growth depends on violent iterations of crisis and recovery.[3]

Successive crises are allowed to continue not least because the financial services sector is in a position of disproportionate power over many nation-states, able to demand billions of taxpayer dollars through government rescue packages. Rescues are typically followed by a flurry of political and media outrage about the lack of oversight in the sector. Each time, in response to the furor, politicians loudly promise change: inquiries are demanded and new legislation is drafted and passed, often alongside calls to enable and support whistleblowers who will prevent the crisis from recurring. In the years that follow, again and again, we see the banking sector gradually regroup as strong lobby organizations complain that the rules are too onerous, that they stymie business and therefore pose a dangerous threat to the nation's economic well-being.

Banks promise to regulate themselves better, and so the cycle continues. We have witnessed this dance repeatedly over the last hundred years.[4]

If crisis is a natural fact of global finance, one that we take for granted, then so also are other aspects, including the advantages of economic liberalization, the neutrality of austerity economics that hides its impacts on ordinary people, and the sector's inherently masculinized, ethnocentric ways of representing and behaving. Because they highlight the extreme and damaging ways these features manifest themselves in organizational practices, perhaps the vicious treatment of whistleblowers is a similarly natural, accepted part of the system. Effectively produced by the dysfunctions and contradictions within global finance, whistleblowers are the embodied and living result of these. Perhaps the ritual destruction of the group of people who are ostensibly paid to speak up is another way that the system persists.

Accepting the modus operandi of global finance as inevitable, and our compliance in reproducing and reinforcing it, contributes to a long-standing wall of silence around wrongdoing and corruption in this sector. This book highlights an integral part of this wall: the aspects of global finance that come together to create a matrix of censorship influencing who can, and cannot, speak out. These dynamics circumscribe what kinds of speech are legitimate, and ensure transgressions are punished. Rather than the work of a single author or source, a vast and dispersed network of forces contribute to this: the global finance organizations and their ostensible regulators but also somewhat surprising elements such as the journalists who report on the sector and recruitment agents within it, in addition to whistleblowers themselves and those they work and live with. This involvement can happen in a number of ways; some participants in this study sought refuge in a treasured identification with the profession of banking, and this is what helped them to speak out. Ironically, it was the authority they were critiquing—financial services—that gave them the strength to do so. This subtle institutional power also influences ordinary citizens, including ourselves, as we work to ensure the survival of an institution we feel we must trust. Perhaps whistleblowers receive such strong reactions from colleagues, friends, and recruiters precisely because they pose a threat to our perceptions of global finance and indeed its very existence. Their presence and their experiences point out some uncomfortable aspects of it that we would rather ignore, including the power-ridden and patri-archal foundations of its institutions and the legacy of gross inequality in the distribution of its wealth that we are left with today. Thus, whistle-blowers threaten to destabilize "our" system. How they are treated high-lights how deeply the system is embedded in our selves.

As the memory of the last global financial crisis fades, we continue to pay for it, and the next one is on the horizon. As usual, increased reg-ulation is proposed and ostensibly implemented. New ways of institu-tionalizing whistleblowing are championed, including an emphasis on speak-up channels that enable people to disclose wrongdoing safely. But if these innovations are applied to a fundamentally dysfunctional system, surely their value in challenging its deep-seated contradictions, and the powerful support that upholds these contradictions, is questionable. These may be mere panaceas as we move toward our next global crisis and get ready to shell out for it too.

What can we do with our angry awareness that, if left unchecked, our children and our children's children, and so on, will be left to pay for future mistakes? Change must come, and as we wait for it, perhaps we can at least challenge the opacity of a system founded on deeply held inequalities. We can begin to highlight who it is that gains from this system and who is left out, so that we might rethink the role of finance in our society. In the meantime, if we feel any affective affiliation and responsibility toward those people who sacrifice so much when they speak out and suffer for it, and if we acknowledge our own complicity in putting them through this, we must recognize whistleblowers as a vul-nerable group of people that needs protecting now.

Appendix: Project Method

THIS STUDY examines the experiences of people who blew the whistle on what they saw as systemic corruption in financial services, who were labeled whistleblower, and who encountered retaliation. I embarked on qualitative, in-depth research into thirteen incidents of speaking out in global finance institutions in the United Kingdom, Ireland, Switzerland, and the United States. Finding these people was not easy, particularly at the outset, and involved searching newspapers and online sources including social media. Something of a snowball process emerged, however; as I got to know and trust particular whistleblowers, they put me in touch with others.[1] Various people working in whistleblower support and advocacy groups such as the U.S. Government Accountability Project and Transparency International Ireland also helped, guiding me toward whistleblowers whose stories had been verified by reliable sources.

Table A.1 contains a summary of the data. I gathered as much documentary information as possible in advance of approaching each person and requesting an interview. This came from online sources, books, newspapers, transcripts of parliamentary debates, public inquiries, and publicly available submissions to these events, along with interviews with industry experts. I used this as backdrop material for each participant. At interview, individuals were invited to reflect on their experiences of whistleblowing, using open-ended questioning.[2] I was aware of the sensitivity of the topics being discussed, and so I spoke with most people a number of times before we met. Interviews were carried out in different places: private areas in restaurants and hotels, the offices of support groups, and over Internet video. In accordance with my university's ethical procedures, I had prepared information on sources of help in the event that an interviewee became upset, although this happened only once, via telephone, when a potential interviewee told me that he was involved in an ongoing court case that he was finding to be very stressful, and he preferred not to take part in the study. In the majority of cases, people had already reflected extensively on their experiences and had formed their own narratives. I found that they were also quite reflexively disposed, open to exploring what had happened to them and questioning it. Other researchers have noted this to be the case when people have spent time in the position of the excluded other; it compels a period of intense self-reflection to make sense of one's new status.[3] For at least two people, repeat interviews were carried out.

Given the concerns of the study, I was interested in people's espoused sense of self and how wider structural and cultural forces influenced this. Interviews typically began with questions about their backgrounds and work in the organization prior to speaking out, moving to the whistleblowing incident itself and its aftermath. I tried when possible to encourage people to reflect on their understanding of their self and how it might have changed over time.[4] Interviews were carried out between April 2011 and May 2014 and each lasted between forty-five minutes and two hours. All were recorded, transcribed verbatim, and checked for accuracy.[5] In some cases interviews were not possible but sufficient secondary interview material was available for analysis.

Some people dropped out of the process after the initial contact, for a variety of reasons including on the advice of lawyers.[6] Another individual was happy to discuss whistleblowing in general but had entered into a confidentiality agreement as part of a settlement with her organization and so could not discuss details. These people are not featured in the study. For my own part, I was quite embedded in the world of whistleblowing while I was carrying out the research, insofar as a mere academic observer can claim to be. For example, I attended many industry events, advised whistleblower advocacy groups in Ireland and the United Kingdom when asked, and assisted journalists who were writing about whistleblowing.[7]

Making Sense of the Data

Data analysis was broadly interpretive and drew on other scholars who study subjectivity in organizations using theories of affect and power. I adopted a broadly thematic analysis that began with immersion in the research data.[8] This involved developing a lengthy document in which empirical topics were organized on the basis of the data categories, without much additional theory to explain them. A draft of this book was printed, bound, and sent to all interview participants in the study for their comments and feedback. I also consulted with industry experts and senior academics in the organization studies, whistleblowing, and sociology fields. People were generous with their time, and many provided thoughtful responses.

Reflecting on these responses and incorporating the feedback and comments into the text, I spent the next year moving between literature that was by now proving helpful in the analysis, including other studies of whistleblowing and those drawing on affective recognition, and the empirical data.[9] This iterative process yielded theoretical insights that are developed in the chapters here. The extended time taken for analysis was valuable because it gave me the opportunity to digest and reflect and to discuss ideas and perspectives with experienced whistleblowing researchers.

When it came to the stage of analyzing the data, I wanted to move away from the normal practices in qualitative social research that involve interrogating interview transcripts and documents to develop categories and data codes, as is done, for example, with strict grounded theory methods.[10] Instead, I was inspired by recent developments in qualitative data analysis that begin from the principles of grounded theory but allow for the incorporation of diverse theoretical frameworks.[11] I drew on other organization scholars who have likewise conducted empirical research informed by an affective recognition approach.[12] These authors use a "politically-engaged theory of performativity" to analyze social settings such as organizations, thus foregrounding both "micro-level" processes of subjectification and the wider systems of power and influence to which these processes relate.[13] Through such work, scholars have described the organizational "signifying economies" that operate to categorize employees, effectively fixing differences between people.[14] This can cause them to occupy normative subject positions that may be painful but that they require because, as organization studies scholar Kathleen Riach and her colleagues describe, "subjective viability and organizational recognition depends on the capacity to maintain a performatively credible conformity to (certain) processes, rules and procedures," not least in our workplaces.[15] When analyzing the materials gathered and the responses from participants, and with my attention on subjection, I focused on how people referred to themselves as "I," how this personal pronoun appeared in talk and text, and how it related to important discursive elements in the particular setting. In other words, I was sensitive to how the I was used as a placeholder that enabled the individual to secure a subject position, even temporarily.[16] For other scholars, this kind of positioning of the self can point to matrices of control that pertain to particular settings, compelling expressions of subjecthood. As organization theorist Nancy Harding notes, "discourses / objects become absorbed into the idiom of the self" in this way.[17]

To make sense of the vast and complex data set, it was necessary to develop codes representing themes that were emerging even as this diminished the inherent richness of what I was finding; such is a limitation of social research although here the process was left open and iterable where possible. Primary themes were specified, and examples of the data were selected to further theorize and clarify these and to enable subthemes to emerge. Each theme forms a chapter in this text.

This process was by no means as neat and orderly as described here; the narratives and my subsequent analysis of them were messy—full of contradiction and paradox. For example, people would often discuss former colleagues who had not blown the whistle with empathy and an understanding of their need to remain silent alongside repulsion and anger that they did not have enough courage to do so. Although the temptation to pretend some kind of coherence is strong within academic research, in the resulting analysis I instead focus on such contradictions and paradoxes, leaving these as they are and exploring what we might learn as a result.[18]

Limitations

This study does not aim to represent an objective view of the experiences of the people that appear here. Just as social life is multifaceted, complex, and subjectively experienced so also are aspects of the research process: the interviews, the reading, the writing, and the theorizing. What is written is colored by my own history and experiences.[19] In the Introduction to this book, I try to reflect upon the choices I made in carrying out this study. Since 2012 I have been writing about whistleblowing, and so my ideas have regularly been reviewed, discussed, and often criticized by academic colleagues and anonymous peer reviewers. These inputs have no doubt informed the findings, as have my own biases, albeit many remain unconscious. I recall that I chose to study the banking sector because of my dismay at being financially liable for its mistakes, as an Irish citizen, during the introduction of post crisis austerity. Other personal factors that influenced the process likely include an earlier attraction to philosopher Michel Foucault's work, not least because of my engagement with critical management studies as a PhD student. This scholarly offshoot of business and management focuses explicitly on the exercise of power and domination within this discipline, both in teaching and in practice.[20] Given critical management studies' explicit concerns with power, Foucault is naturally a popular theorist among scholars. I believe I was initially drawn to this approach because of the comfort it gave me during a difficult time in my professional life prior to joining academia, when I was made redundant from an organization I loved. Foucault helped me understand how micro level experiences such as redundancy, that we often believe to be our own fault, are affected by wider discourses of power. Macro level forces at my old firm included venture capital investors whose injection of funding was contingent on moving our headquarters from Dublin to London. Employees that had helped to found the company some five years earlier were offered a choice between a redundancy package and a transfer to a low-level position in Kensington. Even acknowledging these facts, I felt somehow to blame for my new and stigmatized position of an unemployed person. On Foucault's view I was not necessarily at fault. The acute sense of anxiety I felt did not reflect some inner pathology; instead it was produced by context and by the discursive norms that circulate therein. Building on a part-time master's degree in management studies at University College Dublin, I went on to pursue doctoral and postdoctoral study at Judge Business School in Cambridge. Here, I continued working with Foucault's ideas. During this time I was fortunate to be able to read, have discussions with, and learn from leading thinkers in this area, including Professors John Roberts, Geoff Walsham, and Hugh Wilmott, all of whom were working in the critical management tradition. Through reading around Foucault's ideas on subjectivity, I was drawn to the work of Professor Judith Butler at Berkeley because she builds on his project of examining experiences of the subject under powerful discourses. She develops the project in exciting new directions and continually applies her ideas to her real-life activism around gender and sexuality, to literature and to film. This theoretical affinity was also for personal reasons; her questioning, or "troubling," of powerful norms offered me a new way of understanding my own discomfort with dominant categories.[21] Extending my PhD work in this new direction, I was fortunate to be able to study and learn from scholars who had been valuably developing Butler's ideas to understand organizations in new ways, including Professor Nancy Harding. Since 2010, I have collaborated with Professor Marianna Fotaki on projects to do with the intersection of critical theory, gender studies and organizations, learning from her theoretical expertise and insight. Even given these reflections, I acknowledge that my attempts as a researcher to make explicit my underlying assumptions and biases are largely futile. Most are deeply embedded, unconscious, and inaccessible; however, the preceding reflections can at least, I hope, position me in relation to the ideas presented here, to give the reader a somewhat clearer picture.[22]

In such qualitative studies as this, limitations are many. The researcher can only attempt to paint a reasonably rich and engaging picture of what has been done, allowing the complexities and paradoxes to emerge and trying not to rigidly fix the subjects of inquiry, even as this is difficult to avoid.[23] One way is to involve people in the co-construction of analytic themes that result; for this reason I shared emergent findings with those I interviewed and sought their input.[24] After learning more about how people had been regularly and systematically silenced through retaliatory techniques, I wanted to use peoples' own words and quote verbatim where I could in an attempt to give some small voice to those who took part.

Even with these caveats, it would be foolish to suggest that as an observer, researcher, and writer I am somehow immune to the need for recognition from prevailing discourses. As others have argued, appreciating the subject position of academic as a radically social entity is long overdue.[25] Doing so helps challenge the fantasy of the rigid self-other distinction that typically characterizes scholarly research. It problematizes the ontological violence that comes with imagining that researcher and researched are separate and independent rather than constitutive of each other.[26] Certainly my own sense of self has been inextricably shaped by the encounters described in the chapters of this book, including a recurring guilt about the suffering that others had experienced and a desire to do something about the problems that caused this. As an ek-static academic subject, I have desires to be considered a competent or at least legible scholar, and these no doubt also influenced the analytic choices mentioned previously. Perhaps the norms of academic practice also influence a felt need to write in something of an authoritative voice because this is expected in academic texts, even as I feel the instability of taking such a position. The awkwardness of the academic subject position on offer, and the fantasy of authority that can accompany it, have become clear through the process of doing this research.[27] Even so, articulating such desires is difficult and fraught with risk.

This mutual constitution of researcher and researched was not unidirectional. As a researcher I played a part in generating data through being an interlocutor in interviews. The data therefore comprises accounts that have arisen in very specific settings. In each case the articulations and reflections that emerged might easily have been analyzed and reported differently by another researcher, in a different setting. By asking someone to take part in this study, I am implicitly addressing them as a particular kind of entity, as a whistleblower, and thus already encouraging them to adopt this subject position, which doubtless shapes their responses.[28] In interviews people use available ideas, descriptions, and categories they find helpful, drawing on the discourses that present

Table A.1 Research participants

Person	Position	Country	Original observation	Data sources (no. instances)
Paul Moore	Head of group regulatory risk at banking and insurance company.	UK	Overheated sales culture in mortgage departments risking bank's stability and customer assets	Radio interview TV interview (4) Newspaper article (12) Testimony to banking inquiry (3) Author interview
Bradley Birkenfeld	Banker and wealth manager at investment bank.	US/ Switzerland	Tax evasion schemes that assisted US residents to hide assets in offshore accounts	TV interview (3) Informal discussion with author Radio interview Newspaper article (16)
Eileen Foster	Head of fraud investigation at mortgage lender.	US	Falsification of documents and other misconduct, leading to customers being encouraged to take out bad mortgages	TV interview Public lecture Newspaper article Author interview with advocacy group Author interview
Ian Taplin	Adviser to private clients at retail and commercial bank.	UK	Unfair treatment of customers including maximizing charges and discrimination on the basis of wealth	Author interview Informal discussion with author Personal blog Testimony to banking inquiry (2)
Linda Almonte	Assistant vice president, credit card debt division at investment bank and financial services company.	US	Falsification of documents and poor quality control prior to reselling outstanding loans to debt-collection agencies	Newspaper article (4) Court transcripts Email communications
Martin Woods	Anti-money laundering officer at financial services company.	UK	Billions of dollars of Mexican drug money knowingly laundered by bank via currency exchanges	Author interview TV interview (4) Newspaper article (8)

Name	Position	Country	Description	Sources
Eugene McErlean	Group internal auditor at commercial and corporate bank.	Ireland	Overcharging on fees relating to management time spent with business clients, and share trading malpractice	Radio interview (3) Panel discussion (video) Parliamentary testimony Newspaper article (6)
Olivia Greene	Senior manager and home loans supervisor at member-owned financial institution (building society).	Ireland	Inappropriate mortgage lending practices, and false accusation of a colleague	Author interview TV interview (2) Book excerpts Newspaper article (7)
Michael Winston	Managing director and enterprise chief leadership officer at mortgage lender.	US	Providing misleading and falsified mortgage information to US government departments, mis-selling mortgages to customers, and health and safety violations relating to toxic workplace	TV documentary (2) Newspaper article (5) Author discussion with lawyer Author interview
Rudolf Elmer	Chief operating officer at offshore location, at private bank.	Switzerland/ international	Helping clients evade tax in their countries of residence	Author interview TV interview (3) Newspaper article (8) Advocacy group website
Graham Senior Milne	Internal auditor at retail and commercial bank.	UK	Auditors enabled life insurance companies to conceal billions in liabilities during a bank takeover, depriving policyholders of income due	Author interview Newspaper article (6) Testimony to banking inquiry (1) Court submission
Sherry Hunt	Vice president and chief mortgage underwriter, investment bank and financial services corporation.	US	Supplying US government with misleading information on mortgages and home insurance	Newspaper article (3) TV documentary (2)
Jonathan Sugarman	Risk manager, banking and financial services company.	Italy/Ireland	Repeated liquidity breaches that contravened legal requirements	Author interview Informal communications with author Newspaper article (5)

themselves at that particular moment.[29] When discussing whistle-blowing, it is easy for both researcher and interviewee to resort to commonly available, and romanticized, tropes.[30] These include ones associated with popular narratives depicting the heroic whistleblower struggling against the evil organization. In addition, the stress involved in whistleblowing experiences can heighten people's desire to appear rational and logical post hoc.[31] These limitations are an inescapable aspect of this kind of research; I acknowledge them and have attempted where I can to provide a more reflective, more resonant, account.

The findings presented here are not definitive and are not necessarily generalizable to the wider population of whistleblowers, in global finance or otherwise. They are the product of a research engagement that was of a time and place and that is necessarily infused with biases, agendas, and shifting subject positions, including my own. Such is the nature of this kind of approach to whistleblowing, and I hope that this trade-off is somewhat balanced by rich and detailed accounts that enable insights not available through admittedly more extensive quantitative studies.[32]

Notes

Introduction

1. Ionescu 2015.
2. Winfield 1994.
3. Arguably the most commonly used definition is that of Near and Miceli (1985, 4), who define whistleblowing as "the disclosure by organization members (former or current) of illegal, immoral or illegitimate practices under the control of their employers, to persons or organizations that may be able to effect action." In his widely cited book on the topic, Alford (2001) adds to this definition by noting that many people speak out in their organizations but are not known as whistleblowers, and therefore this label should be reserved for those who experience reprisal as a result. Related to this, some commentators argue that the term *whistleblower* should encompass those outside an organization who observe wrongdoing within it (see Culiberg and Mihelič 2016). However, I follow others (Miceli, Dreyfus, and Near 2014) who differentiate between alerts raised by outsiders (which they call *bell ringing*) and insider disclosures to focus on the latter.
4. The long-run total output loss to the world economy is estimated as at least $60 trillion (Admati and Hellwig 2013, 233)
5. A fuller account of my position in relation to this study is given in the Appendix.

6. Labaton Sucharow 2015.

7. Full details of the study's methodology, data sample, and analytic approach are given in the Appendix.

8. Their details are summarized in Table A.1 in the Appendix.

9. Victor and Cullen 1987; Miethe 1999.

10. Wigand 2011.

11. Devine and Maassarani 2011, 316.

12. Before the financial crisis of 2008, AIG was a global company with about $1 trillion in assets. It collapsed and almost failed due to having engaged in overly risky credit default swaps, but was rescued by the Federal Reserve Bank of New York. The Libor (London Interbank Offered Rate) is a widely-used interest rate. It represents the average of interest rates offered by major banks worldwide. In 2012 it emerged that people in some banks had been falsely adjusting their rates in order to make money from trades, or to give the impression that their institution was more creditworthy than was the case. A third example involves the subprime crisis, which is explained later in this book.

13. Vandekerckhove, James, and West 2013, 6.

14. See also Labaton Sucharow 2015; Public Concern at Work 2013, 4; see also Chapter 3.

15. Specifically, the work of Judith Butler and relatedly Michel Foucault.

16. Epstein 2006.

17. *Economist* 2014; Reinhart and Rogoff 2009.

18. On a conservative estimate this event cost $14 trillion in the five years after: approximately a year's gross domestic product in the United States.

19. Admati and Hellwig 2013.

20. Parliament 2013a, 82.

21. Minsky 1985.

22. Parliament 2013, 104.

23. Thrift 2001.

24. Parliament 2013, 137.

1. Speaking Out

1. Clegg and Bailey 2008.

2. Some exceptions include Public Concern at Work 2013; Kenny 2014.

3. For the United States, see Kohn 2017; for wider analysis see Worth 2013; Webster 2015; Wolfe et al. 2014.

4. Dworkin and Near 1987; Miceli et al. 1999; Lewis 2008; Miceli, Near, and Dworkin 2008, 34.

5. Grant 2002; Glazer and Glazer 1989.

6. This act was introduced by Lincoln during the Civil War as an attempt to curb the theft of railway sleepers, the sale of sick horses and faulty rifles to the army, and other such fraud.

7. Kohn 2017.
8. Labaton Sucharow 2015.
9. Vandekerckhove and Tsahuridu 2010; Vandekerckhove 2006.
10. Near and Miceli 1996.
11. Kenny 2015b.
12. Coleman 2015; FCA 2015.
13. Francis 2013; Lewis and Vandekerckhove 2015.
14. Lewis, Brown, and Moberly 2014, 24; Public Concern at Work 2014; Vandekerckhove and Lewis 2012; ACCA 2016.
15. Lewis and Vandekerckhove 2015; Roberts, Olsen, and Brown 2009.
16. Walden and Edwards 2014.
17. Olsen 2014.
18. Holtzhausen 2009; Near and Miceli 1985.
19. Contu 2014; Vandekerckhove and Tsahuridu 2010; Grant 2002.
20. Devine 2015.
21. Near and Miceli 2016.
22. See Culiberg and Mihelič 2016 for an overview.
23. Skivenes and Trygstad 2014.
24. Miceli and Near 1992.
25. King 1999; Keenan 2000; Miceli and Near 1994; Weiskopf and Willmott 2013.
26. Miceli and Near 1992; King 1999; Victor and Cullen 1988.
27. Near and Miceli 1996.
28. Leys and Vandekerckhove 2014.
29. Glazer and Glazer 1989; Kenny 2015a; Grant 2002.
30. Faunce et al. 2014; P. Roberts 2014.
31. Leys and Vandekerckhove 2014; Olsen 2014; Miceli, Near, and Dworkin 2008.
32. Miceli, Near, and Dworkin 2008, 59. Also see Contu 2014.
33. Rothwell and Baldwin 2006; Mesmer-Magnus and Viswesvaran 2005; Near and Miceli 1996; Miethe 1999.
34. Public Concern at Work 2013.
35. Grant 2002; Near and Miceli 1996.
36. Rothschild and Miethe 1999; Keenan 1995; Near and Miceli 2016.
37. Near and Miceli 1985.
38. Vandekerckhove 2010.
39. Near and Miceli 2016, 107; see also Miceli, Near, and Dworkin 2008; Vandekerckhove 2010.
40. Ethics Resource Center 2012.
41. Near and Miceli 1985.
42. Miceli, Near, and Dworkin 2008.
43. Lewis, Brown, and Moberly 2014.
44. Vandekerckhove, Brown, and Tsahuridu 2014, 315.

45. Rehg et al. 2008; Verschoor 2012.
46. Rehg et al. 2008, 222.
47. Near and Miceli 2016; Ethics Resource Center 2014, 5.
48. Casal and Zalkind 1995; Miceli et al. 1999.
49. Mesmer-Magnus and Viswesvaran 2005; Near, Dworkin, and Miceli 1993.
50. Near and Miceli 1987; Rehg et al. 2008. See also Miceli and Near 1992, 1994; Near et al. 1993; Near and Miceli 1986.
51. Miceli et al. 1999; Rehg et al. 2008; Miceli et al. 1999.
52. Rehg et al. 2008; Near and Jensen 1983; Miethe 1999; Miceli and Near 2002.
53. Mesmer-Magnus and Viswesvaran 2005; Rothschild 2013; Verschoor 2012.
54. Miethe 1999; Lennane 2012; Parmerlee, Near, and Jensen 1982; Rothschild and Miethe 1999; Dworkin and Baucus 1998; Glazer and Glazer 1999; Alford 2001.
55. Devine and Maassarani 2011, 26.
56. Martin and Rifkin 2004.
57. Kenny et al. 2018.
58. Martin and Rifkin 2004; Miethe 1999; General Medical Council 2015.
59. Ewing 1983; Armenakis 2004, 359; Near and Miceli 1985; Alford 2007.
60. Alford 2001, 32.
61. D. Oliver 2003; Alford 2007; Gunsalus 1998.
62. Jackson et al. 2010; Kenny et al. 2018; Peters et al. 2011.
63. Rothschild 2013, 872.
64. Lennane 2012.
65. Devine and Maassarani 2011.
66. See, for example, Glazer and Glazer 1989.
67. Perry 1998.
68. Contu 2014, 394.
69. Rothschild and Miethe 1999, 125; Alford 2001.
70. Thomas 2005, 147.
71. Grant 2002.
72. See also Grant 2002; D. Oliver 2003.
73. Fleddermann 1999.
74. It is interesting to note that whistleblowing policy in the United Kingdom, one of the first nations to implement such laws, has moved away from its initial concern with motives. Whereas whistleblowers previously had to prove that their disclosures were coming from a position of good faith before they could be protected under law, they now merely have to demonstrate that they were acting in the public interest, albeit that this can also be problematic.
75. Vandekerckhove 2010. See, for example, Gabriel 2008; Rothschild and Miethe 1999.
76. Perry 1998.
77. Meyer and Rowan 1977.

78. Perry 1998, 248.

79. Perry 1998, 251.

80. Alford 2001, 99, 6, 22.

81. Vadera, Aguilera, and Caza 2009; see also Grant 2002.

82. Contu 2014, 399.

83. Grant 2002, 396.

84. Grant 2002, 398.

85. Grant 2002, 398.

86. Alford 2001, 3.

87. Alford 2001, 12.

88. Alford 2001, 137.

89. This is described in his so-called third-period seminar in Berkeley, California, in 1983 (Foucault 2006) and in his lectures at the Collège de France in 1984 (Foucault 2009; see also Vandekerckhove and Langenberg 2012).

90. Foucault 2001, 19.

91. Jack 2004, 130.

92. Foucault also describes it as a "subject position" (Foucault, 2005, 318); see also Jack [2004]; Andrade 2015; Jack 2004; Weiskopf and Tobias-Miersch 2016.

93. Foucault 2001, 19; Foucault 2010.

94. Contu 2014; De Maria 2008; Mansbach 2009; Rothschild 2013; Kenny, Fotaki, and Vandekerckhove 2019.

95. Alford 2001, 138.

96. Perry 1998, 239.

97. Brown 2017.

98. Perry 1998, 238; see also Alford 2001.

99. Alford 2001, 38, see also Kenny 2018.

100. Perry 1998, 239.

101. Lewis et al. 2014; Vandekerckhove 2010.

102. Perry 1998, 239.

2. Whistleblowing, the Subject, and Power

1. Lloyd 2007; Hall 2000, 28.

2. For studies into subjectivity and power in organizational settings, see Harding 2003, 2007, 2013; J. Roberts 2005; Fotaki 2013; Borgerson and Rehn 2004; Fotaki and Harding 2013; Fotaki, Metcalfe, and Harding 2014; Kenny and Euchler 2012; Linstead and Pullen 2006; Pullen and Knights 2007; Pullen et al. 2016; Tyler and Cohen 2008; Hancock and Tyler 2007; Riach, Rumens, and Tyler 2014; Borgerson 2005; Ford and Harding 2004; Fotaki 2014; Hodgson 2005; Kenny 2009, 2010; Varman and Al-Amoudi 2016; Ford, 2010; M. Parker 2001, 2002. For labor conditions under capitalism, see

Butler and Athanasiou (2013, 148), who highlight "the arbitrary and violent rhythms of being instrumentalised as disposable labor: never knowing the future, being subjected to arbitrary hirings and firings, having one's labor intensively utilized and exploited . . ." and draw on the ideas described here earlier to theorize the "radical helplessness" that results.

3. Exceptions include Kenny 2018; Fotaki et al. 2015.

4. Butler's interest in normative categories is inspired by Foucault, who famously declared that continuous problematization of what is taken for granted in society is one of the most important tasks for scholars today (Foucault 1991).

5. Butler 1990, 4.

6. Butler 1990, 6.

7. Butler 1990, xxviii.

8. Butler 1990, 24.

9. Weedon 1997, 105.

10. Harding 2003, 7.

11. Foucault 1990, 94–95.

12. Harding 2003, 209. Subjects are both formed by and formative of, discourses of power.

13. Foucault 1990.

14. Foucault 1990.

15. Butler 1997b, 18.

16. Butler 1997b, 18.

17. Foucault 1991.

18. In this, she follows Lacan. See Butler 2009, 3.

19. Butler 2004.

20. Butler 2004, 32.

21. Butler 2004, 31.

22. Borgerson 2005; Butler 1990.

23. This idea draws on Jacques Lacan's concept of the psyche as being fundamentally linguistic; as subjects we cannot escape the necessity to be recognized within the terms of the symbolic order. Butler develops this point in *The Psychic Life of Power* (1997b).

24. Butler 1997b, 19. Reading Foucault's ideas on discursive power via Lacan, Butler is inspired by the latter's refusal of the persistent "ontological dualism" whereby the "inner" psyche and "outer" world are seen as separate.

25. In this, she follows Lacan (see, e.g., Lacan 2006a).

26. Butler 2004, 1.

27. Butler 1997b, 3.

28. Butler 2004, 148; see also Butler 1997b.

29. Butler 2004, 32.

30. Butler (1997b, 169).

31. Butler 2004.
32. Butler 2004, 148.
33. Ford and Harding 2004; Kenny 2010.
34. Butler 1997b, 104.
35. Harding 2007, 1769; see also Hook 2007; Stavrakakis 2002, 2010; I. Parker 2005.
36. Butler 1997b, 7.
37. Thanem and Wallenberg 2014; Linstead and Pullen 2006.
38. Tyler 2012, 66.
39. Riach et al. 2014; Kenny 2010; J. Roberts 2005; Harding 2003.
40. Douglas 1966, 50.
41. Douglas 1966, 112.
42. Douglas 1966, 2.
43. Kristeva 1982.
44. Kristeva 1982, 5.
45. Kristeva 1982, 7. See also Rizq 2013.
46. Butler 1990, 168.
47. Butler 1997b, 132, in which she draws on Freud's notion of melancholia.
48. Butler 1997b, 137.
49. Butler 1997b, 139.
50. Butler 2009, 142.
51. Butler 2004, 25.
52. Butler 1993, 3.
53. Harding 2003, 7.
54. Butler 1990.
55. Butler 1993, 3.
56. Butler 1993, ix.
57. Butler 1990, 170.
58. Butler 1990, 170.
59. Butler 1997a, 50.
60. Butler 1997a, 143.
61. Butler and Athanasiou 2013; Kenny and Fotaki 2015.
62. Butler 1997a.
63. Butler 1997a, 133.
64. Butler 1997a, 141.
65. Harding et al. 2011.
66. Butler 2004, 30.
67. Butler 2004, 25.
68. Varman and Al-Amoudi 2016, 651.
69. Butler 2004, 27.
70. Butler 1990, 175.
71. Butler 1990, 179.
72. Borgerson 2005, 71.

73. Butler 1997b, 30.

74. Butler 1990, 176.

75. Butler 1990, xxiii; 2004, 29.

76. Butler 1990, 176.

77. Blumenfeld and Breen 2001; Borgerson 2005; Rhodes and Pullen 2007; Hodgson 2005; M. Parker 2001, 2002; Kenny 2009.

78. Tyler and Cohen 2008.

79. Political theories of recognition, including those of Nancy Fraser, Axel Honneth, and Charles Taylor, have been influential. These theories also discuss the role played by recognition in identity formation; however, they tend to focus on the normative grounding that this can provide to theories of justice.

80. See critiques of Charles Taylor's and Axel Honneth's work in, for example, McQueen 2015; McNay 2008.

81. See, for example, Levinas 1969; Merleau-Ponty 2002.

82. Butler 2004, 19.

83. Butler and Athanasiou 2013.

84. In addition to Foucault's and Butler's theories described here, see also Haraway 1991; Lloyd 2005; McNay 2008.

85. McNay 1999.

86. Butler 1997b, 3.

87. Butler 2004, 235.

88. Butler 2004, 20.

89. Butler 1997b, 8.

90. Jameson 1984; Lutz 1988.

91. Braunmühl 2012.

92. Glynos and Stavrakakis 2008; Lacan 1958. As Zizek reminds us, "emotions lie" (2006, 229).

93. Butler 1990.

94. Butler 2004.

95. See, for example, Lacan 1988, 1992; Johnston 2010 for a discussion.

96. For example, Butler (1997b, 22) describes how a sense of conscience can be felt (albeit one that emerges as a fantasmatic effect of power) and the drive and desires that for attachments that accompany this.

97. Braunmühl 2012, 232.

98. Laplanche 1999, 167.

99. Butler 2004, 20.

100. Braunmühl 2012, 226.

101. Braunmühl 2012, 227.

102. Kenny and Fotaki 2015.

103. Butler and Athanasiou 2013, ix.

104. Butler and Athanasiou 2013, ix.

105. Butler and Athanasiou 2013.

106. Butler 2009; Kenny and Fotaki 2015.

107. Fotaki 2017.

108. Fotaki 2014; Fotaki and Prasad 2015.

109. Butler 2004, 22.

110. Butler 2004, 235; see also Kenny 2012.

111. Frosh 2010.

112. Butler 2005.

113. A full and detailed account of the methodology adopted is set out in the Appendix.

114. Riach, Rumens, and Tyler 2016, 4.

3. Global Finance

1. Hudson 2011a. For more on Countrywide's organizational culture and practices near this time, see Heffernan 2012.

2. Hudson 2011a.

3. Hudson 2011a.

4. Wite-Out is a white correction fluid similar to Tipp-Ex.

5. "Prosecuting Wall Street" 2011.

6. When, as part of her investigations into fraud, Eileen Foster created a list of problematic loans in these investor packages it created a stir within Countrywide, and her project was dropped.

7. Hudson 2011a.

8. Hudson 2011a, Testimony to Labor Department.

9. OSHA 2011.

10. Hudson 2011b.

11. Chittum 2011.

12. Admati and Hellwig 2013; Salter 2012; O'Brien 2003, 13; O'Brien 2009, 250.

13. Public Concern at Work 2013.

14. Lowenstein 2004; see also Parliament 2013a; Nyberg 2011.

15. FCIC 2011; Parliament 2013a.

16. Salter 2012; Moore, Carter, and Associates 2009.

17. Labaton Sucharow 2015; see also Which? 2013.

18. Martin Woods, interview with the author, video call, 30 October 2012.

19. Woods interview.

20. Upin 2010.

21. Parliament 2013, 14; O'Brien 2009.

22. Fields 2013.

23. Ho 2009; see also Heffernan 2012, 164, for Brad Ruderman on Lehman Brothers.

24. Salter 2012.

25. Ian Taplin, interview with the author, Windsor, UK, 26 August 2012.

26. Graham Senior Milne, interview with the author, Berwick, UK, 22 August 2012.
27. The FSA regulated the UK's financial services industry between 2001 and 2013, when it was abolished and its responsibilities split between two new agencies: the Financial Conduct Authority and the Prudential Regulation Authority.
28. Taplin interview.
29. Taplin interview.
30. Public Concern at Work 2013.
31. Such conflict of responsibility encourages institutional corruption; see Thompson 1995; Kenny 2014.
32. O'Brien 2007; O'Brien and Gilligan 2013. For examples, see the role of internal compliance system failures in the context of Enron's collapse (Froud et al. 2004; O'Brien 2003) and the recent securitization debacle that led to the global financial crisis (O'Brien 2009).
33. Milne interview.
34. BBC 2008.
35. Parliament 2009, 553.
36. *Financial Times* 2009.
37. Woods interview.
38. Woods interview.
39. Woods interview.
40. O'Brien 2009, 13; O'Brien 2007, 3.
41. O'Brien 2003, 6.
42. Turner 2014.
43. Turner 2014, 218.
44. Parliament 2013, 92.
45. In Chapter 4 we see how the UK's HBOS was warned by the FSA about problematic aspects of its mortgage sales, long before the bank entered a crisis.
46. Woods interview.
47. Woods interview.
48. Upon his release, he was awarded a bounty of $104 million by the IRS whistleblower office for his work.
49. Comptroller and Auditor General 2007.
50. Lui 2014.
51. Dorn 2014.
52. O'Brien 2009, 5; Devine and Maassarani 2011, 1; Parliament 2013, 14.
53. O'Brien 2009, 1.
54. Wilson 2012.
55. Fields 2013.
56. O'Brien 2009, 27–31; O'Brien 2003, 2, 13; Ross 2010.
57. Heffernan 2012.

34. Rothschild and Miethe 1999; Devine and Maassarani 2011, 7, 82; Glazer and Glazer 1989.
35. Alford 2001; Devine and Maassarani 2011, 11.
36. Grant 2002, 397.
37. Bryman and Bell 2015; McLain and Keenan 1999.
38. Butler 1997b, 39.
39. Riach, Rumens, and Tyler 2016.
40. Alford 2001.
41. Butler 1997b, 39.
42. See, for example, Alford 2001; Contu 2014; Grant 2002.

5. Whistleblower Retaliation

1. A building society is a member-owned financial institution that lends capital for buying or improving homes. It is similar to a credit union.
2. Ross 2010, 232.
3. Cooper 2010.
4. Ross 2010, 110.
5. Ross 2010, 226.
6. Olivia Greene, interview with the author, Monaghan, Ireland, 14 May 2012.
7. Greene interview.
8. Greene interview.
9. Greene interview.
10. Greene interview.
11. Greene interview.
12. Hudson 2011b.
13. Greene interview.
14. Greene interview.
15. Ethics Resource Center 2012; Lennane 1993; Mesmer-Magnus and Viswes- varan 2005; Rothschild and Miethe 1999; Vandekerckhove, Brown, and Tsahuridu 2014.
16. Devine and Maassarani 2011, 26.
17. Greene interview.
18. Greene interview.
19. Greene interview.
20. Alford 2001; McLain and Keenan 1999.
21. Martin Woods, interview with the author, video call, 30 October 2012.
22. Perry 1998; Devine and Maassarani 2011, 27.
23. Martin and Rifkin 2004; Miethe 1999.
24. Miceli et al. 1999.
25. See Butler 1997a, chap. 4.
26. Butler 1997a, 133.
27. Butler 1997a, 133.

28. Butler 1997, 141,
29. Butler 1997a, 134; see also Kenny 2018.
30. Butler 1997a, 133.
31. Butler 2009.
32. Butler 1993.
33. Butler 1990; Chambers 2007.
34. Butler 2009, 31.
35. For violence in its primary form, see Chambers 2007. For typical violence, see Butler 1990, 2004.
36. Miceli and Near 1985; Rothschild and Miethe 1999.
37. Burrows 2001; Premeaux and Bedeian 2003; Lee and Bjørkelo 2013; Mesmer-Magnus and Viswesvaran 2005; Rehg et al. 2008.
38. Perry 1998.

6. Speaking Out in Public

1. Devine and Maassarani 2011, 18.
2. O'Brien 2009, 5.
3. *Guardian* 2012.
4. O'Toole 2009.
5. Lavery and O'Brien 2005.
6. See O'Toole 2009 for the example of the Depfa / Hypo Real case from the 1990s.
7. Barrington 2010.
8. O'Toole 2009.
9. *Guardian* 2009.
10. LiberteInfo 2011.
11. Vulliamy 2011a.
12. Rudolf Elmer, interview with the author, video call, 7 November 2012.
13. Elmer interview.
14. Elmer 2008.
15. The American Polygraph Association explicitly advises against using the tests for such purposes, although Julius Bär made the unlikely claim that such advisements apply in the United States but not the Caymans (Elmer 2008).
16. Elmer interview.
17. E. Taylor 2005.
18. He was charged with violating in particular Article 47 of the Swiss Banking Act. He was also charged with document forgery and for sending "threatening messages" to staff at Julius Bär. In response to the charges of document forgery, Rudolf reported that he had altered the names of files to make them clearly identifiable. He also wrote letters to tax authorities in which he pretended to be a repentant tax evader confessing the misdemeanor. He

insisted he had not altered the actual contents of any documents. Contacting Julius Bär for a response, the *Guardian* asked the bank to identify a single forged document. They declined to do so (*Guardian* 2009).

19. LiberteInfo 2011.
20. Schumpeter 2014.
21. No member of the Elmer family was questioned by the prosecutor for the canton of Zurich until 2011, when the Federal Court of Switzerland got involved.
22. LiberteInfo 2011.
23. Elmer interview.
24. Elmer interview.
25. LiberteInfo 2011.
26. LiberteInfo 2011.
27. *Economist* 2013.
28. Elmer interview.
29. Elmer interview.
30. LiberteInfo 2011.
31. LiberteInfo 2011.
32. Vulliamy 2011a.
33. Schmitt 2008.
34. His complaint was that Article 47 of Swiss law had left him unprotected. His appeal to the European Court of Human Rights said the level of threats against his family had risen and that they were increasingly afraid.
35. Elmer interview.
36. *Guardian* 2009.
37. *Guardian* 2009.
38. Elmer interview.
39. Elmer interview.
40. Vulliamy 2011a.
41. *Economist* 2012.
42. Balzli and Stark 2008.
43. *Guardian* 2009.
44. Moore 2015.
45. Eileen Foster, interview with the author, phone call, 28 January 2014.
46. Hudson 2011a; 2011b.
47. Vulliamy 2011b.
48. Vulliamy 2011b.
49. Markopolous was the whistleblower in the Bernie Madoff case, in which Madoff, a stockbroker, defrauded clients in a Ponzi scheme.
50. Martin Woods, interview with the author, video call, 30 October 2012.
51. Devine and Maassarani 2011, 48.
52. Butler 1997a, 136.
53. Elmer interview.

54. LiberteInfo 2011.
55. Vulliamy 2011a.
56. *Telegraph* 2011.
57. Jones 2011.
58. Vulliamy 2011a.
59. Rudolf was prosecuted for having threatened Julius Bär that he would go public with the information he had (he admitted he had done this) and also for trying to extort $50,000 from the bank (he denied he had done this).
60. LiberteInfo 2011.
61. LiberteInfo 2011.
62. Vulliamy 2011a.
63. *International Tax Review* 2012.
64. Jones 2011.
65. Vulliamy 2011a.
66. Regarding Martin Woods, see Vulliamy 2011b.
67. See also Heffernan 2012.
68. Martin and Rifkin 2004, 221; see also Devine and Maassarani 2011, 50.
69. LiberteInfo 2011.
70. Elmer interview.
71. LiberteInfo 2011.
72. LiberteInfo 2011.

7. Media, Recruitment, and Friends

1. *The Choice* 2009.
2. UK Treasury 2009.
3. UK Treasury 2009.
4. UK Treasury 2009.
5. Moore 2015.
6. Ebrahimi 2012.
7. Moore 2015, 519.
8. Parliament 2009, 638.
9. BBC 2009.
10. Parliament 2009, 545.
11. UK Treasury 2009.
12. Paul Moore, interview with the author, video call, 1 May 2014.
13. See also Press 2012 for a description of Leyla Wydler's case. After speaking out about corruption at the Stanford Financial Group she was likewise the target of media scrutiny.
14. Molloy 2009.
15. The *Irish Examiner* (2009a) ran a story on his case whose headline, "Whistleblower Had Coloured History with AIB," implied that McErlean was at fault.

16. Dáil Éireann 2009.
17. LiberteInfo 2011.
18. Vulliamy 2011a.
19. *Economist* 2013.
20. Jones 2011.
21. Rudolf Elmer, interview with the author, video call, 7 November 2012.
22. LiberteInfo 2011.
23. Devine and Maassarani 2011, 19.
24. Butler and Athanasiou 2013, ix.
25. Foucault 1980, 39–40.
26. Rabinow 1991, 22.
27. Foucault 1976, 170.
28. Foucault 1980, 39–40.
29. Dreyfus and Rabinow 1982, 361.
30. BBC *Hardtalk* 2009.
31. LiberteInfo 2011.
32. See Chapter 3.
33. LiberteInfo 2011.
34. This is explored further in Chapter 9.
35. BBC 2008.
36. Moore 2015, 467.
37. Hoyos 2012.
38. Butler 1997b; Butler 2004.
39. Butler 1997b, 104.
40. Foucault 1990.
41. Jonathan Sugarman, interview with the author, Dublin, Ireland, 16 April 2012.
42. Sugarman interview.
43. Sugarman interview.
44. Hudson 2011a.
45. Government Accountability Project 2012.
46. Morgensen 2012.
47. Taibbi 2015.
48. Olivia Greene, interview with the author, Monaghan, Ireland, 14 May 2012. Olivia also noted that ambivalence toward hiring her was because of her connection with Irish Nationwide, deemed a fallen company after the scandals that plagued it late in the first decade of the 2000s. That she had spoken out against these problems in her testimony did little to sway potential employers.
49. Smyth 2013.
50. Berlin 2012.
51. Fraser 2012.
52. Vulliamy 2011b.

53. Fraser 2012.
54. Fraser 2012.
55. Fraser 2012.
56. Fraser 2012.
57. Rothschild and Miethe 1999.
58. Horwitz 2012.
59. McErlean 2010.
60. Sugarman interview.
61. Martin Woods, interview with the author, video call, 30 October 2012.
62. Parliament 2013b.
63. Parliament 2009, 435.
64. Rothschild and Miethe 1999; Devine and Maassarani 2011.
65. Rothschild and Miethe 1999; Devine and Maassarani 2011.
66. Labaton Sucharow 2012; 2015.
67. Butler 1997b.
68. Butler 1997b, 139.
69. Butler 1997b, 143.
70. The notion of abjection as developed by Julia Kristeva (1982) and inspired by Mary Douglas (1966) is helpful here.
71. Perry 1998.
72. Alford 2001; Rothschild and Miethe 1999.
73. Perry 1998.

8. Turning Inward

1. Barrington 2009.
2. Barrington 2009.
3. Dáil Éireann 2009.
4. Dáil Éireann 2009, 7.
5. Thompson 1995 describes this phenomenon as "institutional corruption."
6. O'Brien and Gilligan 2013, xvi; for Irish context, see Nyberg 2011; for UK context, see Parliament 2013a.
7. FCIC 2011.
8. Barrington 2009.
9. Dáil Éireann 2009, Deputy Fergus O'Dowd statement.
10. Dáil Éireann 2009. The Basel guidelines, or Basel Accords, are an international set of recommendations for regulation in the banking industry. All Group of Twenty economies are covered by these accords, in addition to major banking hubs like Hong Kong and Singapore. The committee agreeing the recommendations has no authority to enforce them directly, although member countries tend to implement them through their national laws and regulations.
11. Dáil Éireann 2009, 21.

12. *Irish Examiner* 2009b.

13. McErlean 2010.

14. Seanad Ireland Debates 2010.

15. Percival 2009; Oliver 2010.

16. McErlean 2010.

17. Olivia Greene, interview with the author, Monaghan, Ireland, 14 May 2012.

18. Greene interview.

19. Jonathan Sugarman, interview with the author, Dublin, Ireland, 16 April 2012.

20. *The Choice* 2009.

21. *The Choice* 2009.

22. Paul Moore, interview with the author, video call, 1 May 2014. Being "sent to Coventry" is a common expression in the UK that means "being deliberately ostracized."

23. Moore 2015.

24. Alford 2001; Rothschild and Miethe 1999; Kenny, Fotaki, and Scriver 2018.

25. Lee and Bjørkelo 2013; Jackson et al. 2010; Peters et al. 2011; Lennane 1993.

26. Rothschild 2013, 892.

27. Fotaki, Kenny, and Scriver 2015.

28. See Kenny, Fotaki, and Scriver 2018 for a problematization of this use of the discourse of mental health in describing whistleblower experiences.

29. Butler 2004, 32.

30. Butler 1997b, 169.

31. Butler 2004, 31.

32. Butler 1997b, 47.

33. Butler 1997b. For a useful example of this dynamic in contemporary management work, see Harding 2013.

34. Butler 1997b, 112.

35. This point echoes ideas from studies of oppressed groups—for example, within postcolonial studies. As noted by Fanon (1963), Bhabha (2004), and others, the colonized are not necessarily free of the cultural norms of the oppressor, but rather the boundary is blurred. Oppressed people can take on the very exclusionary norms of the culture that they are against, engaging in self-berating (Hook 2008).

36. Devine and Maassarani 2011, 21; Fotaki et al. 2015.

37. UK Treasury 2009, 665.

38. Connolly 2012.

39. Kenny, Fotaki, and Scriver 2018.

40. Kenny, Fotaki, and Scriver 2018.

41. Rudolf Elmer interview with the author, video call, 7 November 2012.

42. Elmer interview.

43. *The Choice* 2009.
44. Devine and Maassarani 2011, 109.
45. Kenny, Fotaki, and Scriver 2018; Corrigan 2005.

9. Coping with Retaliation

1. Arsenault 2012.
2. Currency exchange houses such as those used by Wachovia are a common means for cartels to launder their profits. See Arsenault 2012.
3. Vulliamy 2011b.
4. Arsenault 2012.
5. Upin 2010.
6. Vulliamy 2010.
7. Vulliamy 2011b.
8. Martin Woods, interview with the author, video call, 30 October 2012.
9. Woods interview. This sense of betrayal is explored in Chapter 4.
10. Vulliamy 2011b.
11. Vulliamy 2011b.
12. Vulliamy 2010.
13. Vulliamy 2011b.
14. Vulliamy 2010.
15. Woods interview.
16. Woods interview.
17. Rudolf Elmer, interview with the author, video call, 7 November 2012.
18. Elmer interview.
19. Woods interview.
20. See also Sherry Hunt who spoke out about mortgage fraud at Citi. She was supported by her direct boss Richard Bowen who was fired for doing so, detailed in Lanyon 2016.
21. Milgram 1974, 121.
22. Woods interview.
23. Woods interview.
24. Woods interview.
25. J. Roberts 2005, 636.
26. Butler 1997b, 8.
27. Butler 2004, 235.
28. *The Choice* 2009; BBC *Hardtalk* 2009.
29. On this topic, see also Grant 2002, 397.
30. Milne 2011.
31. Woods interview.
32. *International Tax Review* 2012.
33. Butler 2004, 22.

34. She draws on Lacan's observations on the nature of language as a wider structure for this point.
35. Butler 2004, 1.
36. See also Ford and Harding 2004; Borgerson 2005; Fotaki and Harding 2018.
37. Butler 2004, 148; 1997b.
38. Honneth 1995; C. Taylor 1994.
39. Butler 2004, 20.
40. Alford 2001; Grant 2002.
41. Devine and Maassarani 2011, 11; Rothschild and Miethe 1994.
42. Parliament 2009, 434.
43. Parliament 2009, 434.
44. Parliament 2009, 435.
45. Parliament 2009, 435.
46. *Positive Money* 2012.
47. Arsenault 2012.
48. Woods interview.
49. Woods interview.
50. Woods interview.
51. Vulliamy 2011b.
52. Jonathan Sugarman, interview with the author, Dublin, Ireland, 16 April 2012.
53. Sugarman interview.
54. Devine and Maassarani 2001, 61.
55. Butler 1993.
56. Butler 2004, 2.
57. Rothschild and Miethe 1999, 121.
58. Alford 2001; Grant 2002; Hersch 2002.

10. Small Victories and Making Fun

1. Vulliamy 2011b.
2. Vulliamy 2011b.
3. Wachovia had profits of $12.3 billion in 2009, which means that the fine was less than 2 percent of the bank's profits in one year. Vuillamy 2011b.
4. Vulliamy 2010.
5. Vulliamy 2010.
6. Vulliamy 2011b.
7. See Chapter 7.
8. Martin Woods, interview with the author, video call, 30 October 2012.
9. Woods interview.
10. Woods interview.
11. Woods interview.

12. Woods interview.
13. LiberteInfo 2011.
14. LiberteInfo 2011.
15. Rudolf Elmer, interview with the author, video call, 7 November 2012.
16. Butler 1990, 176.
17. Woods interview.
18. See Foucault 1971 for more on the changing meaning of "madness" in society.
19. *Positive Money* 2012.
20. Paul Moore, interview with the author, video call, 1 May 2014.
21. Moore interview.
22. Eileen Foster, interview with the author, phone call, 28 January 2014.
23. Elmer interview.
24. Butler 1990, xxii.
25. Butler 1990, xxii.
26. Butler 1990, 175.
27. Critchley 2000; Rhodes 2001.
28. Butler 1990, xxviii.
29. Butler 1997b, 30.
30. Parody can also perform such a critical function in the treatment of *contemporary* institutions and organizations (Kenny 2009; Rhodes 2001; Rhodes and Pullen 2007).
31. See also Fotaki 2010a; Kenny 2012.
32. Butler 1997b.
33. Foucault 1990, 11.
34. O'Doherty 2007, 199; see also Collinson 2002; Kavanagh and O'Sullivan 2007.
35. Butler 1990.
36. Butler 1990, 176.
37. Butler 1990, xxvi.

Conclusion

1. See Kenny 2015b.
2. O'Brien and Gilligan 2013; O'Brien 2007, 4, 30, 47; Devine and Maassarani 2011, 103.
3. Habermas 1973.
4. Johnson and Kwak 2010; Rajan 2010.

Appendix

1. It is difficult to gain access to participants in whistleblowing research, and so it is frequently necessary to draw on industry contacts and snowball samples despite the relative limitations of these methods.
2. Judd, Smith, and Kidder 1991; Miles and Huberman 1994.

3. See also Riach et al. 2014, 1683.
4. Miles and Huberman 1994.
5. The personal testimony included in this book has been agreed through the signing of consent forms as part of my university's ethics protocol, or else it comes from the public domain.
6. Some respondents were restricted in what they could say because of pending court cases or settlement agreements with their organizations. Other participants' evidence, such as testimony to public hearings on the banking crisis, has been removed from the public domain, despite other parts of these hearings being available.
7. Articles have been published in the *Guardian*, the *Irish Times,* and the *Financial Times.*
8. Miles and Huberman 1994.
9. Alvesson and Sköldberg (2009) describe this process.
10. Eisenhardt 1989; Miles and Huberman 1994; Strauss and Corbin 1990.
11. Charmaz 2006.
12. Riach et al. 2014; Riach 2016. Harding 2008; Harding et al. 2014.
13. Riach et al. 2016, 2072.
14. Riach et al. 2016, 2073.
15. Riach et al. 2016, 2073.
16. Harding 2008; Parker 2005; Pavon-Cuellar 2010.
17. Harding 2008, 46.
18. Butler 1993; Parker 2005; Hook 2007; Pullen 2006.
19. Geertz 1973; Watson 1994; Van Maanen 1979.
20. See Alvesson and Deetz 2000.
21. Butler 1990, 176.
22. Foucault 1976.
23. Riach et al. 2016, 2073.
24. Ellis 2007.
25. Fotaki and Harding 2013; Pullen 2006; as Butler (1993, 136) notes, there is no such thing as a "neutral . . . omniscient gaze" in such encounters.
26. Pratt 2000; Wray-Bliss 2003; Lutz 1988.
27. Lapping 2010; Parker 2005.
28. See Harding et al. 2011, for a discussion of this aspect of organizational research.
29. Harding 2007.
30. Alford 2001; Brown 2017; Perry 1998.
31. McLain and Keenan 1999.
32. Miceli, Near, and Dworkin 2008.

Bibliography

ACCA. 2016. "Effective Whistleblowing Arrangements." 10 May. http://www
.accaglobal.com/uk/en/technical-activities/technical-resources-search/2016
/may/effective-speak-up-arrangements-for-whistle-blowers.html.

Admati, A., and M. Hellwig. 2013. *The Bankers' New Clothes: What's Wrong with
Banking and What to Do about It.* Princeton, NJ: Princeton University Press.

Alexander, J., and P. Smith. 1993. "The Discourse of American Civil Society: A
New Proposal for Cultural Studies." *Theory and Society* 22 (2): 151–207.

Alford, C. F. 2001. *Whistleblowers: Broken Lives and Organizational Power.*
Ithaca, NY: Cornell University Press.

———. 2007. "Whistle-Blower Narratives: The Experience of Choiceless Choice."
Social Research 74 (1): 223–248.

Alvesson, M., and S. Deetz. 2000. *Doing Critical Management Research.* London:
Sage.

Alvesson, M., and K. Sköldberg. 2009. *Reflexive Methodology.* London: Sage.

Andrade, J. A. 2015. "Reconceptualizing Whistleblowing in a Complex World."
Journal of Business Ethics 128 (2): 321–335.

Annesley, C., and A. Scheele. 2011. "Gender, Capitalism and Economic Crisis:
Impact and Responses across Europe." *Journal of Contemporary European
Studies* 19 (3): 335–347.

Armenakis, A. 2004. "Making a Difference by Speaking Out." *Journal of Management Inquiry* 13 (4): 355–362.

Arsenault, C. 2012. "Dirty Money Thrives Despite Mexico Drug War." *Al Jazeera*, 17 July. http://www.aljazeera.com/indepth/features/2012/06 /201261515312418850.html.

Assassi, L. 2009. *The Gendering of Global Finance*. Basingstoke, UK: Palgrave Macmillan.

Balzli, B., and H. Stark. 2008. "The Cayman Connection: International Tax Evasion Scandal Spreads." *Der Spiegel*, 3 March. http://www.spiegel.de /international/business/the-cayman-connection-international-tax-evasion -scandal-spreads-a-539068.html.

Barrington, K. 2009. "Did the Regulator Fail to Act on AIB?" *Business Post*, 5 April. https://www.businesspost.ie/legacy/did-the-regulator-fail-to-act-on -aib-102476.

———. 2010. "Norris Raises Red Flag at IFSC." *Business Post*, 15 May. https://www .businesspost.ie/legacy/norris-raises-red-flag-at-ifsc-109581.

BBC. 2008. "HBOS Former Head of Regulatory Risk Questions Bank's Controls." Press release, 30 October. http://www.bbc.co.uk/pressoffice/pressreleases /stories/2008/10_october/30/money.shtml.

———. 2009. "Text: HBOS Whistleblower Statement." 10 February. http://news .bbc.co.uk/2/hi/uk_politics/7882581.stm.

BBC *Hardtalk*. 2009. "Sherron Watkins and Paul Moore." Interview by Stephen Sackur. *Hardtalk*. BBC News. 3 April.

Berlin, L. 2012. "JPMorgan Chase Whistleblower: 'Essentially Suicide' to Stand Up to Bank." 7 May. http://www.huffingtonpost.com/2012/05/07/linda -almonte-jpmorgan-chase-whistleblower_n_1478268.html.

Bhabha, H. 2004. *The Location of Culture*. London: Routledge.

Blumenfeld, W., and M. Breen. 2001. "Introduction to the Special Issue: Butler Matters: Judith Butler's Impact on Feminist and Queer Studies since Gender Trouble." *International Journal of Sexuality and Gender Studies* 6 (1–2): 1–5.

Borgerson, J. 2005. "Judith Butler: On Organizing Subjectivities." *Sociological Review* 53 (1): 63–79.

Borgerson, J., and A. Rehn. 2004. "General Economy and Productive Dualisms." *Gender, Work and Organization* 11 (4): 455–474.

Braunmühl, C. 2012. "Theorizing Emotions with Judith Butler: Within and beyond the courtroom." *Rethinking History* 16 (2): 221–240.

Brown, A. J. 2017. "Whistleblowers as Heroes: Fostering Quiet Heroism in Place of the Heroic Whistleblower Stereotype." In *Handbook of Heroism and Heroic Leadership*, edited by S. Allison, G. Goethals, and R. Kramer, 356–376. London: Routledge.

Bryman, A., and E. Bell. 2015. *Business Research Methods*. Oxford: Oxford University Press.

Burrows, J. 2001. "Telling Tales and Saving Lives: Whistleblowing—the Role of Professional Colleagues in Protecting Patients from Dangerous Doctors." *Medical Law Review* 9 (2): 110–129.

Butler, J. 1990. *Gender Trouble: Feminism and the Subversion of Identity.* London: Routledge.

———. 1993. *Bodies That Matter: On the Discursive Limits of "Sex."* London: Routledge.

———. 1997a. *Excitable Speech.* New York: Routledge.

———. 1997b. *The Psychic Life of Power: Theories in Subjection.* London: Routledge.

———. 2004. *Undoing Gender.* New York: Routledge.

———. 2005. *Giving an Account of Oneself.* New York: Fordham University Press.

———. 2009. *Frames of War.* New York: Verso.

Butler, J., and A. Athanasiou. 2013. *Dispossession: The Performative in the Political.* Cambridge: Polity Press.

Casal, J. C., and S. S. Zalkind. 1995. "Consequences of Whistleblowing: A Study of the Experiences of Management Accountants." *Psychological Reports* 77 (3): 795–802.

Chambers, S. A. 2007. "Normative Violence after 9 / 11: Rereading the Politics of *Gender Trouble.*" *New Political Science* 29 (1): 43–60.

Charmaz, K. 2006. *Constructing Grounded Theory: A Practical Guide through Qualitative Data Analysis.* London: Sage.

Chittum, R. 2011. "The Countrywide Fraud Machine: Michael Hudson Tallies Up Dozens of Allegations That Executives Retaliated against Whistleblowers." *Columbia Journalism Review,* 22 September. https://archives.cjr.org/the_audit/the_countrywide_fraud_machine.php.

The Choice. 2009. "Interview with Paul Moore." Interview by Michael Buerk. *The Choice.* BBC Radio 4. 3 November.

Clegg, S., and J. R. Bailey. 2008. *International Encyclopedia of Organization Studies.* Thousand Oaks, CA: Sage.

Coleman, C. 2015. "SEC Guidance Supports Protection for Internal Whistle-blowers." *Lexology,* 31 August. http://www.lexology.com/library/detail.aspx?g=b72f7b2b-73eb-4563-8fc3-e2294a2fe1d2.

Collinson, D. 2002. "Managing Humor." *Journal of Management Studies* 29 (3): 269–289.

Comptroller and Auditor General. 2007. *The Financial Regulator.* Government of Ireland. http://www.audgen.gov.ie/documents/vfmreports/57_FinRegulator.pdf.

Connell, R. W. 1998. "Masculinities and Globalization." *Men and Masculinities* 1 (1): 3–23.

Connell, R. W., and J. Wood. 2005. "Globalization and Business Masculinities." *Men and Masculinities* 7 (4): 347–364.

Connolly, K. 2012. "German Man Locked Up over HVB Bank Allegations May Have Been Telling Truth." *Guardian,* 28 November. http://www.theguardian.com/world/2012/nov/28/gustl-mollath-hsv-claims-fraud.

Contu, A. 2014. "Rationality and Relationality in the Process of Whistleblowing: Recasting Whistleblowing through Readings of Antigone." *Journal of Management Inquiry* 23 (4): 393–406.

Cooper, M. 2010. *Who Really Runs Ireland?* Dublin: Penguin.

Corrigan, P. W., ed. 2005. *On the Stigma of Mental Illness: Practical Strategies for Research and Social Change.* Washington, DC: American Psychological Association.

Critchley, S. 2000. *On Humour.* Routledge: London.

Culiberg, B., and K. K. Mihelič. 2016. "The Evolution of Whistleblowing Studies: A Critical Review and Research Agenda." *Journal of Business Ethics.* https://doi.org/10.1007/s10551-016-3237-0.

Dáil Éireann. 2009. *Joint Committee on Economic Regulatory Affairs: Questions to Eugene McErlean,* Irish Parliament (Oireachtas). March 24.

De Goede, M. 2004. "Repoliticizing Financial Risk." *Economy and Society* 33 (2): 197–217.

———. 2005. *Virtue, Fortune, and Faith: A Genealogy of Finance.* Minneapolis: University of Minnesota Press.

De Maria, W. 2008. "Whistleblowers and Organizational Protesters: Crossing Imaginary Borders." *Current Sociology* 56 (6): 865–883.

Devine, T. 2015. "International Best Practices for Whistleblower Statutes." In *Developments in Whistleblowing Research 2015,* edited by D. Lewis and W. Vandekerckhove, 7–19. London: International Whistleblowing Research Network.

Devine, T., and T. Maassarani. 2011. *The Corporate Whistleblower's Survival Guide.* San Francisco: Berrett-Koehler.

Dorn, N. 2014. *Democracy and Diversity in Financial Market Regulation.* Abingdon, UK: Routledge.

Douglas, M. 1966. *Purity and Danger: An Analysis of Concepts of Pollution and Taboo.* London: Routledge.

Dreyfus, H., and P. Rabinow. 1982. *Michel Foucault: Beyond Structuralism and Hermeneutics.* Chicago: University of Chicago Press.

Duvvury, N., V. Malesevic, and E. Vasquez del Aguila. 2014. "Economic Crisis and Recovery: Gendered Impacts." *Gender, Sexuality and Feminism* 1 (2): 1–4.

Dworkin, T. M., and M. S. Baucus. 1998. "Internal vs. External Whistleblowers: A Comparison of Whistleblowing Processes." *Journal of Business Ethics* 17 (12): 1281–1298.

Dworkin, T. M., and J. P. Near. 1987. "Whistleblowing Statutes: Are They Working?" *American Business Law Journal* 25 (2): 241–264.

Ebrahimi, H. 2012. "KPMG Faces Inquiry over Rescue of HBOS." *Telegraph* (London), 28 April. http://www.telegraph.co.uk/finance/newsbysector/banksandfinance/9233840/KPMG-faces-inquiry-over-rescue-of-HBOS.html.

Economist. 2012. "Swiss Banking Secrecy: Don't Ask, Won't Tell." 11 February. http://www.economist.com/node/21547229.

———. 2013. "Who's the Criminal? The Agony and the Ecstasy of Offshore Whistleblowing." 16 February. http://www.economist.com/news/special

-report/21571558-agony-and-ecstasy-offshore-whistleblowing-whos
-criminal.

———. 2014. "The Slumps That Shaped Modern Finance Financial Crises." 10
April. http://www.economist.com/news/essays/21600451-finance-not-merely
-prone-crises-it-shaped-them-five-historical-crises-show-how-aspects-today
-s-fina.

Eisenhardt, K. 1989. "Building Theories from Case Study Research." *Academy of
Management Review* 14 (4): 532–550.

Ellis, C. 2007. "Telling Secrets, Revealing Lives: Relational Ethics in Research
with Intimate Others." *Qualitative Inquiry* 13 (1): 3–19.

Elmer, R. 2008. *Submission to European Court for Human Rights*, 14 May.
https://wikileaks.org/wiki/Rudolf_Elmer_files_against_Swiss_banking
_secrecy_at_ECHR.

Elson, D. 1996. "Gender-Aware Analysis and Development Economics." In *The
Political Economy of Development and Underdevelopment*. 6th ed., edited by
K. P. Jameson and C. K. Wilber, 70–80. New York: McGraw-Hill.

Epstein, G. 2006. *Financialization and the World Economy*. Cheltenham, UK:
Edward Elgar.

Ethics Resource Center. 2012. *Inside the Mind of a Whistleblower: A Supplemental
Report of the 2011 National Business Ethics Survey*. http://www.ethics.org
/nbes/files/reportingFinal.pdf.

———. 2014. *National Business Ethics Survey*. http://www.ethics.org/nbes.

Ewing, D. W. 1983. *Do It My Way—or You're Fired! Employee Rights and the
Changing Role of Management Prerogatives*. New York: John Wiley.

Fanon, F. 1963. *The Wretched of the Earth*. London: Penguin.

Faunce, T., K. Crow, T. Nikolic, and F. M. Morgan. 2014. "Because They Have
Evidence: Globalizing Financial Incentives for Corporate Fraud Whistle-
blowers." In *International Handbook on Whistleblowing Research*, edited by
A. J. Brown, D. Lewis, R. Moberly, and W. Vandekerckhove, 381–404.
Cheltenham, UK: Edward Elgar.

FCA (Financial Conduct Authority). 2015. *FCA Introduces New Rules on
Whistleblowing*. https://www.fca.org.uk/news/press-releases/fca-introduces
-new-rules-whistleblowing.

FCIC (Financial Crisis Inquiry Commission). 2011. *Final Report of the National
Commission on the Causes of the Financial and Economic Crisis in the United
States*. http://fcic.law.stanford.edu/report.

Fields, G. 2013. "Banking on Tomorrow: Why Today Is Never Good for Financial
Reform." Edmond J. Safra Center for Ethics, 10 May. https://ethics.harvard
.edu/blog/banking-tomorrow.

Financial Times. 2009. "Memorandum from Paul Moore, Ex-head of Group
Regulatory Risk, HBOS Plc." 11 February. https://www.ft.com/content
/fca6a706-f81d-11dd-aae8-000077b07658.

Fleddermann, C. 1999. *Engineering Ethics*. Englewood Cliffs, NJ: Prentice Hall.

Ford, J. 2010. "Studying Leadership Critically: A Psychosocial Lens on Leadership Identities." *Leadership* 6 (1): 1–19.

Ford, J., and N. Harding. 2004. "We Went Looking for an Organisation but Could Find Only the Metaphysics of Its Presence." *Sociology* 38 (4): 815–830.

Fotaki, M. 2010a. "Why Do Public Policies Fail So Often? Exploring Health Policy Making as an Imaginary / Symbolic Construction." *Organization* 17 (6): 703–720.

———. 2010b. "The Sublime Desire for Knowledge (in Academe): Sexuality at Work in Business and Management Schools in England." *British Journal of Management* 22 (1): 42–53.

———. 2013. "No Woman Is like a Man (in Academia): The Masculine Symbolic Order and the Unwanted Female Body." *Organization Studies* 34 (9): 1251–1275.

———. 2014. "Can Consumer Choice Replace Trust in the National Health Service in England? Towards Developing an Affective Psychosocial Conception of Trust in Health Care." *Sociology of Health and Illness* 36 (8): 1276–1294.

———. 2017. "Relational Ties of Love: A Psychosocial Proposal for Ethics of Compassionate Care in Health and Public Services." *Psychodynamic Practice* 27 (2): 181–189.

Fotaki, M., and N. Harding. 2013. "Lacan and Sexual Difference in Organization and Management Theory: Towards a Hysterical Academy?" *Organization* 20 (2): 153–172.

———. 2018. *Gender and the Organization: Women at Work in the 21st Century.* London: Routledge.

Fotaki, M., K. Kenny, and S. Scriver. 2015. "Whistleblowing and Mental Health: A New Weapon for Retaliation?" In *Developments in Whistleblowing Research*, edited by D. Lewis and W. Vandekerckhove, 106–121. London: International Whistleblowing Research Network.

Fotaki, M., S. Long, and H. S. Schwartz. 2012. "What Can Psychoanalysis Offer Organization Studies Today? Taking Stock of Current Developments and Thinking about Future Directions." *Organization Studies* 33 (9): 1105–1120.

Fotaki, M., B. Metcalfe, and N. Harding. 2014. "Writing Materiality into Organisation Theory." *Human Relations* 67 (10): 1239–1263.

Fotaki, M., and A. Prasad. 2015. "Questioning Neoliberal Capitalism and Economic Inequality in Business Schools." *Academy of Management Learning and Education* 14 (4): 556–575.

Foucault, M. 1971. *Madness and Civilization: A History of Insanity in the Age of Reason.* London: Tavistock.

———. 1976. *The Birth of the Clinic, An Archaeology of Medical Perception.* Translated by A. M. Sheridan. London: Tavistock.

———. 1980. *Michel Foucault: Power / Knowledge.* Edited by C. Gordon. Brighton: Harvester Press.

———. 1990. *The History of Sexuality*. Vol. 1, *An Introduction,* translated by R. Hurley. London: Penguin.

———. 1991. "Polemics Politics and Problematizations." In *The Foucault Reader,* edited by P. Rabinow, 381–390. London: Penguin.

———. 2001. *Fearless Speech*. Los Angeles: Semiotext(e).

———. 2005. *The Hermeneutics of the Subject: Lectures at the Collège de France, 1981–1982*. Edited by F. Gros and translated by G. Burchell. Houndmills, UK: Palgrave Macmillan.

———. 2006. *Discourse and Truth: The Problematization of Parrhesia*. https://foucault.info/parrhesia/.

———. 2009. *Cours au Collège de France. 1984. Le courage de la vérité. Le gouvernement de soi et des autres II*. Paris: Gallimard Seuil.

———. 2010. *The Government of Self and Others: Lectures at the Collège de France, 1982–83*. Basingstoke, UK: Palgrave Macmillan.

Francis, R. 2013. *Report on the Mid Staffordshire NHS Foundation Trust Public Inquiry*. London: Stationery Office. http://webarchive.nationalarchives.gov.uk/20150407084003/http://www.midstaffspublicinquiry.com/report.

Fraser, I. 2012. "RBS Accused of Withdrawing Job Offer to Mexico Drug Deals Whistleblower." *Sunday Herald,* 22 July. https://www.ianfraser.org/rbs-accused-of-withdrawing-job-offer-to-mexico-drug-deals-whistleblower/.

Frosh, S. 2010. *Psychoanalysis Outside the Clinic: Interventions in Psychosocial Studies*. London: Palgrave Macmillan.

Froud, J., S. Johal, V. Papazian, and K. Williams. 2004. "The Temptation of Houston: A Case Study of Financialisation." *Critical Perspectives on Accounting* 15 (6–7): 885–909.

Gabriel, Y. 2008. "Spectacles of Resistance and Resistance of Spectacles." *Management Communication Quarterly* 21 (3): 310–326.

Geertz, C. 1973. *The Interpretation of Cultures*. New York: Basic Books.

General Medical Council. 2015. *The Handling by the General Medical Council of Cases Involving Whistleblowers. Report by the Right Honourable Sir Anthony Hooper to the General Medical Council Presented on the 19th March 2015*. http://www.gmc-uk.org/Hooper_review_final_60267393.pdf.

Giddens, A. 1991. *The Consequences of Modernity*. Cambridge: Polity Press.

Glazer, M. P., and P. M. Glazer. 1989. *The Whistleblowers: Exposing Corruption in Government and Industry*. New York: Basic Books.

———. 1999. "On the Trail of Courageous Behavior." *Sociological Inquiry* 69 (2): 276–295.

Glynos, J., and Y. Stavrakakis. 2008. "Lacan and Political Subjectivity." *Subjectivity* 24: 256–274.

Government Accountability Project. 2012. *BofA / Countrywide Whistleblower Eileen Foster Wins Ridenhour Award*. https://www.whistleblower.org/press/bofacountrywide-whistleblower-eileen-foster-wins-ridenhour-award.

Grant, C. 2002. "Whistleblowers: Saints of Secular Culture." *Journal of Business Ethics* 39 (4): 391–399.

Griffin, P. 2013. "Gendering Global Finance: Crisis, Masculinity and Responsibility." *Men and Masculinities* 16 (1): 9–34.

Guardian. 2009. "Isles of Plenty." 13 February. http://www.theguardian.com /business/2009/feb/13/tax-gap-cayman-islands.

———. 2012. "Top Italian Banker to Face Trial over UniCredit Tax Fraud Allegations." 5 June. http://www.theguardian.com/business/2012/jun/05 /italian-banker-trial-UniCredit-tax-fraud.

———. 2017. "Women Bearing 86% of Austerity Burden, Commons Figures Reveal." 9 March. https://www.theguardian.com/world/2017/mar/09/women -bearing-86-of-austerity-burden-labour-research-reveals.

Gunsalus, C. K. 1998. "How to Blow the Whistle and Still Have a Career Afterwards." *Science and Engineering Ethics* 4 (1): 51–64.

Habermas, J. 1973. "What Does a Crisis Mean Today? Legitimation in Late Capitalism." *Social Research* 40 (4): 643–667.

Hall, S. 2000. "Who Needs 'Identity'?" In *Identity: A Reader,* edited by P. du Gay, J. Evans, and P. Redman, 15–31. London: Sage / Open University.

Hancock, P., and M. Tyler. 2007. "Un / doing Gender and the Aesthetics of Organizational Performance." *Gender, Work and Organization* 14 (6): 512–533.

Haraway, D. 1991. *Simians, Cyborgs, and Women: The Reinvention of Nature.* London: Free Association Books.

Harding, N. 2003. *The Social Construction of Management: Texts and Identities.* London: Routledge.

———. 2007. "On Lacan and the 'Becoming-ness' of Organizations / Selves." *Organization Studies* 28 (11): 1761–1773.

———. 2008. "The 'I,' the 'Me' and the 'You Know': Identifying Identities in Organizations." *Qualitative Research in Organizations and Management* 3 (1): 42–58.

———. 2013. *On Being at Work: The Social Construction of the Employee.* New York: Routledge.

Harding, N., H. Lee, J. Ford, and M. Learmonth. 2011. "Leadership and Charisma: A Desire That Cannot Speak Its Name?" *Human Relations* 64 (7): 927–950.

Heffernan, M. 2012. *Willful Blindness: Why We Ignore the Obvious at Our Peril.* London: Simon and Schuster.

Hersch, M. A. 2002. "Whistleblowers—Heroes or Traitors? Individual and Collective Responsibility for Ethical Behaviour." *Annual Reviews in Control* 26 (2): 243–262.

Ho, K. 2009. *Liquidated: An Ethnography of Wall Street.* Durham, NC: Duke University Press.

Hodgson, D. 2005. "Putting on a Professional Performance: Performativity, Subversion and Project Management." *Organization* 12 (1): 51–68.

Holtzhausen, N. 2009. "Organisational Trust as a Prerequisite for Whistle-blowing." *Journal of Public Administration* 44 (1): 234–246.

Honneth, A. 1995. *The Struggle for Recognition: The Moral Grammar of Social Conflicts.* Cambridge: Polity Press.

Hook, D. 2007. *Foucault, Psychology and the Analytics of Power.* Hampshire, UK: Palgrave.

———. 2008. "Postcolonial Psychoanalysis." *Theory and Psychology* 18 (2): 269–283.

Hooper, C. 2001. *Manly States: Masculinities, International Relations and Gender Politics.* New York: Columbia University Press.

Horwitz, J. 2012. "How a Whistleblower Halted JP Morgan Chase's Card Collection." *American Banker,* 15 March. https://www.americanbanker.com /news/how-a-whistleblower-halted-jpmorgan-chases-card-collections.

Hoyos, C. 2012. "The Whistleblowers Club." *Financial Times,* 14 September. https://www.ft.com/content/9e7b9f5e-fd34-11e1-a4f2-00144feabdc0.

Hudson, M. 2011a. "Countrywide Protected Fraudsters by Silencing Whistle-blowers, Say Former Employees." The Center for Public Integrity, 22 September. https://www.publicintegrity.org/2011/09/22/6687/countrywide -protected-fraudsters-silencing-whistleblowers-say-former-employees.

Hudson, M. 2011b. "Mortgage industry whistleblower wins case against Bank of America." The Center for Public Integrity, 15 September. https://www .huffingtonpost.com/the-center-for-public-integrity/mortgage-industry -whistle_b_963882.html.

International Tax Review. 2012. *The Leaders Creating an Impact around the World.* http://www.internationaltaxreview.com/Article/3111667/The-leaders -creating-an-impact-around-the-world.html.

Ionescu, R. 2015. "Whistleblowing and Disaster Risk Reduction." In *Developments in Whistleblowing Research,* edited by D. Lewis and W. Vandekerck-hove, 50–69. London: International Whistleblowing Research Network.

Irish Examiner. 2009a. "Whistleblower Had Coloured History with AIB." 25 March. http://www.irishexaminer.com/ireland/whistleblower-had-coloured -history-with-aib-87605.html.

———. 2009b. "The Persistence of One Good Banker Exposed Bank's Hidden Dealings." 28 March. http://www.irishexaminer.com/ireland/the-persistence -of-one-good-banker-exposed-banks-hidden-dealings-87953.html.

Jack, G. 2004. "On Speech, Critique and Protection." *Ephemera* 4 (2): 121–134.

Jackson, D., K. Peters, S. Andrew, M. Edenborough, E. Halcomb, L. Luck, Y. Salamonson, R. Weaver, and L. Wilkes. 2010. "Trial and Retribution: A Qualitative Study of Whistleblowing and Workplace Relationships in Nursing." *Contemporary Nurse: A Journal for the Australian Nursing Profession* 36 (1–2): 34–44.

Jameson, F. 1984. "Postmodernism, or the Cultural Logic of Late Capitalism." *New Left Review* I (146): 59–92.

Johnson, S., and J. Kwak. 2010. *13 Bankers: Wall Street Takeover and the Next Financial Meltdown*. New York: Pantheon.

Johnston, A. 2010. "Affective Life between Signifiers and Jouis-sens: Lacan's Senti-ments and *Affectuations*" in *Filozofski Vestnik: What Is It to Live?* 30 (2): 113–141.

Jones, B. 2011. "Rudolf Elmer: Whistleblower and Wanted Man." *CNN World,* 17 January. http://edition.cnn.com/2011/WORLD/europe/01/17/rudolfelmer .profile/index.html.

Judd, C., E. Smith, and L. Kidder. 1991. *Research Methods in Social Relations*. Fort Worth, TX: Holt, Rinehart, and Winston.

Kavanagh, D., and D. O'Sullivan. 2007. "Advertising: The Organizational Production of Humour." In *Humour, Work and Organization,* edited by R. Westwood and C. Rhodes, 235–248. Abingdon, UK: Routledge.

Keenan, J. P. 1995. "Whistleblowing and the First-Level Manager: Determinants of Feeling Obliged to Blow the Whistle." *Journal of Social Behavior and Personality* 10 (3): 571–584.

———. 2000. "Blowing the Whistle on Less Serious Forms of Fraud: A Study of Executives and Managers." *Employee Responsibilities and Rights Journal* 12 (4): 199–217.

Kenny, K. 2009. "The Performative Surprise: Parody, Documentary and Critique." *Culture and Organisation* 15 (2): 221–235.

———. 2010. "Beyond Ourselves: Passion and the Dark Side of Identification in an Ethical Organization." *Human Relations* 63 (6): 857–873.

———. 2012. "'Someone Big and Important': Identification and Affect in an International Development Organisation." *Organization Studies* 33 (9): 1175–1193.

———. 2014. "Banking Compliance and Dependence Corruption: Towards an Attachment Perspective." *Law and Financial Markets Review* 8 (2): 165–177.

———. 2015a. "Constructing Selves: Whistleblowing and the Role of Time." In *Developments in Whistleblowing Research 2015,* edited by D. Lewis and W. Vandekerckhove, 70–84. London: International Whistleblowing Research Network.

———. 2015b. "We Need to Protect the Whistleblowers Who Save Our Skins but Pay the Price." *The Conversation,* 12 May. https://theconversation.com/we -need-to-protect-the-whistleblowers-who-save-our-skins-but-pay-the-price -41635.

———. 2018. "Censored: Whistleblowers and Impossible Speech." *Human Relations* 71 (8): 1025–1048.

Kenny, K., and G. Euchler. 2012. "'Some Good Clean Fun': Humour, Control and Subversion in an Advertising Agency." *Gender, Work and Organisation* 19 (3): 306–323.

Kenny, K. and M. Fotaki. 2015. "From Gendered Organizations to Compassionate Borderspaces: Reading Corporeal Ethics with Bracha Ettinger." *Organization* 22(2): 183–199.

Kenny, K., M. Fotaki, and S. Scriver. 2018. "Mental Health as a Weapon: Whistleblower Retaliation and Normative Violence." *Journal of Business Ethics,* 1–15. https://doi.org/10.1007/s10551-018-3868-4.

Kenny, K., M. Fotaki, and W. Vandekerckhove. 2019. "Whistleblower Subjectivities: Organization and Passionate Attachment." *Organization Studies,* forthcoming.

King, G., III. 1999. "The Implications of an Organization's Structure on Whistle-blowing." *Journal of Business Ethics* 20 (4): 315–326.

Knyght, R., N. Kakabadse, A. Kakabadse, and A. Kouzmin. 2011. "When Rules and Principles Are Not Enough: Insiders' Views and Narratives on the Global Financial Crisis." *Journal of Change Management* 11 (1): 45–67.

Kohn, S. 2017. *The New Whistleblower's Handbook: A Step-By-Step Guide to Doing What's Right and Protecting Yourself.* Guildford, CT: Lyons Press

Kristeva, J. 1982. *Powers of Horror: An Essay on Abjection.* Translated by L. Rondiez. New York: Columbia University Press.

Labaton Sucharow. 2012. *Wall Street, Fleet Street, Main Street: Corporate Integrity at a Crossroads.* https://berkleycenter.georgetown.edu/publications/wall -street-fleet-street-main-street-corporate-integrity-at-a-crossroads-united -states-united-kingdom-financial-services-industry-survey.

———. 2015. *The Street, the Bull and the Crisis: A Survey of the US and UK Financial Services Industry.* https://www.secwhistlebloweradvocate.com/pdf /Labaton-2015-Survey-report_12.pdf.

Lacan, J. 1958. *The Seminar of Jacques Lacan Book VI: Desire and its Interpretation.* Translated by Cormac Gallagher. 12 November. http://www .lacaninireland.com/web/wp-content/uploads/2010/06/THE-SEMINAR-OF -JACQUES-LACAN-VI.pdf.

Lacan, J. 1988. *The Seminar of Jacques Lacan: Freud's Papers on Technique.* Vol. 1. Edited by Jacques-Alain Miller. New York: W. W. Norton.

———. 1992. *The Seminar of Jacques Lacan: The Ethics of Psychoanalysis.* Vol. 7. Edited by Jacques-Alain Miller. New York: W. W. Norton.

———. 2006a. "Seminar on "The Purloined Letter." In *Ecrits: The First Complete Edition in English,* edited by B. Fink, H. Fink, and R. Grigg, 6–48. New York: Norton.

Lanyon, C. 2016. "Sherry Hunt Took on One of the World's Biggest Banks and Won." *New York Magazine,* 26 November. http://nymag.com/vindicated /2016/11/sherry-hunt-took-on-one-of-the-worlds-biggest-banks-and-won .html.

Laplanche, J. 1999. *The Unconscious and the Id.* London: Karnac.

Lapping, C. 2010. *Psychoanalysis in Social Research.* London: Routledge.

Lavery, B., and T. O'Brien. 2005. "For Insurance Regulators, Trails Lead to Dublin." *New York Times,* 1 April. http://www.nytimes.com/2005/04/01 /business/worldbusiness/for-insurance-regulators-trails-lead-to-dublin.html.

Lee, R. T., and B. Bjørkelo. 2013. "Workplace Bullying after Whistleblowing: Future Research and Implications." *Journal of Managerial Psychology* 28 (3): 306–323.

Lennane, J. 1993. "'Whistleblowing': A Health Issue." *British Medical Journal* 307 (6905): 667–670.

———. 2012. "What Happens to Whistleblowers, and Why?" *Social Medicine* 6 (4): 249–258.

Lessig, L. 2011. *Republic, Lost: How Money Corrupts Congress—and a Plan to Stop It.* New York: Twelve / Hachette.

Levinas, E. 1969. *Totality and Infinity: An Essay on Exteriority.* Pittsburgh, PA: Duquesne University Press.

Lewis, D. 2008. "Ten Years of Public Interest Disclosure Legislation in the UK: Are Whistleblowers Adequately Protected?" *Journal of Business Ethics* 82 (2): 497–507.

Lewis, D., A. J. Brown, and R. Moberly. 2014. "Whistle-Blowing, Its Importance and the State of the Research." In *International Handbook of Whistle-Blowing Research,* edited by A. J. Brown, D. Lewis, R. Moberly, and W. Vandekerckhove, 1–36. Cheltenham, UK: Edward Elgar.

Lewis, D., and W. Vandekerckhove. 2015. "Does Following a Whistleblowing Procedure Make a Difference? The Evidence from the Research Conducted for the Francis Inquiry." In *Developments in Whistleblowing Research,* edited by D. Lewis and W. Vandekerckhove, 85–105. London: International Whistleblowing Research Network.

Leys, J., and W. Vandekerckhove. 2014. "Whistle-Blowing Duties." In *International Handbook of Whistle-Blowing Research,* edited by A. J. Brown, D. Lewis, R. Moberly, and W. Vandekerckhove, 115–132. Cheltenham, UK: Edward Elgar.

LiberteInfo. 2011. *Rudolf Elmer—the Man Who Defied and Exposed the Dark Side of Global Finance.* http://liberte-info.net/interviews/elmer.html.

Linstead, S., and A. Pullen. 2006. "Gender as Multiplicity: Desire, Displacement, Difference and Dispersion." *Human Relations* 5 (9): 1287–1310.

Lloyd, M. 2005. *Beyond Identity Politics: Feminism, Power and Politics.* London: Sage.

———. 2007. *Judith Butler: From Norms to Politics.* Cambridge: Polity.

Lowenstein, R. 2004. *Origins of the Crash: The Great Bubble and Its Undoing.* New York: Penguin.

Lui, A. 2014. "Protecting Whistle-blowers in the UK Financial Industry." *International Journal of Disclosure and Governance* 11 (3): 195–210.

Lutz, C. 1988. *Unnatural Emotions: Everyday Sentiments on a Micronesian Atoll and Their Challenge to Western Theory.* Chicago: University of Chicago Press.

Mansbach, A. 2009. "Keeping Democracy Vibrant: Whistleblowing as Truth-Telling in the Workplace." *Constellations* 16 (3): 363–376.

Martin, B., and W. Rifkin. 2004. "The Dynamics of Employee Dissent: Whistle-blower and Organizational Jiu-Jitsu." *Public Organization Review: A Global Journal* 4 (3): 221–238.

McErlean, E. 2010. Transparency International Ireland's Alternative to Silence Seminar, Panel Contribution. Transparency International Ireland, 19 January. https://www.transparency.ie/content/event-alternative-silence-whistleblower-protection-ireland-ucd-2010.

McLain, D. L., and J. P. Keenan. 1999. "Risk, Information, and the Decision about Response to Wrongdoing in an Organization." *Journal of Business Ethics* 19 (3): 255–271.

McNay, L. 1999. "Subject, Psyche and Agency: The Work of Judith Butler." *Theory, Culture and Society* 16 (2): 175–183.

———. 2008. *Against Recognition.* Cambridge: Polity.

McQueen, P. 2015. *Subjectivity, Gender and the Struggle for Recognition.* London: Palgrave Macmillan.

Merleau-Ponty, M. 2002. *Phenomenology of Perception.* Translated by C. Smith. Oxford: Routledge.

Mesmer-Magnus, J., and C. Viswesvaran. 2005. "Whistleblowing in Organizations: An Examination of Correlates of Whistleblowing Intentions, Actions, and Retaliation." *Journal of Business Ethics* 62 (3): 277–297.

Meyer, J. W., and B. Rowan. 1977. "Institutional Organizations: Formal Structure as Myth and Ceremony." *American Journal of Sociology* 83 (2): 340–363.

Miceli, M., S. Dreyfus, and J. P. Near. 2014. "Outsider 'Whistleblowers': Conceptualizing and Distinguishing 'Bell-Ringing' Behavior." In *International Handbook on Whistleblowing Research,* edited by A. J. Brown, D. Lewis, R. E. Moberly, and W. Vandekerckhove, 71–94. Cheltenham, UK: Edward Elgar.

Miceli, M. P., and J. P. Near. 1985. "Characteristics of Organizational Climate and Perceived Wrongdoing Associated with Whistle-Blowing Decisions." *Personnel Psychology* 38 (3): 525–544.

———. 1992. *Blowing the Whistle: The Organizational and Legal Implications for Companies and Employees.* New York: Lexington Books.

———. 1994. "Whistleblowing: Reaping the Benefits." *Academy of Management Executive* 8 (3): 65–72.

———. 2002. "What Makes Whistle-Blowers Effective? Three Field Studies." *Human Relations* 55 (4): 455–479.

Miceli, M. P., J. P. Near, and T. M. Dworkin. 2008. *Whistleblowing in Organizations.* New York: Routledge.

Miceli, M. P., M. Rehg, J. P. Near, and K. Ryan. 1999. "Can Laws Protect Whistle--Blowers? Results of a Naturally Occurring Field Experiment." *Work and Occupations* 26 (1): 129–151.

Miethe, T. D. 1999. *Whistleblowing at Work: Tough Choices in Exposing Fraud, Waste, and Abuse on the Job.* Boulder, CO: Westview.

Miles, M., and A. Huberman. 1994. *Qualitative Data Analysis.* Thousand Oaks, CA: Sage.

Milgram, S. 1974. *Obedience to Authority.* New York: Harper Perennial.

Milne, G. 2011. "Whistleblowing About the Scottish Widows Demutualization." http://www.happywarrior.org/widows/widows01.htm. Accessed 10 September 2018.

Minsky, H. 1985. "The Financial Instability Hypothesis: A Restatement." In *Post Keynesian Economic Theory,* edited by P. Arestis and T. Skouras, 24–53. Armonk, NY: M. E. Sharpe.

Molloy, T. 2009. "Stockbrokers 'Hid AIB Deals Behind Secret Tax Havens.'" *Independent* (Ireland), 25 March. http://www.independent.ie/irish-news/stockbrokers-hid-aib-deals-behind-secret-tax-havens-26523551.html.

Moore, Carter, and Associates. 2009. *The RiskMinds 2009 Risk Manager's Survey: The Causes and Implications of the 2008 Banking Crisis.* http://www.moorecarter.co.uk/RiskMinds%202009%20Risk%20Managers%27%20Survey%20Report.19March2010.pdf.

Moore, P. 2015. *Crash Bank Wallop: The Memoirs of the HBOS Whistleblower.* London: New Wilberforce Media.

Morgensen, G. 2012. "He Felled a Giant, but He Can't Collect" *New York Times,* 30 June. https://www.nytimes.com/2012/07/01/business/countrywide-ex-executive-still-awaiting-3-8-million-award.html.

Near, J. P., T. M. Dworkin, and M. P. Miceli. 1993. "Explaining the Whistle-Blowing Process: Suggestions from Power Theory and Justice Theory." *Organization Science* 4 (3): 393–411.

Near, J. P., and T. Jensen. 1983. "The Whistle-Blowing Process: Retaliation and Perceived Effectiveness." *Work Occupations* 10 (1): 3–28.

Near, J. P., and M. P. Miceli. 1985. "Organizational Dissidence: The Case of Whistleblowing." *Journal of Business Ethics* 4 (1): 1–16.

———. 1986. "Retaliation against Whistleblowers: Predictors and Effects." *Journal of Applied Psychology* 71 (1): 137–145.

———. 1987. "Whistleblowers in Organizations: Dissidents or Reformers?" In *Research in Organizational Behavior.* Vol. 7, edited by B. M. Staw and L. L. Cummings, 321–368. Greenwich, CT: JAI Press.

———. 1996. Whistle-Blowing: Myth and Reality. *Journal of Management* 22 (3): 507–526.

———. 2016. "After the Wrongdoing: What Managers Should Know about Whistleblowing." *Business Horizons* 59 (1): 105–114.

Nyberg, P. 2011. "Misjudging Risks: The Causes of the Systemic Banking Crisis in Ireland." Houses of Oireachtas Commission of Investigation into the Banking Crisis in Ireland, 19 April. http://www.bankinginquiry.gov.ie.

O'Brien, J. 2003. *Wall Street on Trial: A Corrupted State?* Chichester, UK: John Wiley and Sons.

———. 2007. *Redesigning Financial Regulation: The Politics of Enforcement.* Chichester, UK: John Wiley and Sons.

———. 2009. *Engineering a Financial bloodbath: How Sub-prime Securitization Destroyed the Legitimacy of Financial Capitalism.* London: Imperial College Press.

O'Brien, J., and G. Gilligan, eds. 2013. *Integrity, Risk and Accountability in Financial Markets: Regulating Culture.* Oxford: Hart Publishing.

O'Doherty, D. 2007. "Heidegger's Unfunny and the Academic Text: Organization Analysis on the Blink." In *Humour, Work and Organization,* edited by R. Westwood and C. Rhodes,. 180–204. Abingdon, UK: Routledge.

Oliver, D. 2003. "Whistle-Blowing Engineer." *Journal of Professional Issues in Engineering Education and Practice* 129 (4): 246–256.

Oliver, E. 2010. "Whistleblower McErlean to Get Official Apology from Regulator." *Independent,* 5 October. http://www.independent.ie/business/irish/whistleblower-mcerlean-to-get-official-apology-from-regulator-26687072.html.

Olsen, J. 2014. "Reporting versus Inaction: How Much Is There, What Explains the Differences and What to Measure." In *International Handbook on Whistle-Blowing Research,* edited by A. J. Brown, D. Lewis, R. Moberly, and W. Vandekerckhove, 177–206. Cheltenham, UK: Edward Elgar.

OSHA. 2011. "Letter to M. Weil." U.S. Department of Labor. 13 September. http://www.corporatecrimereporter.com/documents/fosterosha.pdf.

O'Toole, F. 2009. *Ship of Fools: How Stupidity and Corruption Sank the Celtic Tiger.* London: Faber and Faber.

Parker, I. 2005. *Qualitative Psychology. Introducing Radical Research.* Maidenhead, UK: Open University Press.

Parker, M. 2001. "Fucking Management: Queer Theory and Reflexivity." *Ephemera* 1 (1): 36–53.

———. 2002. "Queering Management and Organization." *Gender, Work and Organisation* 9 (2): 146–166.

Parliament. 2009. *Banking Crisis.* Vol. 2, *Written Evidence.* HC 144-II. https://publications.parliament.uk/pa/cm200809/cmselect/cmtreasy/144/144ii.pdf.

———. 2013a. *Changing Banking for Good: Report of the Parliamentary Commission on Banking Standards.* Vol. 1. HL Paper 27-I, HC 175-I. http://www.parliament.uk/documents/banking-commission/banking-final-report-volume-i.pdf.

———. 2013b. *An Accident Waiting to Happen: Fourth Report of Session 2012–13.* HL Paper 144, HC 705. Parliamentary Commission on Banking Standards .https://publications.parliament.uk/pa/jt201213/jtselect/jtpcbs/144/144.pdf.

Parmerlee, M. A., J. P. Near, and T. C. Jensen. 1982. "Correlates of Whistle-blowers" Perceptions of Organizational Reprisals." *Administrative Science Quarterly* 27 (1): 17–34.

Pavon-Cuellar, D. 2010. *From the Conscious Interior to an Exterior Unconscious: Lacan, Discourse Analysis and Social Psychology.* London: Karnac.

Percival, G. 2009. "Former AIB Internal Auditor Accepts Apology from Bank and Has 'Moved On.'" *Irish Examiner,* 22 May. http://www.irishexaminer.com /business/former-aib-internal-auditor-accepts-apology-from-bank-and-has -moved-on-92327.html.

Perry, N. 1998. "Indecent Exposure: Theorizing Whistleblowing." *Organization Studies* 19 (2): 235–257.

Peters, K., L. Luck, M. Hutchinson, L. Wilkes, S. Andrew, and D. Jackson. 2011. "The Emotional Sequelae of Whistleblowing: Findings from a Qualitative Study." *Journal of Clinical Nursing* 20 (19–20): 2907–2914.

Positive Money. 2012. "The HBOS Whistleblower: Paul Moore." Interview by Positive Money. 2 March. Available *http://positivemoney.org/2012/03/video -hbos-whistleblower-paul-moore/*

Pratt, M. 2000. "The Good, the Bad, and the Ambivalent: Managing Identification among Amway Distributors." *Administrative Science Quarterly* 45 (3): 456–493.

Premeaux, S., and A. Bedeian. 2003. "Breaking the Silence: The Moderating Effects of Self-Monitoring in Predicting Speaking Up in the Workplace." *Journal of Management Studies* 40 (6): 1537–1562.

Press, E. 2012. *Beautiful Souls: Saying No, Breaking Ranks, and Heeding the Voice of Conscience in Dark Times.* New York: Farrar, Straus and Giroux.

"Prosecuting Wall Street." 2011. *60 Minutes,* episode 44. CBS, 4 December. http://www.cbsnews.com/news/prosecuting-wall-street/.

Public Concern at Work. 2013. *Silence in the City? Whistleblowing in Financial Services"?.* London: Public Concern at Work.

———. 2014. *Code of Practice.* London: Public Concern at Work.

Pullen, A. 2006. "Gendering the Research Self: Social Practice and Corporeal Multiplicity in the Writing of Organizational Research." *Gender, Work and Organization* 13 (3): 277–298.

Pullen, A., and D. Knights. 2007. "Editorial: Organizing and Disorganizing Performance." *Gender, Work and Organization* 14 (6): 506–511.

Pullen, A., T. Thanem, M. Tyler, and L. Wallenberg. 2016. "Sexual Politics, Organizational Practices: Interrogating Queer Theory, Work and Organization." *Gender, Work and Organization* 23 (1): 1–6.

Rabinow, P. 1991. *The Foucault Reader.* London: Penguin.

Rajan, R. 2010. *Fault Lines: How Hidden Fractures Still Threaten the World Economy.* Princeton, NJ: Princeton University Press.

Rehg, M. T., M. P. Miceli, J. P. Near, and J. R. Van Scotter. 2008. "Antecedents and Outcomes of Retaliation against Whistleblowers: Gender Differences and Power Relationships." *Organization Science* 19 (2): 221–240.

Reinhart, C. M., and K. S. Rogoff. 2009. *This Time Is Different: Eight Centuries of Financial Folly.* Princeton, NJ: Princeton University Press.

Rexrode, C. 2012. "Bank of America Sued for 'Brazen' Fraud at Countrywide." *Christian Science Monitor,* 24 October. http://www.csmonitor.com/Business /Latest-News-Wires/2012/1024/Bank-of-America-sued-for-brazen-fraud-at -Countrywide-video.

Rhodes, C. 2001. "D'oh: The Simpsons, Popular Culture and the Organizational Carnival." *Journal of Management Inquiry* 10 (4): 374–383.

Rhodes, C., and A. Pullen. 2007. "Representing the D'other: The Grotesque Body and Masculinity at Work in *The Simpsons.*" In *Humour, Work and Organization,* edited by R. Westwood and C. Rhodes, 161–179. Abingdon, UK: Routledge.

Riach, K., N. Rumens, and M. Tyler. 2014. "Un / doing Chrononormativity: Negotiating Ageing, Gender and Sexuality in Organizational Life." *Organization Studies* 35 (11): 1677–1698.

Riach, K., N. Rumens, and M. Tyler. 2016. "Towards a Butlerian Methodology: Undoing Organizational Performativity through Anti-narrative Research." *Human Relations* 69 (11): 2069–2089.

Rizq, R. 2013. "States of Abjection," *Organization Studies* 34 (9): 1277–1297.

Roberts, J. 2005. "The Power of the "Imaginary" in Disciplinary Processes." *Organization* 12 (5): 619–642.

Roberts, P. 2014. "Motivations for Whistleblowing: Personal, Private and Public Interests." In *International Handbook on Whistleblowing Research,* edited by A. J. Brown, D. Lewis, R. Moberly, and W. Vandekerckhove, 207–229. Cheltenham, UK: Edward Elgar.

Roberts, P., J. Olsen, and A. J. Brown. 2009. *Whistling While They Work: Towards Best Practice Whistleblowing Programs in Public Sector Organisations.* Brisbane, Australia: Griffith University.

Ross, S. 2010. *The Bankers.* Dublin: Penguin Ireland.

Rothschild, J. 2013. "The Fate of Whistleblowers in Nonprofit Organizations." *Nonprofit and Voluntary Sector Quarterly* 42 (5): 886–901.

Rothschild, J., and T. Miethe. 1994. "Whistleblowing as Resistance in Modern Work Organizations." In *Resistance and Power in Organizations,* edited by J. Jermier, J, D. Knights and W. Nord, 252–73. London: Routledge.

Rothschild, J., and T. D. Miethe. 1999. "Whistle-Blower Disclosures and Management Retaliation." *Work and Occupations* 26 (1): 107–128.

Rothwell, G., and J. N. Baldwin. 2006. "Ethical Climates and Contextual Predictors of Whistle-Blowing." *Review of Public Personnel Administration* 26 (3): 216–244.

Salter, M. 2012. "How Short-Termism Invites Corruption—and What to Do about It." *Harvard Business School Working Knowledge,* 7 June. http://hbswk.hbs .edu/item/7015.html.

Schmitt, D. 2008. "Clouds on the Cayman Tax Heaven." WikiLeaks, 15 February. https://www.wikileaks.org/wiki/Clouds_on_the_Cayman_tax_heaven.

Schumpeter. 2014. "Swiss Bank Secrecy: A Whistleblower's Woes." *Economist,* 19 July. http://www.economist.com/blogs/schumpeter/2014/07/swiss-bank -secrecy.

Seanad Ireland Debates. 2010. Vol. 202, no. 12. 10 May. http://oireachtasdebates .oireachtas.ie/debates%20authoring/debateswebpack.nsf/takes /seanad2010051800004?opendocument.

Sievers, B. 2010. "Beneath the Surface of the Financial Crisis: The Psychoanalytic Perspective." In *Psychoanalytic Perspectives on a Turbulent World,* edited by H. Brunning and M. Perini, 117–137. London: Karnac.

Skivenes, M., and S. C. Trygstad. 2014. "Wrongdoing: Definitions Identification and Categorizations." In *International Handbook on Whistleblowing Research,* edited by A. J. Brown, D. Lewis, R. Moberly, and W. Vandekerck-hove, 95–114. Cheltenham, UK: Edward Elgar.

Smyth, J. 2013. "Ireland's Lonely Whistleblowers." *Financial Times,* 25 November. https://www.ft.com/content/e5c1cf4e-4876-11e3-a3ef-00144feabdc0.

Stavrakakis, Y. 2002. "Encircling the Political: Towards a Lacanian Political Theory." In *Jacques Lacan: Critical Evaluations in Cultural Theory.* Vol. 3, edited by S. Žižek, 274–305. London: Routledge.

———. 2010. "Symbolic Authority, Fantasmatic Enjoyment and the Spirits of Capitalism: Genealogies of Mutual Engagement." In *Lacan and Organ-ization,* edited by C. Hoedemaekers and C. Cederstrom, 59–100. London: Mayfly Books.

Strauss, A., and J. Corbin. 1990. *Basics of Qualitative Research.* Thousand Oaks, CA: Sage.

Taibbi, M. 2015. "A Whistleblower's Horror Story." *Rolling Stone,* 18 February. https://www.rollingstone.com/politics/news/a-whistleblowers-horror-story -20150218.

Taylor, C. 1994. "The Politics of Recognition." In *Multiculturalism and the Politics of Recognition,* edited A. Gutman, 25–74. Princeton, NJ: Princeton Univer-sity Press.

Taylor, E. 2005. "Julius Bär Says Unit's Client Data Were Stolen." *Wall Street Journal,* 16 June. http://online.wsj.com/news/articles/SB111887029173960737 ?mg=reno64wsj&url=http%3A%2F%2Fonline.wsj.com%2Farticle%2FSB1118 87029173960737.html.

Telegraph, 2011. "WikiLeaks to target wealthy individuals," 17 January. https://www.telegraph.co.uk/news/worldnews/wikileaks/8264179 /WikiLeaks-to-target-wealthy-individuals.html.

Tett, G. 2010. *Fool's Gold: The Inside Story of J. P. Morgan and How Wall St. Greed Corrupted Its Bold Dream and Created a Financial Catastrophe.* New York: Free Press.

Thanem, T., and L. Wallenberg. 2014. "Just Doing Gender? Transvestism and the Power of Underdoing Gender in Everyday Life and Work." *Organization* 23 (2): 250–271.

Thomas, P. G. 2005. "Debating a Whistle-Blower Protection Act for Employees of the Government of Canada." *Canadian Public Administration* 48 (2): 147–184.

Thompson, D. 1995. *Ethics in Congress: From Individual to Institutional Corruption.* Washington: Brookings Institution.

Thrift, N. 2001. "'It's the Romance, Not the Finance, That Makes the Business Worth Pursuing': Disclosing a New Market Culture." *Economy and Society* 30 (4): 412–432.

Turner, John. 2014. *Banking in Crisis: The Rise and Fall of British Banking Stability, 1800 to the Present.* Cambridge: Cambridge University Press.

Tyler, M. 2012. "Glamour Girls, Macho Men and Everything in Between." In *Dirty Work,* edited by R. Simpson, N. Slutskaya, P. Lewis, and H. Höpfl, 65–90. Basingstoke, UK: Palgrave.

Tyler, M., and L. Cohen. 2008. "Management in / as Comic Relief: Queer Theory and Gender Performativity in *The Office.*" *Gender, Work and Organization* 15 (2): 113–132.

UK Treasury. 2009. *Supplementary Memorandum from Lord Stevenson of Coddenham.* http://www.publications.parliament.uk/pa/cm200809/cmselect /cmtreasy/144/144iii16.htm.

Upin, C. 2010. "Getting Dirty Money Clean." *Need to Know.* PBS. 1 June. http://www.pbs.org/wnet/need-to-know/economy/getting-dirty-money -clean/1121/.

Vadera, A. K., R. V. Aguilera, and B. B. Caza. 2009. "Making Sense of Whistle-Blowing's Antecedents: Learning from Research on Identity and Ethics Programs." *Business Ethics Quarterly* 19 (4): 553–586.

Vandekerckhove, W. 2006. *Whistle-Blowing and Organisational Social Responsibility: A Global Assessment.* Hampshire, UK: Ashgate.

———. 2010. "European Whistleblowing Polices: Tiers or Tears?" In *A Global Approach to Public Interest Disclosure,* edited by D. B. Lewis, 15–35. Cheltenham, UK: Edward Elgar.

Vandekerckhove, W., A. J. Brown, and E. E. Tsahuridu. 2014. "Managerial Responses to Whistleblowing." In *International Handbook on Whistleblowing Research,* edited by A. J. Brown, D. Lewis, R. Moberly, and W. Vandekerckhove, 298–327. Cheltenham, UK: Edward Elgar.

Vandekerckhove, W., C. James, and F. West. 2013. *Whistleblowing: The Inside Story—a Study of the Experiences of 1,000 Whistleblowers.* London: Public Concern at Work.

Vandekerckhove, W., and S. Langenberg. 2012. "Can We Organize Courage? Implications of Foucault's Parrhesia." *Electronic Journal of Business Ethics and Organisation Studies* 17 (2): 35–44.

Vandekerckhove, W., and D. Lewis. 2012. "The Content of Whistleblowing Procedures: A Critical Review of Recent Official Guidelines." *Journal of Business Ethics* 108 (2): 253–264.

Vandekerckhove, W., and E. E. Tsahuridu. 2010. "Risky Rescues and Whistle-blowing." *Journal of Business Ethics* 97 (3): 365–380.

Van Maanen, J. 1979. "Reclaiming Qualitative Methods for Organizational Research: A Preface," *Administrative Science Quarterly* 24 (4): 520–527.

Varman, R., and I. Al-Amoudi. 2016. "Accumulation through Derealization: How Corporate Violence Remains Unchecked." *Human Relations* 69 (10): 1909–1935.

Verschoor, C. C. 2012. "Retaliation for Whistleblowing Is on the Rise." *Strategic Finance* 95 (5): 13–15.

Victor, B., and J. B. Cullen. 1987. "A Theory and Measure of Ethical Climate in Organisations." *Research in Corporate Social Performance and Policy* 9 (1): 51–71.

———. 1988. "The Organizational Bases of Ethical Work Climates." *Administrative Science Quarterly* 33 (1): 101–125.

Vulliamy, E. 2010. "The Wachovia Whistleblower." *The Nation,* 9 December. http://www.thenation.com/article/156986/wachovia-whistleblower

———. 2011a. "Swiss Whistleblower Rudolf Elmer Plans to Hand Over Offshore Banking Secrets of the Rich and Famous to WikiLeaks." *Guardian,* 16 January. https://www.theguardian.com/media/2011/jan/16/swiss-whistleblower-rudolf-elmer-banks.

———. 2011b. "How a Big US Bank Laundered Billions from Mexico's Murderous Drug Gangs." *Guardian,* 3 April. https://www.theguardian.com/world/2011/apr/03/us-bank-mexico-drug-gangs.

Walden, S., and B. Edwards. 2014. "Whistleblower Protections in International Government Organizations." In *International Handbook on Whistleblowing Research,* edited by A. J. Brown, D. Lewis, R. Moberly, and W. Vandekerckhove, 430–456. Cheltenham, UK: Edward Elgar.

Wall Street Journal. 2008. "Dodd and Countrywide: The Senator Should Take the Witness Stand." Wall *Street Journal,* 10 October. https://www.wsj.com/articles/SB122360116724221681.

Watson, T. 1994. *In Search of Management: Culture, Chaos and Control in Managerial Work.* London: Routledge.

Webster, A. 2015. "Developments in Whistleblowing." *Business Law International* 16 (1): 65–75.

Weedon, C. 1997. *Feminist Practice and Poststructuralist Theory.* Oxford: Blackwell.

Weiskopf, R., and Y. Tobias-Miersch. 2016. "Whistleblowing, Parrhesia and the Contestation of Truth in the Workplace." *Organization Studies* 37 (11): 1621–1640.

Weiskopf, R., and H. Willmott. 2013. "Ethics as Critical Practice: The 'Pentagon Papers,' Deciding Responsibly, Truth-Telling, and the Unsettling of Organizational Morality." *Organization Studies* 34 (4): 469–493.

Wheatley, J. 2013. "Six Things You Need to Know about Raghuram Rajan." *Financial Times,* 6 August.

Which? 2013. *Here to Help? Bank Staff Reveal the Truth about Working for Britain's Big Banks.* http://www.which.co.uk/documents/pdf/banking-staff -research-pdf-305345.pdf.

Wigand, G. 2011. Foreword to *The Corporate Whistleblower's Survival Guide,* edited by T. Devine and T. Maassarani, xi–xv. San Francisco: Berrett-Koehler.

Wilson, H. 2012. "'Banks Are "Too Big to Prosecute,' says FSA's Andrew Bailey." *Telegraph,* 14 December. http://www.telegraph.co.uk/finance/newsbysector /banksandfinance/9743839/Banks-are-too-big-to-prosecute-says-FSAs -Andrew-Bailey.html.

Winfield, M. 1994. "Whistleblowers as Corporate Safety Net." In *Whistleblowing: Subversion or Corporate Citizenship?,* edited by G. Vinten, 21–32. New York: St. Martin's.

Wolfe, S., Worth, M., Dreyfus, S. and Brown, A.J. 2015. *Breaking the Silence: Strengths and Weaknesses in G20 Whistleblower Protection Laws, Blueprint for Free Speech.* https://blueprintforfreespeech.net/wp-content/uploads/2015 /10/Breaking-the-Silence-Strengths-and-Weaknesses-in-G20-Whistleblower -Protection-Laws1.pdf.

Worth, M. 2013. *Whistleblowing in Europe: Legal Protections for Whistleblowers in the EU, Transparency International.* http://www.transparency.org /whatwedo/publication/whistleblowing_in_europe_legal_protections_for _whistleblowers_in_the_eu.

Wray-Bliss, E. 2003. "Research Subjects / Research Subjections: The Politics and Ethics of Critical Research." *Organization* 10 (2): 307–325.

Žižek, S. 2006. *The Parallax View.* Cambridge: MIT Press.

Acknowledgments

Thanks to the whistleblowers who have shared their experiences with me over the past number of years, many of whom feature here. I am in awe of your perseverance and courage.

While writing this book I was collaborating with Marianna Fotaki on a number of projects related to whistleblowing. Our conversations were invaluable in developing these ideas. I am also grateful to Meghan Van Portfliet for her help in producing this book and for discussions that are ongoing. Nancy Harding's continual development of organization theory was a further source of inspiration.

A number of friends and colleagues were kind enough to comment on earlier drafts of this text, or to offer advice and guidance. Sincere thanks to: Emma Bell, Fergal Crehan, Parisa Dashtipour, Tom Devine, John Devitt, Robert Dudley, Ricca Edmondson, Bea Edwards, Gregg Fields, Michael Fish, Philip Flynn, Ian Fraser, Susan Gates, Dana Gold, Joan Gorman, David Hazard, Muhammad Irfan, Sean Leonard, Kieran O'Malley, Didem Derya Ozdemir, Philip Roscoe, Malcolm Salter, Cathy Scharf, Mark Stein, Scott Taylor, John Turner, Eda Ulus, Wim Vandekerckhove, and Michael Winston. Thanks also to Thomas LeBien, my editor at Harvard University Press, for his continued encouragement, and to Kathleen Drummy and Sherry Gerstein for help in the production process.

I am grateful for the support provided by Queen's University Belfast and my colleagues there, and for a two-year fellowship at Harvard University's Edmond J. Safra Center for Ethics. The research for this book was assisted by funding from the Safra Center and from National University of Ireland, Galway's Millennium Research Fund.

Finally, thanks to my family, whom I love very much.

Index

abjection, 41, 42–44, 48. *See also* coping with exclusion; exclusion; internalization of exclusion; isolation; scapegoating

affect, 51–54

affective recognition: and understanding whistleblowing, 3–4, 8–9, 32–34, 54–55, 209–213; and contingent norms, 34–37; and ek-static recognition, 37–39; and injurious norms, 39–46; and subjection, 40–44, 210–211; and performative norms, 46–48; emotion and, 49–54; and coping with exclusion, 179–184, 192–193

AIG, 7, 228n12

Alford, C. Fred, 21, 24–25, 26–27, 28, 102, 227n3

Allied Irish Bank, 5, 76–77, 142–143, 160–164. *See also* McErlean, Eugene

Almonte, Linda, 152, 154, 224t

anger, displaying, 170–171. *See also* emotion

Assange, Julian, 130

Athanasiou, A., 231n2

autonomous individual, 38

BaFin, 119–120

Bank of America, 64–65, 80, 99, 129. *See also* Countrywide Financial

banks and banking: new financial culture in, 10–11; trust for, 82–83, 210–211. *See also* financial crisis; financial services, corruption in; global finance

Basel Accords, 244n10

Birkenfeld, Bradley, 15, 76, 127–128, 148, 224t

Bizet, Frederic, 121

blacklisting, 21, 143, 151–154. *See also* employment, exclusion from

Blum, Jack, 127

bonuses, 67–68, 93–94. *See also* compensation

bounties, 14–15, 212–213
Bowen, Richard, 246n20
Brown, Gordon, 75
bullying, 106–108, 113–114, 164, 201
Butler, Judith: and affective recognition, 33; on normative categories, 34, 36–37, 232n4; on ek-static recognition, 37, 38–39; on exclusion, 42, 43; on guilt and violence, 45–46; on performative norms, 46, 47; criticism of, 48–49; poststructural reading of psychoanalysis, 51–53; on subjection, 100, 167, 182; on deviation and censorship, 111, 113, 131; on violence, 114; on individualism, 145, 150; on melancholia, 156–157; on subject formation, 185; on integration of self, 186; on parody, 203; on labor under capitalism, 231n2; on Lacan and discursive power, 232n24; on conscience, 234n96; on academic as social entity, 249n25

Cayman Islands, 120–123, 125, 128. *See also* Elmer, Rudolf; Julius Bär
censorship, 44, 111–113, 130–132, 136
Christensen, John, 134
Churchill, Winston, 183
clients, overcharging, 161–162
Coca-Cola, 45
colonialism, 245n35
compensation: for whistleblowers, 14–15, 212–213; linking of compliance and, 74. *See also* bonuses
complicity: of society, 81–86, 155–159; impacts of, 86–87; norms of, 167, 168; of coworkers, 187–192
complicity, culture of: in finance industry, 60, 66; organizational contexts fostering, 66–71; at Halifax Bank of Scotland, 91–94; at Allied Irish Bank, 161–162; and whistleblowing as social act, 212–213
contingent norms, 34–37, 59
Contu, Alessia, 26

coping with exclusion, 173, 192–194; through professionalism, 177, 180, 188, 211; through friends and family, 177–178, 180, 181–182, 183–184, 185; through mutual-support partnerships, 178–179, 181, 185, 193, 201–202; affective recognition and, 179–184, 192–193; ek-static recognition and, 185–186; and distinguishing self from silent others, 186–192; through humor, 200–207
corporate bond funds (CBFs), 90–94, 238n2
Countrywide Financial, 60–66, 76, 80, 86–87, 129. *See also* Bank of America; Foster, Eileen; Winston, Michael
Coutts, 152–153, 197–198
creative compliance, 74
critical management studies, 221–223. *See also* organization studies
Crosby, Sir James, 95–96, 139
Cummings, Peter, 141

Dayen, David, 80
Derrida, Jacques, 46–47
Devine, Tom, 130, 171
différance, 46–47
discourse, and contingent norms, 35–37
Douglas, Mary, 40–41
drug money, 67, 173–176, 196–197, 246n2
Dugan, John, 129–130

Einstein, Albert, 183
ek-static recognition, 37–39, 48, 52, 145, 185–186
Elmer, Rudolf: prosecution of, 76, 122, 124, 134, 135, 240–241n18, 242n59; as public whistleblower, 120–130; censorship of, 130–131; and legitimate speech, 133–136; faces scrutiny for public whistleblowing, 143–144, 147–148; excluded from employment in desired sector, 152; and controlling emotion, 170–171; copes with

exclusion, 177–178, 180, 181–182; on whistleblowing and personal legacy, 184; *reconceptualization of, as* whistleblower, 198–199, 202; as research participant, 225*t*

emotion: poststructuralist approach to, 49–50; and passionate attachments, 51–54; controlling, 170–172

emotional health, and internalization of exclusion, 166–169, 170–172. *See also* mental health

employment, exclusion from, 150–154. *See also* blacklisting

Employment Act, 153

exclusion: and affective recognition, 40–44; as form of violence, 114–116; from employment in desired sector, 150–154, 243n48; by friends and colleagues, 154–155; understanding, following public whistleblowing, 155–159. *See also* abjection; coping with exclusion; individualization; internalization of exclusion; isolation; scapegoating

external whistleblowing, 19–20, 117–120, 133–135; success in, 120, 133. *See also* financial regulator

faith, coping with exclusion through, 183

False Claims Act, 15, 228n6 (chap. 1)

family, and coping with exclusion, 178, 181–182, 183–184, 185

Financial Conduct Authority (FCA), 15–16

financial services, corruption in, 87–88; Eileen Foster's experience with, 60–66; and culture of complicity, 66–71; and institutional and regulatory norms, 71–81; and societal complicity, 81–86; and impact of complicity, 86–87. *See also* global finance

financial crisis, 7, 10, 59–89, 110, 118, 128, 141, 155, 213–215

financial regulator, 15, 64, 66, 69–71, 75–78, 79, 91, 96, 119–120, 143, 162–163. *See also* external whistleblowing

Financial Services Authority (FSA), 70, 75, 91, 92, 139–140, 236n27

Fingleton, Michael, 105–107, 110–111

Fitzgibbon, Brian, 105, 178

Foster, Eileen: experience of, as whistle-blower, 60–66; retaliation against, 73, 108; and impact of complicity, 86, 87; motivation of, 99; gains valid subject position, 129, 135; excluded from employment in desired sector, 151; copes with exclusion, 178; *reconceptu-alization of, as* whistleblower, 201–202, 206; as research participant, 224*t*

Fotaki, Marianna, 53

Foucault, Michel: and disciplinary norms, 21; and parrhesia, 27; and affective recognition, 33; and power / knowledge, 35; and norm reproduction, 36; on subjectification, 49, 180–181; on contingent norms, 59; on fostering trust, 82–83; on individu-alism, 145–146; on critique and subversion of norms, 207; on norma-tive categories, 232n4; on industry-specific language and training, 237n73

friends: exclusion by, 154–155; and coping with exclusion, 177–178, 180, 181–182

gender: as normative category, 34–35; and performative norms, 46, 47; and norms of silence in financial services, 83–86; theory, 114, 203

Giddens, Anthony, 83

Glass-Steagall Act, 79

global finance: whistleblowers in, 4–7, 10–11; culture of silence in, 66, 213–215; as structurally gendered, 83–86. *See also* banks and banking; financial services, corruption in

Goffman, Erving, 111
Gold, Dana, 96
Government Accountability Project, 7
Grant, Colin, 26–27, 101
Greene, Olivia: experience of, as whistle-blower, 105–110; retaliation against, 111–115; excluded from employment in desired sector, 152, 243n48; internalizes exclusion, 164–165, 169; copes with exclusion, 178; reconceptualization of, as whistleblower, 201, 206; as research participant, 225t
guilt, 167–169

Halifax Bank of Scotland (HBOS), 72–73, 89–98, 139–142, 187–188. *See also* Moore, Paul
Harding, Nancy, 35, 39, 42
health, and internalization of exclusion, 166–169, 170–172
Ho, Karen, 69
Holder, Eric, 78
homophobia, 41–42
Hudson, Michael, 66, 129
humor, coping through, 200–207
Hunt, Sherry, 15, 225t, 246n20

impact of whistleblowing, 21–22
impossible speech, 44, 111–113, 130–132, 136, 156
importance of whistleblowing, 2, 86–87, 213–215
individualization, 144–147. *See also* abjection; coping with exclusion; exclusion; internalization of exclusion; isolation; scapegoating
institutional norms, 71–81
interest-only mortgages, 106–107
internalization of exclusion: whistle-blowers' experiences with, 160–166; impact of, 166–169; and controlling emotion, 169–172
Internal Revenue Service, 126, 128, 149, 175, 196

intersubjective recognition, 181
Irish bank bailout, 4, 118–120
Irish Nationwide Building Society (INBS), 105–112. *See also* Greene, Olivia
isolation, 108–110, 144. *See also* abjection; coping with exclusion; exclusion; internalization of exclusion; scapegoating

J. P. Morgan, 152
Julius Bär, 120–127, 128–130, 133–134, 143–144. *See also* Elmer, Rudolf

Kelly, Morgan, 82
KPMG, 90, 139–141, 142, 144–145, 148, 165
Kristeva, Julia, 41

Lacan, Jacques, 232nn23–24
legislation, protecting whistleblowers, 14–16, 79–80, 96, 153, 212, 213, 228n6
Levin, Carl, 126, 130
Libor (London Interbank Offered Rate), 7, 228n12
light-touch regulation, 75–78, 91
Lloyds Bank, 183
lobbying, 79–81

Madoff, Bernie, 130, 241n49
malpractice, rewarding, 67–69
Markopolous, Harry, 130, 241n49
Martin, B., 135
McErlean, Eugene: author's first encounter with, 5; and regulatory inaction, 76–77; gains valid subject position, 135; faces scrutiny for public whistleblowing, 142–143; excluded by friends and colleagues, 154; whistle-blowing experience of, 160–163; internalizes exclusion, 163–164, 169; as research participant, 225t
media attention, isolation for whistle-blowers amplified by, 146–150

megabanks, 78

melancholia, 41, 42, 156–157

mental health: and whistleblowing, 21–22, 50, 123, 200; internalization of exclusion, 166–169, 170–172

method, 4–9, 54–55, 101–102, 217–227; position of researcher in, 4–6, 221–226

Miceli, Marcia, 19, 227n3

Miethe, T., 191

Milgram, Stanley, 178, 193

Milne, Graham Senior, 69–70, 72, 183, 225t

Mollath, Gustl, 170

money laundering, 67–68, 173–176, 188–189, 196–197, 246n2. *See also* Wachovia; Woods, Martin

Moore, Paul: and regulatory inaction, 72–73; experience of, as whistleblower, 89–96; retaliation against, 95–96, 108, 111; motivation of, 96–99; gains valid subject position, 129, 141–142; faces scrutiny for public whistleblowing, 139–142, 144–145, 146; media support for, 148, 149; excluded by friends and colleagues, 155; internalizes exclusion, 165, 166; mental health of, questioned, 170; and controlling emotion, 171; copes with exclusion, 182, 183; on complicit coworkers, 187–188, 190, 191; reconceptualization of, as whistleblower, 200–201, 206; as research participant, 224t

moralized narcissism, 27, 28

Mozilo, Angelo, 62

mutual-support partnerships, 178–179, 181, 185, 193, 201–202. *See also* support for whistleblowers

Near, Janet, 19, 227n3

norms: normative categories, 34, 36–37, 232n4; contingent, 34–37, 59; and ek-static recognition, 37–39; injurious, 39–46, 150–206; performative, 46–48, 51; of silence, 66, 167, 168; institutional and regulatory, 71–81; professional

recognition under dominant, 100; power of, 102; whistleblowing as deviation from, 111–113; normative violence, 114, 115; of individualism, 144–145; of complicity, 167, 168; dependence of whistleblowers on, 167–168; confirmation of existence through, 180–181; reconceptualization of whistleblowers and subversion of, 204–207; and affective recognition, 211

Obama, Barack, 128

O'Brien, Justin, 74

oppressed groups, self-berating of, 245n35

organizations: and speak-up systems, 16; position of whistleblowers in, 22–25. *See also* institutional norms

organization studies, 8, 13–14, 33, 35, 40, 44, 47, 220. *See also* critical management studies

overcharges, 161–162

parody, 47–48, 200–207, 248n30

parrhesia, 27–28

passionate attachments, 51–54, 182; to global finance, 155–159

payment protection insurance (PPI) scandal, 75

performativity, 46–48, 51, 219–220

Perry, Nick, 23–24, 29

Pettifor, Ann, 82

potted palm gambit, 20, 109

power/knowledge, 35

power relations: and normative categories, 36; and instilling norms of silence and compliance, 111–113; interlinking of subjection and, 181

PPI scandal, 75

professionalism of whistleblowers: Paul Moore and, 89–96; as motivation for whistleblowing, 96–103, 176; and dealing with retaliation, 108; and coping with exclusion, 177, 180, 188, 211

subjection: to discourse, 36–37; and affective recognition, 40–44, 210–211; and motivation of whistleblowers, 96–102; and professionalism, 97–101; bad conscience in, 167; as exclusionary process, 191

subject positions: gaining valid, 129–130, 133, 135, 141–142, 180–181; created by censorship, 131, 136; variation in performance of, 132; of Rudolf Elmer, 133, 134–135

subprime mortgages, 60–65, 86–87. *See also* 2008 subprime mortgage crash

Sugarman, Jonathan: as public whistle-blower, 118–120, 132; media support for, 148; excluded from employment in desired sector, 150–151; excluded by friends and colleagues, 154–155; internalizes exclusion, 165, 169; copes with exclusion, 182; on complicit coworkers, 189–190; as research participant, 225*t*

support for whistleblowers: lack of from society, 28–29, 54, 158, 192, 212–215; importance of, 126–129; high-profile helpers, 130–135, 141, 147–148; from media, 148–149; from friends, family and colleagues, 177–178, 193; from whistleblower and advocacy organizations, 179; from online helpers and faith, 182–186

Swiss bank secrecy, 122, 124, 127–128, 133–136. *See also* Elmer, Rudolf

Taplin, Ian, 69, 70, 182–183, 224*t*

tax evasion, 120, 122, 125–128, 131, 133, 134, 143–144, 199. *See also* Elmer, Rudolf

Thrift, Nigel, 84

2008 subprime mortgage crash, 10–11, 85, 86–87

Tyler, M., 40

UBS, 127, 148. *See also* Birkenfeld, Bradley

UniCredit, 118–120, 182. *See also* Sugarman, Jonathan

violence: and affective recognition, 44–46; as response to speaking out, 110–116, 130, 156; and self, 167–169; and complicity, 221; in research, 223

Volker Rule, 79

Wachovia, 67–68, 129–130, 173–176, 196–197, 247n3. *See also* Woods, Martin

watchdogs, 60, 71–75, 238n32

whistleblower(s): defined, 2; as collective entity, 186, 210–212; characteristics of, 5–6, 8, 18; positive and negative associations with, 6–7; compensation for, 14–15, 212–213; legal and organizational protections for, 14–16; legislation protecting, 14–16, 79–80, 96, 153, 212, 213, 228n6; ambivalence surrounding, 22–25, 210–211, 214–215; self of, 25–30; motivation of, 26–28, 89, 96–103; tendencies shared by, 27–28; as hero figures, 28–29; as victim, 29–30; mutual support among, 178–179, 181, 185, 193, 201–202. *See also* profession-alism of whistleblowers; reconceptuali-zation of whistleblowers

whistleblowing: consequences of, 1–2; questions regarding, 2–3; affective recognition and, 3–4, 8–9, 32–34, 209–213; new theory of, 3–4; author's study of, 4–7, 217–226; scholarship on, 7–8, 13–14, 59, 101; complexity of, 11; in organizations, 16–22; factors influencing, 17–18; likelihood of, 17–18; process perspective of, 18–20; personal impact of, 21–22; ambiva-lence surrounding, 22–25, 210–211, 214–215; theorizing, in organizations, 22–30; as social act, 212–213; defined, 227n3. *See also* importance of whistleblowing; public whistleblowing